# WRITING AWAY

# WRITING AWAY
## The PEN Canada Travel Anthology

Edited by

## CONSTANCE ROOKE

**Canadian Cataloguing in Publication Data**
Main entry under title:
Writing away : the PEN Canada travel anthology
ISBN 0-7710-6956-1
1. Voyages and travels - Literary collections. 2. Authors, Canadian (English) - 20th century - Journeys.* 3. Canadian literature (English) - 20th century.* I. Rooke, Constance, 1942- . II International P.E.N. Canadian Centre.

PS8323.T7W7 1994    C810.8'0355    C94-931118-9
PR9197.28.T7W7 1994

Typesetting by M&S, Toronto

The publishers acknowledge the support of the Canada Council and the Ontario Arts Council for their publishing program.

The support of the Government of Ontario through the Ministry of Culture, Tourism and Recreation is acknowledged.

Printed and bound in Canada on acid-free paper

Thanks to Tony Urquhart for allowing the one-time reproduction of four of his drawings.

All written material and artwork are the property of their respective contributors. Photographs, unless otherwise credited, are the property of the authors.

No written material, artwork, or photographs may be reproduced without permission.

English translation of "Between the Freud Video Club and the Jung Café" by Nicole Brossard © 1994 by Sheila Fischman.

McClelland & Stewart Inc.
*The Canadian Publishers*
481 University Avenue
Toronto, Ontario
M5G 2E9

1 2 3 4 5   98 97 96 95 94

# CONTENTS

*Introduction* by Constance Rooke, Editor     vii

*"Without Let or Hindrance"* by Salman Rushdie     xi

✳ MARGARET ATWOOD · The Grunge Look     1

PIERRE BERTON · River of Ghosts     12

DIONNE BRAND · Just Rain, Bacolet     19

NICOLE BROSSARD · Between the Freud Video Club
and the Jung Café     31

JUNE CALLWOOD · Swimming Around the Planet     37

GEORGE ELLIOTT CLARKE · To Paris, Burning     43

LEONARD COHEN · Two Poems     54

✳ ROBERTSON DAVIES · Getting There     56

✳ TIMOTHY FINDLEY · Barbados: The Very Pineapple of
Perfection     61

GEORGE GALT · Night Pictures in Peru     71

GRAEME GIBSON · Notes from a Cuban Journal     77

PETER GZOWSKI · Up the Liard by Magic Carpet     94

JACK HODGINS · Il Porcellino     98

ISABEL HUGGAN · Notes from the Philippines     109

✳ JANICE KULYK KEEFER · Kiev, November 1993     123

THOMAS KING · The Open Car     147

MYRNA KOSTASH · Table Manners     156

ALBERTO MANGUEL · After Carthage     164

DAVID MCFADDEN · Mr. Looney     173

ROHINTON MISTRY · Searching for Stevenson     187

DANIEL DAVID MOSES · Rain in Hawaii     199

ALICE MUNRO · What Do You Want to Know For?     203

MICHAEL ONDAATJE · Six Photographs     221

✳ P. K. PAGE · Settling In     227

NINO RICCI · Things Fall Apart     248

DAVID ADAMS RICHARDS · Travel     259

JOHN RALSTON SAUL · Subversion in the North     263

CAROL SHIELDS · Travelwarp     276

LINDA SPALDING · Others     281

SUSAN SWAN · Corfu: Visiting Lawrence Durrell's
White House (from My Greek Journals)     295

JUDITH THOMPSON · No Soy Culpable     307

JANE URQUHART · Returning to the Village     317

ARITHA VAN HERK · Death in Vienna     326

RONALD WRIGHT · The Painted Cave     335

*About the Contributors*     349

*Breaking the Silence* by Alison Gordon, President,
PEN Canada     362

# Introduction

## by

## Constance Rooke, Editor

This book came into being because PEN Canada is in trouble. PEN is running dangerously low on funds needed to carry our words around the world. We're not thinking on this occasion about the words that shape themselves into novels and such, words that are transmutable (with a lucky break) into royalties and fame as well as the gold available to all those who choose to read. At issue on this occasion are the words we hope will translate into literal freedom: the thousands of urgent, strategic communications that PEN sends out – and must, somehow, continue to send out – to writers in prison all over the world, and to the people who have put them there. The crime of these writers was to speak their minds, and we cannot ever let them pay the price for that without protesting. Our noise-making skills, our powers of persuasion, are called for and must be exercised at once.

We need seeds in the rattle, quick.

McClelland & Stewart, in the redoubtable person of Avie Bennett, came to the rescue with the suggestion that M&S publish a book whose proceeds would go to PEN. The idea of a travel anthology was Avie's, too: he felt sure readers would buy a book like this one, and that, after all, was the point. But it made sense for other reasons too.

Writers travel constantly. They cannot help it. At home or away, they are always making tracks. It may be that travel is the most telling metaphor for what writers do. Over and over, they move; and they go back, partly because the world is moving too. Inventing multiple, branching itineraries, assigning stars to bits we must not under any circumstances miss, they move ahead of us – and confess repeatedly (the best of them do) to all the places in which they cannot serve as expert guides. They speak of rewards and punishment, of a world that beguiles and eludes us. The perilous, exhilarating journey out of everyday, the taste of the world's skin, the jolt of difference, the need to register what the world speaks or declines to speak to us: all of that is the writer's need as much as the traveller's.

A travel book called *Writing Away* made sense for PEN and the many writers in Canada who support the work of PEN, because that's what they do: they write away, and often toward that other place in which matters of importance are going on, some of them pig-ugly. They write for beauty too, and for the love of life. And they travel, literally – for reasons of work or pleasure or discovery – more than most people do, so that it was feasible (just barely) for them to say yes to a travel anthology when I called up and begged. These extraordinarily busy, wonderfully talented people, almost all of whom were deep in other projects, said yes in astonishing numbers when they knew it was PEN that needed help. (I had to stop asking too soon, since almost no one declined PEN's irresistible offer to take their work for free.) Given absurd deadlines of a month or so, and informed that the work donated to this cause must be unpublished, they kept on saying yes in droves. Once in, they were obliged to start – writing away.

There were no other specifications: the piece could be funny or not, work-related or not, political or not, recent or not, short or not. I did ask to be told which places the writers were considering, so that I could try to dampen one enthusiasm and whet another if too many of our company happened to be travelling to Venice, for example, or Down Under. ("You'd really better ask," Alice Munro advised. "You don't want a pot-luck supper where everyone brings lasagne.") The assortment, however, largely took care of itself. I asked for snapshots too, if they had some handy.

One other rule was that you had to be Canadian, unless you were Salman Rushdie. But if there is truth in buttons, those categories are not mutually exclusive. Witness the number of Canadians wearing a pin that says I AM SALMAN RUSHDIE, just to confound the enemy – and speak our solidarity. For it was on the stage of Toronto's Winter Garden Theatre, in December 1992, that Salman Rushdie was for the first time welcomed and passionately supported by a head of government. (Good for you, Bob Rae.) Only a handful of PEN board members knew that our most famous writer-in-prison would be making a surprise appearance at the PEN benefit; the rest of us could not account for the extraordinary backstage rash of men in trenchcoats, all of whom (to judge from the gadgets on their ears) were severely hard-of-hearing. I will remember forever how a friend said, "Come with me a minute. There's someone I want you to meet," and we went into a broom closet, and there he was – Salman Rushdie, huddled in a closet, waiting for intermission and the brief bittersweet surprise party we would have backstage. On stage he spoke, and read a story for us – just as any other writer might – and all over the Winter Garden there blossomed the pins that said I AM SALMAN RUSHDIE. In about an hour, the real Rushdie – the free Rushdie – had disappeared once more.

So here's the book some Canadian writers made for PEN and for all writers in prison all over the world. Thanks so much to them, and to those at McClelland & Stewart who contributed to the final editorial, design, and production stages – Peter Buck, Tania Charzewski, Mark Delvecchio, Trish Lyon, Sharmila Mohammed, Kong Njo, Krystyna Ross, Alex Schultz, Ellen

Seligman, and Andrew Skuja – and the numerous others in the sales, promotion, and distribution departments, whose efforts are greatly appreciated. Thanks also to Louise Dennys and Esta Spalding – and to the real Salman Rushdie for the words of introduction that follow mine.

# *"Without Let or Hindrance"*

by

Salman Rushdie

My first, Indian, passport permitted me to travel only to a very few countries, which were carefully listed on the second right-hand page. If I wanted to go anywhere else – Canada, for example, or almost anywhere one might want to go – special application would have to be made, and, it was suggested, permission would not be particularly easy to get.

I used this passport to travel to England as a schoolboy, and I remember that when I became a British citizen some years later, the words in the British passport which "request and require" all countries to allow the bearer to pass "without let or hindrance" made a deep impression on me. Since then I have made a point of passing through a large number of countries, nor were there very many lets or hindrances.

(There were a few, though. The first time I visited the United States I was young, had long hair and a Zapata moustache, and quite possibly I was wearing a long-collared purple shirt with red crushed-velvet trousers. In the immigration hall I saw the following sign: A FEW MINUTES EXTRA IN THIS HALL IS A SMALL PRICE TO PAY TO SAVE YOUR CHILDREN FROM THE MENACE OF DRUGS. An American gent with a wide, red neck turned to me with a kindly smile and said, "Buddy, I sure feel sorry for you, because even if you ain't got nothing, they'll find something." They did their best, exploring me as thoroughly as I had hoped to explore America, and by the time I hit the street (they found nothing) I was something of a wreck. Then, in the bus queue, a little old lady who looked like the little old lady in "The Beverly Hillbillies" asked me what the matter was (that's how dreadful I looked), and I found myself telling her everything. She heard me out gravely and then, clasping her hands together, she drew herself up to her full height and made a formal apology to me on behalf of the United States of America. Amazingly, this worked. I stopped shaking and dreaming of dark revenges, and began to enjoy my stay.

Five years ago, however, the Ayatollah Khomeini did his best to turn my British passport into something rather like my old Indian one. In these five years, I was three times refused permission to enter France – even though, as a European citizen, I have the absolute right to do so – and as many times politely requested not to enter America. Both these bans have since come to an end, but I did spend a while wondering if they would. Airlines, which happily carry anyone from Gerry Adams to Carlos the Jackal, became reluctant to carry me. (Coming to Canada, for example, proved very, very tricky.) And when I did manage to go places, I gained the impression that the normal population had been wholly replaced by men in police uniform.

"How is it for you, nowadays?" a journalist asked me the other day. "Can you fly?"

"Not without using an aeroplane," I replied.

All of which is by way of saying that I am at present just about the worst person who could have been asked to introduce a book of travel writing. I have learned a lot about motorcades, it's true. In Paris they closed the Place de la Concorde to let my convoy cross it. "Wouldn't it have been safer," I asked, "to have brought me through the backstreets in a secondhand Citroën?" The security men looked at me as if I was mad. In New York I found out

xii

what it's like to be in a thirteen-vehicle motorcade rushing at speed through Harlem (pretty nice). "It's what we'd do for Arafat," I was told. And what would you do if it were the President, I asked. "For the President we'd shut down a lot of these side roads here, but in your case we thought that would look too conspicuous." Whereas the sirens, the motorbikes, the twelve police cars, and my white limo were, of course, very low-profile . . .

Things will improve. Things may even be improving. Until the end of all lets and hindrances, however, I will content myself with reading about other people's journeys, in the real world, and feeling sick with jealousy.

February 25, 1994

MARGARET ATWOOD

# The Grunge Look

I first went to Europe on May the 13th, 1964. I had been told I was going to do this five months earlier by a male psychic working out of a Toronto tea shop. "You will be going to Europe in May," he said.

"No I won't," I said.

"Yes you will," he said, smugly reshuffling his cards.

I did.

Fleeing a personal life of Gordian complexity, and leaving behind a poetry manuscript rejected by all, and a first novel ditto, I scraped together what was left after a winter of living in a Charles Street rooming-house and writing *tours-de-force* of undiscovered genius while working by day at a market research company, borrowed six hundred dollars from my parents, who were understandably somewhat nervous about my choice of the literary life by then, and climbed onto a plane. In the fall I would be teaching grammar to Engineering students at eight-thirty in the morning in a Quonset hut at the University of British Columbia, so I had about three months. In this period of time I intended to become – what? I wasn't sure exactly, but I had some notion that the viewing of various significant pieces of architecture

1

would improve my soul – would fill in a few potholes in it, get rid of a few cultural hangnails, as it were. Here, I had been studying English literature for six years – I even had an M.A., which had got me rejected for employment by the Bell Telephone Company on the grounds of overqualification – and I had never even seen, well, things. Stonehenge, for instance. A visit to Stonehenge would surely improve my understanding of Thomas Hardy. Or someone. Anyway, a lot of my friends from college had already run to England, intending to be actors and the like. So England was my first stop.

The truth is that I didn't have much idea of what I was really doing. Certainly, I had almost no idea at all of where I was really going, and how much it had changed since I'd last checked in via the pages of Charles Dickens. Everything was so much smaller and shabbier than I had imagined. I was like the sort of Englishman who arrives in Canada expecting to find a grizzly bear on every street corner. "Why are there so many *trucks?*" I thought. There were no trucks in Dickens. There weren't even any in T. S. Eliot. "I did not know Death had undone so many," I murmured hopefully, as I made my way across Trafalgar Square. But the people there somehow refused to be as hollow-cheeked and plangent as I'd expected. They appeared to be mostly tourists, like myself, and were busy taking pictures of one another with pigeons on their heads.

My goal, of course, was Canada House, the first stop of every jet-stunned, impecunious young Canadian traveller in those days. But before I go on, let me say a few words about those days. What sort of year was 1964?

It was the year after 1963, in which John Kennedy had been so notably shot. It was the year before the first (to my knowledge) anti-Viet Nam peace march; it was roughly four years before the great hippie explosion, and five years before the onset of the early-seventies wave of feminism. Miniskirts had not yet arrived; pantihose were approaching, but I don't believe they had as yet squeezed out the indigenous population of garter-belts and stockings. In hair, something called the bubble-cut was favoured: women rolled their hair in big bristle-filled rollers to achieve a smoothly swollen look, as if someone had inserted a tube into one of their ears and blown up their heads like balloons. I indulged in this practice too, though with mixed results, since my hair was ferociously curly. At best it resembled a field of weeds gone over with a lawn roller – still squiggly, though somewhat mashed. At worst it looked as if I'd stuck my finger in a light socket. This silhouette was later to become stylish, but was not so yet. As a result I went in for head scarves, of the Queen-Elizabeth-at-Balmoral type. Paired with the slanty-eyed, horned-rimmed glasses I wore in an attempt to take myself seriously, they were not at all flattering.

Come to think of it, neither was anything in my suitcase. (Hitchhiking backpackers had not yet overrun Europe, so it was, still, a suitcase.) Fashion-wise, 1964 was not really my year. Beatniks had faded, and I hadn't discovered the romantic raggle-taggle gypsy mode; but then, neither had anyone else. Jeans had not yet swept all before them, and for ventures to such places as churches and museums, skirts were still required; grey-flannel jumpers with Peter-Pan-collared blouses were my uniform of choice. High heels were the norm for most occasions, and about the only thing you could actually walk in were some rubber-soled suede items known as Hush Puppies.

Lugging my suitcase, then, I Hush-Puppied my way up the imposing steps of Canada House. At that time it offered – among other things, such as a full shelf of Geological Surveys – a reading room with newspapers in it. I riffled anxiously through the Rooms To Let, since I had no place to stay that night. By pay telephone, I rented the cheapest thing available, which was located in a sub-urb called Willesden Green. This turned out to be about as far away from everything as you could get, via the London Under-ground, which I promptly took (here at last, I thought, looking at my intermittently-bathed, cadaverous and/or dentally-challenged fellow passengers, were a few people Death had in fact undone, or was about to). The rooming-house furnishings smelled of old, sad cigarette smoke, and were of such hideous dinginess that I felt I'd landed in a Graham Greene novel; and the sheets, when I finally slid between them, were not just cold and damp, they were wet. ("North Americans like that kind of thing," an Englishwoman said to me, much later. "Unless they freeze in the bathroom they think they've been cheated of the English experience.")

The next day I set out on what appears to me in retrospect a dauntingly ambitious quest for cultural trophies. My progress through the accumulated bric-a-brac of centuries was marked by the purchase of dozens of brochures and postcards, which I col-lected to remind myself that I'd actually been wherever it was I'd been. At breakneck speed I gawped my way through Westminster Abbey, the Houses of Parliament, St. Paul's Cathedral, the Tower of London, the Victoria and Albert Museum, the National Por-trait Gallery, the Tate, the house of Samuel Johnson, Buckingham Palace, and the Albert Memorial. At some point I fell off a double-decker bus and sprained my foot, but even this, although it slowed me down, did not stop me in my headlong and reckless pursuit. After a week of this, my eyes were rolling around like loose change, and my head, although several sizes larger, was actually a good deal emptier than it had been before. This was a mystery to me.

Another mystery was why so many men tried to pick me up. It was hardly as if I was, in my little grey-flannel jumpers, dressed to kill. Museums were the usual locale, and I suppose there was something about a woman standing still with her head tilted at a ninety-degree angle that made solicitation more possible. None of these men was particularly rude. "American?" they would ask, and when I said Canadian, they would look either puzzled or disappointed, and would proceed only tentatively to the next question. When they got no for an answer, they simply moved along to the next upstretched neck. Possibly, they hung around tourist lodestones on the theory that female travellers travelled for the same kinds of sexual-adventure reasons they would have travelled, had they been travelling themselves. But in this there was – and possibly still is – a gender difference. Ulysses was a sailor, Circe was a stay-at-home with commodious outbuildings.

When not injecting myself with culture, I was looking for something to eat. In England in 1964, this was quite difficult, especially if you didn't have much money. I made the mistake of trying a hamburger and a milkshake, but the English didn't yet have the concept: the former was fried in rancid lamb fat, the latter fortified with what tasted like ground-up chalk. The best places were the fish-and-chip shops, or, barring that, the cafés, where you could get eggs, sausages, chips, and peas, in any combination. Finally, I ran into some fellow-Canadians, who'd been in England longer than I had, and who put me onto a Greek place in Soho, which actually had salads, a few reliable pubs, and the Lyons' Corner House on Trafalgar Square, which had a roast-beef all-you-can-eat for a set price. A mistake, as the Canadian journalists would starve themselves for a week, then hit the Lyons' Corner House like a swarm of locusts. (The Lyons' Corner House did not survive.)

It must have been through these expatriates that I hooked up with Alison Cunningham, whom I'd known at university and who was now in London, studying modern dance and sharing a second-floor flat in South Kensington with two other young women. Into this flat, Alison – when she heard of my wet-sheeted Willesden Green circumstances – generously offered to smuggle me. "Smuggle" is appropriate; the flat was owned by aristocratic twins called Lord Cork and Lady Hoare, but as they were ninety and in nursing homes, it was actually run by a suspicious dragon of a housekeeper; so for purposes of being in the flat I had to pretend I didn't exist.

In Alison's flat I learned some culturally useful things that have stuck with me through the years: how to tell a good kipper from a bad one, for instance; how to use an English plate-drying rack; and how to make coffee in a pot when you don't have any other device. I continued with my tourist program – stuffing in Cheyne Walk, several lesser-known churches, and the Inns of Court – and Alison practised a dance, which was a reinterpretation of *The Seagull*, set to several of the Goldberg Variations as played by Glenn Gould. I can never hear that piece of music without seeing Alison, in a black leotard and wearing the severe smile of a Greek caryatid of the Archaic period, bending herself into a semi-pretzel on that South Kensington sitting-room floor. Meanwhile, I was not shirking in the salt-mines of Art. Already, my notebook contained several new proto-gems, none of which, oddly, busied itself with the age-old masterworks of Europe. Instead, they were about rocks.

When things got too close for comfort with the dragon house-keeper, I would have to skip town for a few days. This I did by cashing in some miles on the rail pass I had purchased in Canada – one of the few sensible preparations for my trip I had managed to make. (Why no Pepto-Bismol, I ask myself; why no acetamino-phen with codeine; why no Gravol? I would never think of leaving the house without them now.) On this rail pass you could go anywhere the railways went, using up miles as you did so. My first journeys were quite ambitious. I went to the Lake District, overshooting it and getting as far north as Carlisle before I had to double back; whereupon I took a bus tour of the Lakes, viewing them through fumes of cigar smoke and nausea, and, although surprised by their smallness, was reassured to hear that people still drowned in them every year. Then I went to Glastonbury, where after seeing the Cathedral, I was waylaid by an elderly lady who got five pounds out of me to help save King Arthur's Well, which – she said – was in her backyard and would be ruined by a brewery unless I contributed to the cause. I made it to Cardiff with its genuine-ersatz castle, and to Nottingham and the ancestral home of the Byrons, and to York, and to the Brontë manse, where I was astonished to learn, from the size of their tiny boots and gloves, that the Brontës had been scarcely bigger than children. As a writer of less than Olympian stature, I found this encouraging.

But as my rail pass dwindled, my trips became shorter. Why did I go to Colchester? To the Cheddar Gorge? To Ripon? My motives escape me, but I went to these places; I have the postcards to prove it. Julius Caesar visited Colchester, too, so there must have been something to it; but I was driven by frugality rather than by the historicist imperative: I didn't want any of my rail pass miles to go to waste.

Around about July, Alison decided that France would be even more improving for me than England had been, so in the company of a male friend of mine from Harvard, in full retreat from a Southern girlfriend who had brought several ball gowns to a student archeological graveyard excavation, we took the night boat-train. It was an average Channel crossing, during which we all turned gently green. Alison bravely continued to discourse on intellectual matters, but finally turned her head and, with a dancer's casual grace, threw up over her left shoulder. These are the moments one remembers.

# Benefits of European Travel

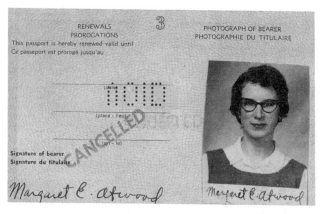

BEFORE
(*photo credit: unknown*)

DURING
A Pre-Ralphaelite pose
(*photo credit: photo machine,
Gare du Norde, Paris*)

AFTER
Montreal, 1968
(*photo credit: Jim Polk*)

By the time we'd been two days in Paris, where we subsisted on a diet of baguettes, *café au lait*, oranges, pieces of cheese, and the occasional bean-heavy bistro meal, I was in an advanced state of dysentery. We were shunting around from cheap *pension* to cheap *pension*; the rooms were always up gloomy flights of stairs, with lights that went off when you we're halfway up and cockroaches that rustled and crackled underfoot. None of these establishments allowed you to stay in them during the day; so I lay moaning softly on hard French park benches, in gravelly French parks, while Alison, with a sense of duty Florence Nightingale would have envied, read me long improving passages from Doris Lessing's *The Golden Notebook*. Every fifteen minutes a policeman would come by and tell me I had to sit up, since lying on the park benches was forbidden; and every half hour I would make a dash for the nearest establishment with a toilet, which featured, not the modern plumbing that has taken over today, but a hole in the ground and two footrests, and many previous visitors with imperfect aims.

A diet of bread and water, and some potent French emulsion, administered by Alison, improved my condition, and I dutifully hiked around to Notre Dame, the Eiffel Tower, and the Louvre. In Paris, the men bent on pickups didn't bother to wait until you had stopped and were craning your neck; they approached at all times, even when you were crossing the street. "Americaine?" they would ask hopefully. They were polite – some of them even used the subjunctive, as in "Voudriez-vous coucher avec moi" – and, when refused, would turn away with a beagle-like melancholy which I chose to find both existential and Gallic.

When we had only a week and a half left, the three of us pooled our resources and rented a car, with which we toured the Châteaux of the Loire, viewing a great many eighteenth-century gilded chairs and staying in youth hostels, and living on more cheese. By this time I was supersaturated with culture; water-logged, so to speak. If someone had stepped on my head, a stream of dissolved brochures would have poured forth.

Then, for some reason now lost in the mists of history, I decided to go to Luxembourg. On the way there, a middle-aged conductor chased me around the train compartment; when I explained that I was not in fact American, as he had supposed, he shrugged and said "Ah," as if that explained my reluctance. By this time I was getting somewhat fed up with the excess of dog-and-fire-hydrant male attention, and I let my irritation spill over onto the cultural agenda; when I finally got to Luxembourg, I did not go to visit a single church. Instead, I saw *Some Like It Hot*, with subtitles in Flemish, French, and German, where I was the only person in the theatre who laughed in the right places.

This seemed an appropriate point of re-entry to North America. Culture is as culture does, I thought to myself, as I returned to England, steered myself and my Hush Puppies towards the plane, and prepared for decompression.

At that moment my trip in retrospect felt a lot like stumbling around in the dark, bumping into heavy, expensive pieces of furniture, while being mistaken for someone else. But distance adds perspective, and in the months that followed, I tried hard for it. Had my soul been improved? Possibly, but not in the ways I'd anticipated. What I took back with me was not so much the churches and museums and the postcards of them I'd collected, but various conversations, in buses, on trains, and with the pickup men at the museums. I remembered especially the general bafflement when it turned out that I was not what I appeared to be; namely, an American. For the Europeans:, there was a flag-shaped blank where my nationality should have been. What was visible to me was invisible to them; nor could I help them out by falling back on any internationally-famous architectural constructs. About all I had to offer as a referent was a troop of horsy policemen, which hardly seemed enough.

But one person's void is another person's scope, and that was where the new poems I'd brought back squashed at the bottom of my suitcase would come in, or so I thought. Speaking of which, my grey-flannel wardrobe – I could see it now – definitely had to go. As a deterrent to stray men it was inadequate, as a disguise irrelevant, as a poetic manifesto incoherent. I did not look serious in it, merely earnest, and also – by now – somewhat grubby. I had picked up a brown suede vest, on sale at Liberty's, which, with the addition of a lot of black and some innovation with the hair, would transform me into something a lot more formidable; or so I intended.

I did get to Stonehenge, incidentally. I felt at home with it. It was pre-rational, and pre-British, and geological. Nobody knew how it had arrived where it was, or why, or why it had continued to exist; but there it sat, challenging gravity, defying analysis. In fact, it was sort of Canadian. "Stonehenge," I would say to the next mournful-looking European man who tried to pick me up. That would do the trick.

# River of Ghosts

The river of my childhood is a devious river. It rises in the peaks of the Coastal Range, just fifteen miles from the Pacific Ocean, and then, like a prospector desperately seeking paydirt, embarks on a long search for that same Pacific water, coiling in a vast 2,200-mile arc over the entire Yukon and Alaska before spending itself in the Bering Sea.

Every river has a personality, but the Yukon has more than most, because its character changes as it grows, broadening and maturing on its long journey to the ocean. The Mackenzie is a bore. It flows directly into the Arctic almost in a straight line, with scarcely a curve and rarely a twist, moving resolutely on beside a long line of mountains. It is much the same with the St. Lawrence and the Saskatchewan, which define the horizontal nature of our country. But the Yukon is more human. It has moments of uncertainty and frivolity, as it changes from baby blue near its source to a sullen grey at its delta. It skitters back and forth, hesitates, changes its mind, charges forward, then retreats. There are few dull moments on the Yukon. New vistas open up at every bend.

It is not practical to travel the Yukon River in a single season. My own advice for cheechakos is to settle for the first four hundred miles – the stretch from Whitehorse to Dawson – and to drift with the current, watching the forest unfold. The trip need not take longer than ten days or two weeks. Outfitters in Whitehorse can supply rubber Zodiacs, which are the safest and most comfortable method of travel. On this stretch the river moves through history, for this is the water highway of the gold-seekers of 1898, and the marks of their passage are everywhere.

The river of my childhood is also a river of ghosts. You can travel for twenty-four hours and never encounter a single human being. Moose raise their snouts from the marshes at the mouths of tributary creeks; black bears scuttle up the hillsides; lynx peer out from the willows at the river's edge like big tawny cats. But the signs of human passage all belong to the past – to the days when the river was the only highway to the city of gold. Ghost towns are dotted along the entire length of the Yukon – ghost cabins, ghost steamboats rotting in the willows, ghostly cemeteries, and, of course, the artifacts left by those who came before.

I can remember sitting on the bank one evening, looking out on the empty river and on the endless hills drifting off to the

north, ridge upon ridge, all the way to the sullen Arctic. There
was no hint of man – no boat upon those swift waters, golden now
in the rays of the late evening sun, no smudge of smoke staining
the far horizon, where the spiky spruces met the pale sky, not even
a clearing in the forest or an old blaze on a tree. But there, hidden
in the mosses, I spotted a little aluminum pot complete with
handle, and recalled that the previous day we had come upon a
wooden rocking horse in the woods.

On a deserted bank near the ghost settlement of Lower
Laberge, I spotted a little white table sitting all by itself as if waiting for guests to arrive. Furniture in the wilderness! One finds it
all along the Yukon.

For fifty years, before the Alaska Highway changed the pattern,
this was steamboat country. The ghosts of those brave days still
haunt the Yukon valley. Near Lower Laberge, the hull of the old
*Casca*, like a vast, wooden whale, looms out of the willows. It is
hard to connect this rotting hull with the proud sternwheeler,
pennants flying, whistle sounding, paddle wheel whirling, that
rounded the Dawson bluffs in my childhood. On an island near
the mouth of the Teslin River, the remains of another steamer, the
*Evelyn*, can still be seen. She has been sitting there, slowly rotting
away, since 1922. And five miles downriver from the ghost community of Big Salmon, the original *Klondike* lies in its watery
grave, nothing more than a hull-shaped ripple in the whispering
river. (A newer *Klondike* is now a monument in Whitehorse.)

At Little Salmon – an Indian village wiped out by the influenza
epidemic of 1919 – the rotting cabins rise out of a blaze of
fireweed. Here, the graves are as numerous as the cabins. They
are, in fact, like small dwellings, a village of spirit-houses with
sloping roofs, glass windows, and curtains, containing dried flowers, teapots, and plates for the use of the dead.

Some communities have vanished without a trace. Only the

presence of tall blue delphiniums and bright Arctic poppies spattering the grass tells us that there was a time when families lived here, and men and women tended flourishing gardens.

The one live community left on the river is Carmacks, now nothing more than a truck stop at the point where the Alaska Highway touches the Yukon. This, too, is historic ground, named for George Carmack, who ran a trading post here and mined soft coal before he found the nugget that touched off the great stampede. The seams of coal can still be seen on the riverbank, just before the famous Five Fingers rapids. Here, the river, caught between two cliffs, seems to be blocked by a wall of broken rock. Through that barrier, the water has torn five narrow channels or "fingers." The rock itself is conglomerate, composed of various small shales forced together like bricks by the pressure of time. These four pinnacles, jagged and misshapen, are rendered more grotesque by the trees and shrubs that grow out from them. Between and around these flower-pot islands, the river races savagely. In the old days, the steamboats on the downstream run used to slip through the right-hand channel and over the ledge of rock in a matter of minutes, but the struggle upriver, especially in low water, was a different matter. It took hours to winch the boat through, so slowly that it seemed to make no headway at all in its struggle with the ten-mile current.

Five Fingers rapids is the only real impediment on the Yukon for all of its 2,200 miles. The easiest way through is by the steamboat passage on the right. On the high bank above, you can see a white smear about a foot beneath the topsoil, uncovered by erosion. This is a layer of volcanic ash, about a foot deep, known locally as Sam McGee's Ashes. It runs for many miles through the great valley of the Yukon. Centuries ago this entire region was smothered in ash from what must have been an awesome volcanic explosion.

Geologically, the Yukon valley is very ancient. The interior plateau was too dry to support much rainfall, most of which fell on the other side of the Coastal Mountains. Thus the Ice Age, which covered so much of the country, did not intrude upon the Yukon. The original drainage pattern is still to be seen in the series of terraces that rise like gigantic steps from the river to the hilltops. Ages ago, when the Yukon was young and these great valleys did not yet exist, this was unstable land, forever tilting, heaving, and rumbling. These various upheavals produced the wonder of the present broad valley, where the benchland drops off in successive steps. Looking up at the hills through half-closed eyes, one seems to be gazing on a gigantic staircase.

On the old steamboat charts, every bend in the river has a name – Vanmeter Bend, Keno Bend, Fourth of July Bend, Steamboat Bend. This last bend coils around a long peninsula, and here, in the old days, the steamboat would stop to let off those passengers who wanted to cross the neck of the peninsula, pick flowers, and enjoy the fresh air. An hour or so later they would join the steamboat on the far side.

There is something new to see around every bend, for the river itself changes and shifts from year to year. Islands vanish, reappear, change shape, diminish, or join onto others, depending on the vagaries of the weather, the current, or the season. At Fourth of July Bend there is an immense escarpment – Dutch Bluff – and at the mouth of the Pelly, a spectacular wall of rock – a sheer cliff of columnar basalt that rises 450 feet to a poplar-topped plateau. It runs for eighteen miles downriver to Twin Falls, looking as if it were fashioned by some monstrous hand.

The oldest community on the river is found at the point where the tawny Pelly pours into the Yukon. Founded as a Hudson's Bay Company post in 1848 by Robert Campbell, Fort Selkirk was destroyed by the Chilkat Indians in 1852, forcing Campbell to make the longest snowshoe journey on record – three thousand miles to the railhead at Crow Wing, Minnesota. The post was never rebuilt, but in my day Selkirk was a lively community. Today, the police post, the Taylor and Drury store, two abandoned churches, and a mission school are still standing. It was to this point in 1898 that the Yukon Field Force of 203 soldiers was dispatched by the Canadian government to show the flag and prevent the Yukon territory from falling into American hands. The outlines of the old parade square can still be found, and the military cemetery not far away is kept in good condition.

The Yukon, which was once light green upriver from Whitehorse, and then baby blue, becomes a rich brown after the Pelly joins it. It changes colour again when the White River pours in on the left. This great stream is choked, as its name implies, with glacial silt and probably volcanic ash from the Kluane Range of mountains. The mouth of the White is blocked by islands formed from that same silt, their wet and colourless flanks encumbered by the bleached trunks and branches of dead trees swept downstream in the high water and left in heaps on the sandbars. These "snags" clog the river for miles, a menace to small boats, some of which have been caught in their clutches and swamped. The same danger can also occur at the mouth of the Stewart, which pours in from the right. What remains of Stewart City – a thriving settlement in the days when steamboats pushed barges of silver ore down from the mines at Keno Hill – can be found on an island in the main stream. I remember when Stewart had a Northern Commercial store, a post office, a telegraph station, servicing facilities, and a cluster of trappers' cabins. But the river has eaten away half of the island – the buildings that have survived have been moved well back from the crumbling bank – and the population is down to four.

Dawson City lies a day's journey downriver from Stewart City. Beneath the boat one now hears a rasping, hissing sound, as if some strange river creature was whispering to itself beneath the waters. In reality, it's the sound of the silt scraping softly against the bottom of the Zodiac. It adds to the spectral quality of the river.

In Dawson, the old buildings still stand, teetering like drunken miners along the main streets. A good many, however, have been restored by the federal government, for Dawson City itself has become a heritage site. It is, in my view, the single most interesting community in Canada, but then I am biased, for it was here that I was raised, in the days when the river was a broad highway linking us to the outside world, when the familiar sound of the steamboat whistle echoed over the rounded hills, when the *chug-chug* of the paddle wheel was as soothing as a lullaby, and no ghosts yet haunted the river of my childhood.

DIONNE BRAND

# Just Rain, Bacolet

Back. Here in Bacolet one night when the rain falls and falls and falls and we swing the door wide open and watch the rainy season arrive I think that I am always travelling back. When the Chaca-laca bird screams coarse as stones in a tin bucket, signalling rain across this valley, when lightning strafes a blue-black sky, when rain as thick as shale beats the xora to arrowed red tears, when squat Julie trees kneel to the ground with the wind and I am not afraid but laugh and laugh and laugh I know that I am travelling back. Are you sure that this is not a hurricane, Faith and Filo ask. No, I say, with certainty, it's just rain. I know this, it's just rain . . . just rain, rain is like this here. You can see it running toward you. And this too, don't fight the sea and don't play with it either that shell blowing means there's fish in the market and yes I'd forgot-ten the water from young green coconuts is good for settling the stomach, you have to cut or scrape the skin off shark before you cook it otherwise it's too oily, this prickly bush, susumba, the seed is good for fever, and the bark of that tree is poison. . . . Though knowing is always a mixed bag of tricks and so is travelling back.

On one side of this island is the Atlantic and on the other the Caribbean sea, and sometimes and very often or if you drive up, up the sibilances of Signal Hill to a place called patience, yes Patience Hill, you can see both. There are few places that you can go to without seeing the sea or the ocean, and I know the reasons. It is a comfort to look at either one. If something hard is on your mind and you are deep in it, if you lift your head you will see the sea and your trouble will become irrelevant because the sea is so much bigger than you, so much more striking and magnificent that you will feel presumptuous.

Magnificent Frigate drapes the sea sky, Magnificent Frigate. Bird is not enough word for this . . . nor is it enough for the first day just on the top of the hill at Bacolet that red could draw a flamboyant against such blue and hill and cloud and the front end of the car floats between them . . .

. . . at first I went alone, was brought, arrived, came, was carried, was there, here, the verb is such an intrusive part of speech, like travelling, suggesting all the time invasion or intention not to leave things alone, so insistent, you want to have a sentence without a verb, you want to banish verb.

Anyway I was carried by the way they'd cut the road, fast and narrow and with magic because always it was impossible for two cars to pass each other but it happened and magic because one afternoon cutting through the rain forest on Parlatuvier Road to Roxborough but right in the middle of the rain forest a woman and soft in the eyes and old like water and gentle like dust and hand clasped over the hand of her granddaughter little girl appeared, walking to Roxborough. So we stopped, seeing no house nearby which she may have come from or be going to. The road was treed and bushed all sides, epiphytes hung from the Palmiste and immortelle and we stopped to her "Thank you darling, thank you. What a sweet set of children! I going just down the road. Thank you darling." To be called darling and child, we knew that it was magic because no one, no stranger in the last

twenty-four years of my life and in all of Faith's living in the city
we had left, had called us child and darling. We stared at her grinning. We settled into her darling and child just like her granddaughter settled into her lap. Magic because she had appeared on
the road with her own hope, a hope that willed a rain forest to
send a car with some women from North America eager for her
darling, her child, or perhaps she wasn't thinking of us at all but of
walking to Roxborough with her granddaughter to buy sugar or
rice and her darling and child were not special but ordinary, what
she would say to any stranger, anyone, only we so starved for
someone to call us a name we would recognise loved her instantly.

One day we are standing in a windmill, no, standing in a windmill trying to avoid the verb to meet which is not enough for
things which exist already and shadow your face like a horizon.
We climbed to the top of the windmill at Courland Bay with S.
The wooden banisters have been eaten away by termites. They've
eaten the insides of the wood, ever existing, trying to avoid the
verb to meet, as I, we. We learn that you cannot hold onto the
banisters though the outside looks as it might have looked then.
She had told us what year, some year in another century, 1650 or
perhaps 1730. We climbed to the top passing through bedrooms
the windmill now holds, the bats' droppings in the abandoned
rooms, then outside to the top, up the iron stairs. That is when she
said that it had been here, a sugar mill, a plantation, and there
were the old buildings, traces of them, there since then. That is
when she showed us the old building, near the caretaker's house,
near the cow roaming on her thick chain, near the governor plum
tree, tangled up in mimosa and razor grass, but not covered and
not all of it there. We learn that you cannot come upon yourself so
suddenly, so roughly, so matter of factly. You cannot simply go to a
place, to visit friends, to pick mangoes on your way to the beach
and count on that being all. You cannot meet yourself without

Faith at Parlour on the Windward Road

being shaken, taken apart. You are not a tourist, you must understand, you must walk more carefully because you are always walking in ruins and because at the top of a windmill one afternoon on
your way to the beach near Courland Bay you can tremble. At the
top of a windmill one afternoon on your way to bathe in the sea
when you stop off to pick some mangoes you might melt into your
own eyes. I was there at the top of the windmill taken apart, crying for someone back then, for things which exist already and
exist simply and still. Things you meet. I am afraid of breaking
something coming down. Something separates us.

   We leave the top of the windmill and the owner who is still
talking about carving it up and selling it in American dollars and
go to talk to the caretaker who feels more like home, more like
people. He knows the kind of talk we need, talk about the rich
and the poor, talk about why you can weep when looking at this

place, talk that sounds quiet in the trembling and razor grass, as if he understands that there are spirits here listening and we must wait our turn to speak or perhaps what they are saying is so unspeakable that our own voices cut back in the throat to quietness. This is where it happened and all we can do is weep when our turn comes, when we meet. Most likely that is the task of our generation, to look and to weep, to be taken hold of by them, to be used in your flesh to encounter their silence. All over there are sugar mills even older, filled with earth and grass. Now everything underfoot is something broken.

Faith went to the Rex last night. It was Friday, the latest Robert Redford movie. Not because she likes Robert Redford but because it's the only cinema and she loves the movies. She loves the Rex with its hand-painted sign, freshly painted every Wednesday when the movie changes. I am scared of the movies. Scared since I was small. Scared because I was afraid of people and because the movies was new and something you had to learn to go to and take care of yourself when you were there. Going to the cinema, you needed money and you needed to dress up and you were in public where people could see if you were dressed up or had the money. And if you didn't have enough money you had to sit in pit where there were a lot of rough boys who made rude remarks about girls and tried to touch you and went to the cinema just to do this and to heckle the screen or imitate the star boy if it was a Western. I was fearful too that what I would see on the screen would confirm the place we occupied in the world. We were going to see how much better white people lived than us and how far away the reach to that living was because we would have to reach into white skin to live it. The re-enactments always came up slightly short. The lipsticked white beauties and the slicked back white macho twisted us into odd shapes on tropical streets; made us long for black turtlenecked sweaters, blue jeans and leather jackets and cowboy hats. So having only this memory of cinema in the Caribbean I didn't go to the Rex with Faith to see *Indecent Proposal* and she went because she didn't believe me, being much more adventurous than I and having grown up when the movies wasn't new or scary but the first primer of the culture as much as the primary text of mine was the British canon. When she came back she said it was lovely, yes lovely, that the whole cinema heckled Robert Redford and Demi Moore and the guy from *White Men Can't Jump*. They laughed and jeered at American romanticism. Perhaps something in a Black cinema in a Third World country makes a screen full of white patriarchy and desire as money seem silly, unlikely and grotesque – unbelievable. Nobody was buying it and not just because it was a silly-ass movie in any terms but nobody was buying the general screen. She said she finally felt a whole audience feeling like her and more. Outside of the screen and critical, belonging to another intellectual cosmos that was not craziness but sense. And nothing that ever came on the screen at the Rex would be seen with anything other than this sense. She had spent so much of her life in lonely deconstruction of the American movie text that the Rex was home, the true meeting of the hegemonic and the counter hegemonic and the counter hegemonic made more than sense, it was normal. But deeper, they were laughing. The crowd, probably blue-jeaned and longing in every other way for America, found America laughable. So I changed my mind about the Rex but I still never went, still so fearful that she went every Friday by herself or with a woman we'd met waiting tables in a restaurant. One Friday night I met her on the street in between a double bill. She was looking for coffee, the street which circled the harbour was packed brightly with young women and men, liming, hanging. Her face came luminous and teary in the crowd. I went to meet her. I thought that she might have been lonely because I hadn't gone with her but it wasn't loneliness, it was ordinariness that moved her. She wanted to keep walking in the crowd on Friday night and going to the Rex.

Travelling is a constant state, you do not leave things behind or take them with you, everything is always moving, you are not the centre of your own movement, everything sticks, makes you more heavy or more light as you lurch, everything changes your direction. We were born thinking of travelling back. It is our singular preoccupation, we think of nothing else. I am convinced. We are continually uncomfortable where we are. We do not sleep easily, not without dreaming of travelling back. This must be the code written on the lining of my brain, go back, go back, like a fever, a pandemic scourging the Diaspora. Go back, the call words waiting for an answer. How complicated they can get all the journeys to the answer, all the journeys, physical and imaginary, on airplanes, on foot, in the heart and drying on the tongue. Faith and I glimpse it here. When we first get off the airplane and slip into our skin the gravity of racial difference disappears. But it is this and more, a knowledge we slip into, a kind of understanding of the world which will get us through. Here we only have to pay attention to what we do. One night Vi called; said, do you want to see a leatherback turtle, she's laying her eggs on Turtle Beach. We went. I felt called as I do for every event here. Surrounded so by spirits, history, ancestors, I give over to their direction. I realize that I live differently in Canada. I live without connection to this world with its obligations, homage, significances, with how you are in the soul.

A woman told me a story last week of how a man from Quebec who had laid floors for a living had all his money stolen on the beach by thugs. "He show me his knees from working and he knees mash up," she said, "and when I look at them knees I say to myself if that man ever kneel down on them knees and pray for that thief, put a light on that thief, God help him. Is so people does look for trouble." She understood the power in his knees in ways that the man from Quebec could not. Knees like that were a weakness where he came from.

So I was called to a great thing. The leatherback turtle came up on the beach like this that night. Every May they come up on Turtle Beach to lay hundreds of eggs, I had forgotten. And when the eggs hatch after six weeks, tiny turtles scramble to the sea under the predaceous swooping of pelicans and frigates. The hotel, its light and customers, intrude on this beach but this part of the sea is inscribed on all the generations of leatherbacks, so they come even as investment and real-estate brokers gobble up the sand and water. One came making circles and digging her back fins into the sand and then she left without laying. The sand there was too hot, Vi said. So she went back into the sea waiting for another time. Later down the beach we came on another. When my eyes became accustomed to the dark I saw her. She was ancient, her head larger than a human's but somehow human-like and her eyes full of silver tears, her skin, black with tiny white spots, wrinkled. She dug a nest in the sand behind her, measuring, measuring the length of her fin. Then I heard her sigh, a sound like an old woman working a field, a sound more human than human and old, like so much life or so much trouble and needing so much rest. This is how old I'd like to be, so old I'll cry silver, sigh human. But I must say here truly how I felt as if she was more than I or more than human, higher on the evolutionary ladder, beyond all surmising or calculation, nothing that we could experience, greater than us not because we had said so but because she was. I watched her for over an hour, dig and measure, dig and measure and then lay her eggs. I went closer to see them and remembered eating one as a child on another beach – "I've seen this before," I told Vi, "when I was little" – eating something it had taken the leatherback fifty or sometimes seventy years to make, delicate and soft after more than half a century. I remembered the torch lights cutting shadow along that other beach and my grandfather digging for the eggs of this now endangered species. She was seventy by her size, broad as the span of my arm and as tall as I am laying down and when she was done and sighed again she covered the hole in the sand and began circling, camouflaging the place she had laid her eggs, making other places looking the same until I could not tell where she had laid them. A leatherback turtle cries on a night like this, her tears are silver and when she is done circling, doing all that she can do she heads laboriously for the sea. She seemed tired. She spun down to the shore, waited for a wave and then plunged, washed, splendid, rode into the sea.

We are so eager to return, our powers of recognition isolate only evidence in support of a place. So I did not mention the unnecessary clutter of tourists and cameras which had to be policed and. . . . So I took this as a gift, this intimacy I intruded on at Turtle Beach, with the tourists, the ones we had to shush, and the lights and the hotel and the cigarette-smoking man Vi told "have a little respect." I measured only the space that the leatherback and I occupied. I took it as part if not all the answer to going back.

We drank Carib up to the last drinking spot on the Northside Road to Moriah, Castara, and Parlatuvier. We stopped, asking for my grandmother's people in Moriah. She was born in Moriah to Angelina Noray and a man named Bobb. I asked an old big gentle man coming down the road where the Norays lived, knowing that all I needed to do was mention a last name and whether they had vanished or were still alive the name would conjure them. "Well, the ones on the hill or on the flat?" he asked. "I'm looking for my grandmother's people, she leave here long, long ago. She had a brother name Dan." "A long time ago. Daniel. Well is the ones on the flat you want then." We looked to where he pointed in the high lush valley that is Moriah. I did not go to the shelf in the hill to see them, just said thank you, comforted, and pointed the car up the Northside Road, remembering his arm pointing to the luxuriant bamboo where my people came from.

"See, see Moriah, Moriah, Moriah, See, see Moriah, Moriah, Moriah, Dingolay lay lay lay lay oh . . ." See Moriah. This children's song comes back to us and Vi and I speculate as to what it might have meant. We hope it was a place to escape to. We know that they do a wedding dance here, only ceremonial now, dating back to the nineteenth century. "See see Moriah Moriah Moriah. See see Moriah, Moriah Moriah Moriah. Dingolay lay lay lay lay oh dingolay one boy one girl . . ." Marriages not being allowed to property, we speculate that perhaps the enslaved ran to this high valley to dance the wedding dance as a sign of revolt and self-affirmation.

Just last night in the Scarborough public library we listened to an architectural anthropologist from the University of Florida talk about the way the French built sugar mills and the way the British built sugar mills and the way the Spanish built sugar mills, how they used the wind and the water, their drains and ditches, the proximity of their great houses to the mills. . . . He said nothing about the people who built them and worked them because he was an architectural anthropologist and not concerned with people but he did make an attempt to appease us by saying that the Moriah wedding was a blend of the European and the African cultures. It never occurred to him that it was in poor taste and perhaps even foolhardy to stand before us and call European conquest and African enslavement a blend. It didn't occur to him to think of the Moriah wedding as a mask, a more than simple duality suggesting mockery, irony, picong, self-affirmation, absence, change, recognition, and antimony. Later, he introduced his protégé, also from the University of Florida, who was a social anthropologist who said that he in fact was interested in the

Dionne and friend on the Windward Road

people who worked in the mills and that at Courland Bay he had found English crockery in a place that he had identified as slave quarters. This suggested to him that the slaves and the master had a relationship of cordiality. He led us to believe that at Courland Bay, which used to be one of the largest slave plantations boasting hundreds of acres and hundreds of slaves, the master let his slaves drink from imported English teacups. He beamed in a kind of self-absolution, a kind of brotherhood, and sat down to the grateful applause of the representatives of the local and island government and the historical society.

"That is what does happen when you let people into your business." Parlatuvier, Parlatuvier, Parlatuvier, old talk, old talk or furnace pipe what is the meaning, Castara, Castara cast away, cast away, next to Englishman's Bay. I'd rather the mystery of names and I'll keep to myself all the women on the island and where we met them. These maps are for passing word of mouth, the way to another place like Moriah for purposes of dancing and lovemaking. And we left some conversations for lesbian anthropologists who also read looks and movement and the inclination of figures and the shortness and silence of this passage as cryptic as the signals for escape.

A long time ago I think I fled this because flight is as strong as return; the same, often. One is not the end of the other or the beginning of the next and often when we go back all we can think of is flight. And in flight. . . . But this time I wanted to stay. We wanted to stay. This ease we slip into leaves us stranded once we have to disappear again. The closer we get to home the more we disappear, contemplating immigration lines and police lines and bank lines and just bullshit lines.

"I know why we don't want to go home. What we have to deal with is not understandable, it's crude and mean-spirited."

"We live with hatred all around us don't we? Exploding the skin."

"It damages us. Damages every part of us but mostly your soul."

"We have to live so small there; here at least there is the simple, simple assumption of goodwill."

NICOLE BROSSARD

# Between the Freud Video Club and the Jung Café

*(Translated by Sheila Fischman)*

"Here the space shudders wildly, like a lunatic."
— Alejan Ira Pizarnik

Between Montreal and Buenos Aires there is a ten-hour flight, there are hundreds of phrases and a few sensations, always the same ones, that converge towards fiction. I cannot compare my thoughts with the sea. My thoughts are transitory. They fly past at full speed between the airport and Salguero Street, where I shall be living during the next three weeks. Tomorrow morning I'll drink my first coffee in Liliana's garden. A tiny garden where the scent of roses mingles with Liliana's perfume. I have often tried to describe that green space, whose indescribable silence rekindles in me a joy so intense that words disappear as they hug the vines and roots that run along the wall and cause the flagstones on the ground to crack. In this garden the *portena* in me experiences, inexplicably, a strong sensation of existing.

Around ten o'clock, when the sun is already high and the word "torrid" settles into my thoughts, I shall cross the street to buy a newspaper, *Pagina 12*, then I'll go to the Sandwicheria for my

A Sunday morning tango, San Thelmo

Plaza Mayo

second coffee. The waiter will have aged four years. He will have the same smile, he'll repeat after me "*una media luna*" to be quite certain that I want a croissant. I'll light a cigarette as I look out the window at the yellow light that is circulating among the taxis.

Then I'll open my notebook. For the hundredth time, I'll try to understand why Buenos Aires has entered my life like a riddle to be decoded, like the plan for a novel.

During the day, images will stream by, with their sensations: the display put on by the jacaranda trees in blossom, the infernal pollution of Santa Fé Avenue, the tango – a melody, the blade of a knife.

Around five o'clock, on Guemez Plaza, I'll sit among the children and the passersby. Then, walking slowly, I'll return to the house. Between the Freud Video Club and the Jung Café perhaps I'll meet the poet Victor R. and his wife, a psychoanalyst. It is said that this neighbourhood is home to a great many psychoanalysts, so that part of the identity of Argentina drifts, impalpable, between walls, doors, alcoves. In the end it has exerted over me a strange fascination in the men and women walking by, causing me to imagine their clandestine colour, their obscure fears, their persistent desire for life. The word "couch" is always with me. And at night my dreams are woven of Spanish words, of Montreal landscapes and women's faces. The words and the faces are intertwined amid a turbulent scenario, then they converge – procession or process – towards a long sentence that in my half-sleep I try every time to transcribe in the notebook that lies on the table by my bed for just that purpose.

I sometimes think that if Buenos Aires is to exist, it must pass through the filter of fiction. And so I won't say much here about my own obsession with the city. I'm jealously keeping that for my next novel. I won't tell about the city until the day when one of my characters saunters onto Corrientes Street to hang around the bookstores and cafés that give you an urge to write and to dream; the day when after spending a long time looking at the houses of San Telmo, my narrator enters a church. It will be Palm Sunday.

In the garden of Liliana

The church will be packed. The strong smell of incense will suffuse people's clothes. The priest will talk that day about the woman taken in adultery. My narrator will be amazed to hear *mujer* and *mujeres* so often in the mouth of a bald old man who is haranguing the faithful as priests did in the days of my childhood in Montreal.

Tomorrow, I'll go walking in the cemetery at La Recoleta. Walk slowly, like the young woman in the novel who is conversing with a disturbingly beautiful woman. The two women stand there in the gentle morning light. They talk about Borges and Silvina Ocampo. Later, one of them will suggest going to Lola's for lunch. The other will prefer a little Italian restaurant on La Placita where Borges and other writers used to meet. I won't be able to describe La Placita, because whenever I've gone there I've been so engrossed in conversation I've seen nothing but the great trees that cast their petals and their shadows on the faces of my hosts.

Between Montreal and Buenos Aires are New York, Miami, the Caribbean, Rio de Janeiro, Montevideo. And yet my thoughts head straight for Buenos Aires. Today is Thursday. Plaza de Mayo. I march in silence behind a tall woman someone says is Hebe Bonafini. A slight breeze lifts her white head scarf. I can see the nape of her neck, the place where thoughts make the link between heart and memory. The nape is frail and powerful. The daylight is brilliant. As I look at her nape, I see them, some in jeans, others completely naked, the women in torn dresses. One by one the *desaparecidos* fall into my gaze and into the sea. Violently, they are swallowed up by the waves of Rio. Now I am walking next to Bonafini. On her cheeks, spindrift or memory, the sea is a child.

Little by little I lose myself in my thoughts, in the place where I am vulnerable and desiring. Now my thoughts are flying full speed towards Montreal. Tomorrow I'll drink my first coffee at my own worktable. I'll be excited, troubled, obsessed with desire for Buenos Aires. Despite the early hour, the whole house will be taken over by Piazzola's tangos. I shall feel the heat. I shall be afraid to start the novel. I shall have aged four years. Outside, the snow. *

---

*Later that night, when the snow has given the night the glimmers and the creases of a Northern landscape, I'll write to Connie Rooke and apologize for sending such a short text about Buenos Aires. I'll tell her: "Connie, sorry, all the words went back to my novel. Maybe I should have written about Eden Mills, September 12, 1993, when we all gathered to read, to talk, to listen under the trees, close to the water and the mill, maybe, Connie, I should have written about this wonderful Eden Mills Writer's Festival day when readers' and writers' shoulders touched slightly, enough so they could enter fiction while the clouds and the sun alternated over their thoughts.

"Could it be that places we've deeply felt for always surface as fiction: between a sentence and a set of images?"

JUNE CALLWOOD

# Swimming Around the Planet

As a child I lived in Belle River, a village on Lake St. Clair, which is part of the Great Lakes chain. I learned to swim there, and when I was ten and we moved to Kitchener, I was delighted to find that the municipal pool was two blocks from our house. Like almost everyone in the neighbourhood, I hung out at the pool all summer long. I made the city's swimming team, won some ribbons for backstroke and diving, and worked a bit as a lifeguard. The love of swimming has never left me; when I travel I want water.

I don't mean a hotel swimming pool with deck chairs set out on Astroturf and a concentration of chlorine that makes the eyes burn. I once swam in a pool on the roof of a hotel in the Latin Quarter of New Orleans, and that was all right, and outside Phoenix are hotel pools with waterfalls, but what I'm after is a stretch of blue ocean with whitecaps rolling over to hiss in the sand.

For some years after our older children left home, in a time when travel was cheap, my husband, Trent Frayne, and I could afford to explore much of the globe. Nowadays we rarely venture beyond motoring distance, but once we were a footloose pair, considering the fact we were freelance writers with a bank overdraft. I savour most the places where I could swim.

Bermuda is the best, the very best. The sand there is the texture of talcum powder, and the sea is the improbable colour of blue ink. Horseshoe Bay on the south shore of Bermuda has the finest beach on the planet, a curve of sand between arms of rock that hold back rough waves. As you wade out to swim, the water is so clear you can see your shadow on the white sand of the sea's bottom. When you submerge you are in warm, weightless heaven.

The adjacent swimming area belonging to the magnificent and very expensive Southampton Princess Hotel is less appealing, but Horseshoe Bay has a public beach spacious enough to provide everyone with a cone of privacy. The next-best beach in Bermuda is at the Coral Beach and Tennis Club down the road. Once, exploring the tiny coves that are accessible only by water, I disturbed hundreds of crabs sunning themselves on the face of the cliff. A cascade of dry-clicking crabs hurled themselves in panic into the sea at about the same velocity at which I departed.

Swimming in the open sea necessarily involves my reluctant acceptance of the reality that other living things inhabit the water where I perform my Australian crawl, *circa* 1935. Once, off Fort Lauderdale, Florida, blissfully stroking along a goodly distance from shore, I was bumped by a large and solid *thing* that slipped away after knocking me upright. The lifeguard didn't want to tell me it might have been a shark. "A barracuda?" he suggested.

Fort Lauderdale's famous broad beach has an area at the south end where I have spent entire days. I bring with me a folding chair, a towel, a beach mat, an apple, some trail mix, a mini-bottle of wine, and a nineteenth-century novel. I swim, I read, I watch the shorebirds glaring at one another, and I close my eyes for long stretches of time to listen to the surf unknotting my soul.

Fort Lauderdale also has the biggest swimming pool I've ever known. Olympic-size, with an Olympic diving pool, it is a training site for American college teams, which thrash the length of it tirelessly. When the steroid-jumped hulks are gone, quiet descends, and the placid lap swimmers take over, each scrupulously respectful of the other's lane.

You can't swim in Tokyo or Beijing or London or Madrid or Hong Kong, or at least I didn't find anywhere, but those places offer other pleasures. Paris, however, has a huge floating piscine moored on the left bank of the Seine. It seems to be a haven for sunbathers, men and women in string bikinis with splendid young bodies; serious swimmers upset the sultry mood of pre-coital display.

If you are in Lisbon you can go to Estoril, a noble resort on the Atlantic, where people change right on the beach, squirming inside portable tents that look like a tube of shower curtain.

Leave nothing in your car at Estoril, even if you lock it tight. Thieves broke into a rental that we parked by the beach and stole the prettiest party dress I have ever owned.

If you are in Rome you are informed that you can swim at its ancient port, Ostia, but don't do it. The beach is a vile black, and human excrement floats in the water.

Don't swim at Dubrovnik either, even if peace descends on Yugoslavia. The hotels are on cliffs, and you descend from the lobby at street level to a swimming dock far below, where the Adriatic heaves and subsides dramatically. I was clinging to a ladder on the cliff wall, preparing to launch myself into the surging water, when I noticed floating around me a profusion of Pepsi cans and used condoms tied in bow knots.

The French riviera has famous beaches, but the Mediterranean isn't a paradise for swimmers, The water somehow doesn't seem fresh, and many beaches are stony. While I was swimming at Nice on a day of crashing waves, my bathing suit filled with pebbles. At Nice and Cannes, the waterside restaurants are the real draw. They are located right on the beach, and you can rent luxurious sun lounges under sparkling umbrellas and be tended by a hovering waiter. Changing rooms and toilets are convenient, and when you are hungry you can repair to the restaurant for a delicious lunch. Topless, if you wish.

Portugal's Algarve is wonderful. The beach stretches below towering chalky cliffs which throw back the sound of the somnambulant sea. One afternoon there, I was approached by a saleswoman with a basket of tablecloths on her head. I selected one, deep blue with white, hand-stitched embroidery and twelve matching napkins, and indicated to her that I would have to go back to the hotel for the money. She thrust the tablecloth at me and marched away up the beach. I watched her till she was out of sight, amazed, then went to my room and got my wallet. I waited a long time for her to reappear so I could pay her.

Whenever I use the cloth I think of that day, and the stranger who trusted me.

Antigua has beautiful beaches dotted with thatched roofs set on stilts through which the warm wind rattles. We stayed at the Anchorage, where we had breakfast on a patio with a view of the sea and fed crumbs from our muffins to tiny yellow birds no bigger than flowers. At night we dressed in our finest and, holding our shoes in our hands, walked barefoot through the surf under a full moon to an exquisite French restaurant on the sand, where we dined gloriously on freshly caught fish.

Once I stayed at Las Brisas in Acapulco in a Barbie-doll fantasy of a pink cottage with a white tile floor and its own private pool on which flowers floated. The pool was only dipping size, so real swimmers rode down the mountain in a pink jeep to the hotel's swimming area – a bay on the beach. The swimming was fine, but leaving the water was a challenge; ankle-biting fish lurked on the submerged stairs.

The beaches near Honolulu in Hawaii are a challenge for swimmers, being more suited to surfers, but Cuba offers some terrific swimming. In general, I find, island beaches provide more variety than can be found on mainland coasts. Nantucket, for instance, gives swimmers a choice: either the wild, exhilarating waves on the shore that faces the sweep of the Atlantic, or the staid, family-style beaches of the sheltered harbour. Swimming in the sedate sea one moonless night, I was enchanted by the phosphorus in the water that glowed behind me with an eerie light as I moved through it.

Nantucket is sophisticated. On the final day there one year, when we were celebrating the vacation with a split of champagne and a beach picnic, the cork of the sun-warmed champagne popped with the sound of gunfire and flew through the air, coming down on a man who was lying on his back basking in the sun. He sat up, startled, checked the brand name on the cork, and lay back again.

The warmest water for swimming in my experience was a shallow lagoon in St. Lucia late in the season, and the coldest, without question, was Clear Lake, Manitoba, in June 1944. My husband was raised in Brandon, and Clear Lake represented to him boyhood delights. We went there for our honeymoon, though it was so early in the season that most of the resort was still closed. He went out on some errand and I slipped into my bathing suit, ran down to a dock, noted that the depth was safe for diving, and plunged in. The shock of the frigid glacial waters, from which the ice had only recently melted, almost stopped my heart.

The happiest swimming I know is less than two hours from where we live in Toronto. At least once a summer, the whole family disperses itself in as many cars as we need and drives to Port

Dover, a fishing village on Lake Erie. We start with a hamburger at the Arbor, an open-air stand that has been there most of this century, and then set up the day's headquarters on blankets spread a few feet from the water's edge, the better to watch our toddlers.

Someone has to make sorties to the sidewalk stand that sells fried perch or shrimp, and someone has to walk the younger children the length of the pier to the lighthouse, but mostly we loaf and swim, loaf and swim. At Port Dover the lake is safe; it is so shallow that a child can be far from shore, a distant figure dancing in the breakers, and still be only up to her knees.

When the heat gets to us, the adults wade and wade and wade and *wade*, and finally can flop in the water at a depth sufficient to take a stroke without scooping sand. Sailboats bob about, the gulls are fat on the remains of hotdog rolls, and small children squeal as they throw themselves on the waves.

Life doesn't offer anything sweeter; not my life, anyway.

# GEORGE ELLIOTT CLARKE

# To Paris, Burning

## *Approaches to Paris*

As an eight-year-old, growing up in the hellish North End of Halifax, I saw Paris burning, the City of Light as a city of flames. In May 1968, barricades had gone up in the streets there, while Pierre Trudeau loped towards a landslide, Bobby Kennedy towards martyrdom, and the Soviets towards Prague. Blurred photos of students tossing molotov cocktails at bizarrely helmeted police swam up at me from the glossy pages of *Life* magazine. Paris was just one more metropolis ablaze – like Memphis, like Montreal.

At seventeen, while Halifax policed my quarter criminally, I crammed my skull with fugitive Funkadelic sounds and crackling Malcolm X raps on scratchy vinyl. I wanted firebombs. My *tricolore* was the pan-Africanist red, black, and green. Paris seemed just another smouldering, white capitol.

Then, I began to pore over sheets of Black American poetry. Suddenly, I found Paris looming before me, beckoning. Under the blues influence of Conrad Kent Rivers' poem "Four Sheets to the Wind and a One-Way Ticket to France," I dreamt the city as an oasis of gorgeous freedom:

*As a child*
*I bought a red scarf and women told me how beautiful it looked,*
*wandering through the sous-sols as France wandered through me.*

I bought a thousand long scarves and longed to trace the paths of Black American exiles. Richard Wright lounged in Paris in the 1940s, James Baldwin followed in the 1950s. Duke Ellington and Miles Davis waged jazz on the Left Bank. Charlie Parker's version of "April in Paris" knifed my heart. Voluptuous images of Josephine Baker, the Siren of the Cubists, disturbed my sleep. Black art seduced me into loving Paris. I met the city as inevitably as poetry.

Twice now I've dropped everything and skipped to Paris – in 1985 and again just before CNN's "War in the Gulf" began to air. The following paragraphs and poems are my memories.

## 2 July 1985

I come with all my Black Baptist piety, all my Nova Scotian loneliness, to Paris, burning. Every book is kindling, every painting brimstone and tar. Is all we do instant dust and fire?

I fold my brain *sous les étoiles* and then awake to a cold morning of dreams, suburbs sliding past the train window. In Gare du Nord, the train station near Montmartre, I repack my knapsack while two drunks try to fleece me of my change. One of them, gawky and pop-eyed, jabs a big thumb and its yellow nail hard against my pants pocket, jiggling it, making coins clank like chains. I free myself of a useless Dutch guilder.

July 19, 1985. The city seems an open-air museum; history breathes from every stone. In the square across from the Cathedral of Notre Dame, my eyes trip over a plaque to the memory of Perrin André, a policeman who was gunned down by the S.S., in Occupied Paris, on July 19, 1944.

On the stone wall of the cathedral, the slogan of the French Revolution, *"Liberté! Egalité! Fraternité!,"* fades. What is eternal? A saxophonist flings jazz against the wind.

It shocks me to shift from the burning sunlight of July to the black coolness of the cathedral, a small, dark city of candles, a spiritual maze. The sun and moon of Time have no meaning here. All awaits the ever-imminent Apocalypse. Smells of tallow, burning flesh. Amid casual, heaped-up splendour, I yearn for the homely simplicity of a white, clapboard African Baptist church confronting the Atlantic. All the Latin in the world can't put God and humanity back together again.

Standing beside rain-pitted, rooftop gargoyles, a grey-haired Black man, speaking a mellifluous French, shepherds tourists into the bell tower. As he relates the history of the bells, he charms them into indelible music. When the visitors applaud, he jokes, *"Je suis Quasimodo."*

I tramp along the Seine. Vines reach down stone walls, brush the river. *Les bouquinistes* – riverside vendors of prints, postcards, paintings, and mom-and-pop porno – pray silently for buyers. I descend stone steps to the river – a turbid, green-brown, liquid energy as seething and sad as T. S. Eliot's Thames or Muddy Waters' blues. Packed with bloodthirsty tourists, double-decked boats drone past. The pleated water swells with tears.

Everywhere is exchange. Everything is exchange. Tour boats gutter by. I remember Langston Hughes: *"My soul has grown deep like the rivers."*

In the labyrinthine Latin Quarter, I scrounge a room at Résidence Coubertin, rue Lhomond, for sixty-three francs a night. When the reedy *concièrge* takes my passport, she scolds, "Don't you speak French in Canada?" *"Un peu,"* I answer, *oui*, a little too tired to explain the whole French-English crisis again.

I open the old, white doublepane windows onto a blue and

orange Gauguin dusk, stare at a sea of jumbled rooftops. Black birds almost jump past me into the room. The wooden chair and table look as though they've leapt out of a van Gogh. I lie down and read the love poems of Irving Layton. I think of C., her lonely visit here in 1980.

I wander into a corner bar-restaurant, write fragments of the same poem, dreaming Gauloises cigarettes, fearing my return to the pittances, the grudging dispensations of Gottingen Street, where white Haligonians creep to paw their black whores and white drugs. The soft night falls upon my eyes and skin. After three shots of Pernod, I love the Paris of imagination.

The gilt cathedrals blacken at night. Behind their backs, the red-light districts gleam.

At the Sorbonne, marbled academe, I open old wooden, brass-handled doors, expecting to free revolution. May 1968 may come again – but not yet. Under the library's high blue ceiling, students bow before the small lamps that blaze over long rows of wooden tables. A bell strikes every quarter-hour.

In May 1968, someone scrawled this message on the walls: *Les larmes des Philistins sont le nectar des dieux*. Now, *Le Pen Nazi* appears everywhere.

At the Musée de l'Armée, I peer down upon Napoleon's massive tomb. Could he rise from under all that black marble? The French must feel naked without a mantle of magnificence. Two white American women ask me who is buried in the tomb. After I tell them, they snap pictures of it.

After the display of death-camp uniforms, the photographs of Auschwitz skeletons, some still living, I drift, shell-shocked, from the Musée, walk past the Canadian Embassy. Should I enter? Will the staff recognize a *Black* Nova Scotian? I decide not to chance it.

J.W.S.C.

Walking again along the Seine, I spy two watercolour scenes of the Cathedral of Notre Dame in the windows of Editions Ephi. In the tiny store, I meet Donna, the beautiful, black-haired, Laotian owner. She likes my slow, mystical French, wants to show me Paris. I buy the two watercolours by Huertas, a local artist who paints scenes for restaurant menus, for three hundred francs.

At the Résidence Luxembourg, rue Jacques, I meet two students from Turkey. We break spring rolls at a Vietnamese restaurant, drink Tsingtao beer and jasmine tea, speak bits of English and French, pasting words into collages of phrases. When I say Canada, they say the Rockies. All else is mystery.

I buy red wine and ride the Métro to the Arc de Triomphe. I stand under the Arc, under stars, shivering, while a *gendarme* snaps back and forth around the monument. I lean against the stone with two Algerians. We split the wine and the night with curses, their tales about the white French hating their Arabic. I think of Nova Scotia, its petty hatreds. The *gendarme* yaps at my dummied French – too much darkness within the dark.

I walk down the Champs-Elysées, a boulevard strung with flags and electric lights, pick my way back to the Seine through thick, muggy night. I pass beneath a bridge where shapes huddle in the shadows. A flashlight beams at me. The Mona Lisa is a bag lady.

I hound poems from musty books and wine. I fall asleep with the full moon in my eyes.

At the Musée Delacroix, the well of impressionism, shimmering pastels spark to blazing colours. Haunted by Africans, Delacroix limns a Black character in each of his *Hamlet* drawings. *La Liberté guidant le peuple*.

A white American couple from Massachusetts assume I'm American. Then, they question my accent.

At the Louvre, I spend a single, holy hour with Egyptian art – temple paintings of black or brown figures, a blue frog on a pink-brown branch, a fish-scale dress, and a jagged-toothed underwater fox. Torch the Pompidou Centre but spare these delicate, African images.

*Ce soir*, I again visit the river, this sordid memory of the Atlantic, and perch on a floating dock. Pouring verses from red wine, I watch the tour boats drift like bright sepulchres of light. I want to wail all of my province – *Nova Scotia, Provence*. I dream of it – crow country, Black voices crying.

Amplified by rain, an alarm howls through my soul. I gut my brain on poetry, weep into flowers. Graffiti demands democracy for Algeria.

Returning to Gare du Nord, I stumble upon Montmartre. Roses, lettuce, vines spill from backyard plots. In a small square, smelling of urine and roses, I dodge dog shit to lie down on a bench. Spent cigarettes, matches, like rotted tears, litter the cobblestones. Spraypainted manifestos cover church walls. Old, wrought-iron lampposts glisten. The sun glares upon every beautiful thing. Everything is light.

## Five Psalms of Paris

### I

A poet thumbs Gauloises cigarettes, stabs air
With phrases that don't even speak for him,
Watches *une femme* brandish a voluble
Bottle of cuss, guzzle strong, bootleg jazz,
And fill her mouth with poems that judge every
Lover wanting. *Je veux six francs de vin*,
*Douze grammes de Zola*, to forget the black
Taste of money and espresso, the sour
Odour of love rotting in littered beds,
The brandy smear of prattle and gossip,
The stiletto politics this *Gaulliste*
Practises in splayed and broken *rues*,
Strict with differences, where *littérature*
Is blues skittered across Notre Dame's square.

### II

These streetlamps bowed, showered Hitler with light,
When he, in dark *triomphe*, captured these *rues*
His art had missed, light years before, when his
Watercolours had blazed and he had stooped
In damp garrets, to fatten on Beauty,
Devouring landscapes like Napoleon.

### III

There's a trick with a verb that I'm learning
To do, splintering French and hand language
With *deux Algériens*, whose history
Is frontiers, curried currencies, white sex,
And contraband cigs steeped enough to swill.
We watch traffic curve around the Arc de

Triomphe like light passed through gravity, like
Colonies pasteurized, bled white, by France.

### IV

*Dans le café*, students drink and go,
Contrasting Le Pen and Steven Biko.

### V

In Montmartre, American Vandals,
Bristling with cameras as lewd as missiles,
Slouch by like a dying civilization.
Meanwhile, the sun sluices down backyard plots
Stuffed with roses, shadows, grapes, and lost time.
I crumble cheese, eat apricots, chew dates,
Water everything with apple juice and wine,
While workmen scrape these stones for love. After
The hue and cry of *francs*, *la Bourse*, damn fools
Trying desperately to keep their coins,
Soon I will taste only oranges and water
Aboard a midnight train to fogged Dunkerque.


## December 1990–January 1991

Driving down the night from Amsterdam, I arrive as stars pale.
The smell of oranges mixes with the perfume the broom-wielding
green men stir up, sweeping shit off the sidewalks. I peruse strewn
streets, find coffee near Gare du Nord, keep nodding toward sleep.

Dawn erupts in Paris, shocks its citizens awake. My loud
thoughts startle birds; they knot upward into bluing light.

At the Grand Hôtel Central, 120, rue de Meaux, in the *XIX^e
arrondissement*, the owner, an old Parisian, practises a baroque

floridity. Flowers occupy his office and colonize his bedspreads, wallpaper, and tablecloths. He has pinned butterflies to the walls.

I rest all day, then feast on vegetables. Wine laughs in my throat. Light rain chills. I see the wind.

To see Paris in a soft, grey light is the right gloom. Time is tiring: I carry more and more years on my head. I think of C. Does love last longer than memory?

At the Louvre, I study Mme. Benoist's painting *Portrait d'une négresse*, admiring the ebon woman, her white headdress and white gown, the indigo fabric she sits upon. *La Liberté continue guider le peuple*.

I return to Editions Ephi, the shop near the Seine. Donna remembers me. I buy a single Huertas watercolour, a scene of the strange, sepulchral beauty of the Cathédral du Sacré Coeur. Donna invites me to a Laotian New Year's Eve Dance.

After weak but persuasive wine, rain chomps at my face. I slip inside the cavernous darkness of the Cathedral of Notre Dame. Candles – like faith – make little dents in the gloom.

January 1, 1991. I take my funny accent to the Eiffel Tower. The city explodes in light. I avoid tourists – the looks on their faces like civil war.

I scribble in my journal a thousand love poems. Conversation arches into poetry.

In the Hôtel Dorée on rue Barbès, an original but ugly oil painting of a nude stares at my bed. On the television, a bare-breasted woman sells nylons.

I riffle a *Newlook* magazine to view the recovered Dallas morgue photographs of Jack Kennedy, discover that several pages uncover Sylvie, all black lace under blue denim.

Near Château-Rouge, I find l'Étoile de Tunisie, where I order a huge sandwich filled with beef, tomato, onion, and potato, a bottle of cider, and sweet mint tea for a few sous. Tunisian wails twine with Motown soul.

In Montmartre, Cathédral du Sacré Coeur, wan light shimmies through stained glass. The sun is Christ's heart.

Africans on the white steps of Sacré Coeur sell gold tinted by barter and banter. They cook a callaloo of currencies into francs.

I go to Place du Tertre, watch artists painting tourists photographing artists. Some artists paint the same scenes and portraits amid anarchies of easels, pigeons. The marble winter enrages what's left of elms.

I wander into the little square I slept in five years ago – at the corner of rue du Mont-Cenis and rue Cortot. Spicy rain garnishes the cobblestones.

A French woman in a flower store asks me if I'm American. My accent is a dead giveaway. The air is roses.

I find the Seine again. The river is at a fever pitch. An old man fishes for truth.

In a station of the Métro, a Chinese woman plays guitar and cries blues in French. The apparition of jazz in Coltrane's "Trane's Blues" and Davis's "Ballads" at Place Saint-Michel: rain strumming the Seine.

Canada recedes slowly. The issue isn't broken promises. It's a broke and broken country.

One more time I walk streets which marble angels excoriate and judge. The white moon enflames the Seine. The *International Herald Tribune* threatens war.


## April in Paris

I wander among the graves of poets,
Stalk inspiration with a loaded pen,
And collect bunches of fresh, cold lilies.

I exult in sprays of green – vines and leaves
Vaulting over walls, flooding *avenues*.
*Une beauté* peels a newspaper from wind.

    Yet, I'm thinking of you, so, so lovely,
Rambling the ramparts of the Citadel
Of Québec. I yearn to drape you in silks,
Array you in gaudy blue-and-white flags,
But you've kept me drifting all of this time.

    If you will offer me another home –
A balcony where I may type this poem,
I will bring you wine and albescent honey.
I'll name you with the most beautiful nouns:
*Carnation, orchid, rose, iris, trillium, anemone.*

# LEONARD COHEN

## ROBERT APPEARS AGAIN

Well, Robert, here you are again talking to me at the Café de Flore in Paris. I haven't seen you for a while. I have several versions of that sonnet I wrote after your death but I never got it right. I love you, Robert, I still do. You were an interesting man, and the first friend I really quarrelled with. I'm slightly stoned on half-a-tab of speed I found in this old suit, it must be twenty years old, and I took it with a glass of orange juice – it couldn't possibly work after all this time, but here we are, talking again. I'm glad you don't tell me what it's like where you are because I have no interest in the afterlife. You're a little pissed-off as usual as if you've just come from something immensely boring. Here we are, talking about the lousy deal we negotiated for ourselves. What are you saying? Why are you smiling? I'm still working hard, Robert. I can't seem to bring anything to completion and I'm in real trouble. The speed is wearing off, or the mood, and I can't tell you an amusing story about my trouble, but you know what I mean. Of all my friends you know what I mean. Well, goodbye, Robert, and fuck you too. Your disembodied status entitles you to a lot of privileges, but you might have excused yourself before disappearing again for who knows how long.

ON THE PATH

On the path of loneliness
I came to the place of song
and tarried there
for half my life
Now I leave my guitar
and my keyboards
my drawings and my poems
my new Turkish carpets
my few friends and sex companions
and I stumble out
on the path of loneliness
I am old but I have no regrets
not one
though I am angry and alone
and filled with fear and desire
Bend down to me
from your mist and vines
O high one, long-fingered
and deep-seeing
Bend down to this sack of poison
and rotting teeth
and press your lips to the light of my heart

*The drawing on previous page is by Leonard Cohen*

# ROBERTSON DAVIES

## Getting There

I DISLIKE TRAVEL. Have, indeed, disliked it from my eleventh year, when in the company of my parents I made my first ocean voyage. I was miserably seasick and would gladly have stayed in Europe rather than attempt the return voyage. But of course I was not my own master. In my experience of travel, I have rarely been my own master. I have travelled much, and almost always at somebody else's bidding, or to go somewhere to do something for somebody, or to give somebody else pleasure.

I had my reservations about travel even before that awful voyage. I did not like travelling on trains. My father, on the contrary, liked nothing better. He was a newspaper man, and knew people everywhere, as it seemed to me, and no sooner had we boarded a train than he set out to walk its length, to see what acquaintances might be offering on the green plush seats, amid the dust and soot of the railway cars. I did not go with him. I was told to sit still and look out of the window, and that after a while he would return. I did as I was told, but in terror. Figures of authority – the brakeman or, most awesome of all, the conductor – appeared at my side and looked at me with what I now suppose was benevolence, but which seemed to me to be the questioning glances of mighty officials who could put me off the train if I had no ticket. And I had no ticket. My father always had all the tickets and all the money and was not in the least awed by men in caps with stiff peaks and ponderous silver watch chains.

My father's most disquieting habit was to leap from the train whenever it entered a station in order to buy a newspaper – for in those days newspapers had many editions, and the latest contained the most up-to-the-minute news. Would he be left behind? I agonized. Certainly not, but it was his debonair habit to swing up onto the steps of the last car on the train as it moved out of the station, while I sat in the green plush seat (the plush penetrating my shorts and teasing my skin) dying a thousand deaths. No ticket; no money; what would become of me?

Later in life I had to make many sea voyages alone, and there was a time when I crossed the Atlantic several times, reaching the icy harbour of Halifax in mid-December, and leaving its unwelcoming arms in mid-January. The North Atlantic in winter is wretchedly cold and stormy. The captains of the ships – those CPR Duchesses that made this Boreal Voyage at that time of year – knew that their decks were dangerous, because in a high sea they might suddenly be awash, and a passenger would at least get very wet, or perhaps break a leg or – Oh, horror! – be swept over the side. Therefore the decks were fitted with canvas sides, so that anyone so foolhardy as to want to walk on deck did so in semi-darkness, breathing the smell of icy wet canvas. But did anybody want to walk the deck? Not I, certainly. I could not have done so anyway, because I was too unwell, and lay in my berth for never less than three of the five days of the voyage. Lay in my berth in the misery known only to the bad sailor, which is a combination of physical nausea that culminates in a fit of vomiting about once every hour, and a dark despair that comes of knowing that nothing – nothing whatever – would make it possible for him to find a stable, plumb place to put himself on the ship. Only leaping over the side would bring about any change, and, though wretched, I drew the line at suicide.

Hopeful, as youth so mercifully is, I always imagined that I could distract myself from the motion of the ship by reading something absorbing. Not fiction. No, no, it had to be something meaty, something that would seize and hold the attention, bringing oblivion to the torments of the sea.

On one such voyage, I sought this sort of relief in a book – excellent, I am sure, but I have never since had the resolution to attempt to read it again – called *The Road To Xanadu* by John Livingston Lowes. It is a detailed examination of what Samuel Taylor Coleridge had read which might have formed the background for "The Rime of the Ancient Mariner." Meaty stuff indeed, and I was almost forgetful of the torments of the ship's heaving and rolling, when suddenly my porthole burst open and a very considerable part of the North Atlantic burst in, flooding my cabin, wetting everything in my trunk, and leaping upon the bunk like a romping dog, soaking me to the skin and drenching John Livingston Lowes. I have the book still, warped by seawater. I rang for the steward – I was in no condition to budge out of the drenching berth – who somehow managed to close the porthole and make it fast.

There was a great old row about that. The steward was determined that I had interfered with ("monkeyed" was his word) the fastening of the porthole, thus causing the accident. I was firm in my assertion that I had done nothing of the kind and would, in my prostrate condition, have been unable to do anything so mischievous. The purser gave the steward a piece of his mind, then gave me another piece – leaving him poorly equipped even for a purser on one of those ships – and it ended in a draw. This excitement did nothing for my seasickness.

After two or three days of this, I was usually able to totter to the dining saloon for a few bites to eat. Furious vomiting does, in the end, promote hunger. On those mid-winter voyages there was nobody on board who had not been compelled by some necessity to travel, and they did not make lively company. I recall a man who travelled to Europe to market British Columbia apples; he was a remorseless talker, and to this day I know more about apples than I really need. Another traveller who sticks in my mind was a young Scots engineer. He was rather a curiosity for, though he was not a priest and was over thirty, he was a virgin and wanted to talk about it.

His condition, he said, was because he had never found The Girl. That there was such a Girl he was confident, and no interim candidate or purchased companion would do. He was Saving Himself, he said. He was by no means without knowledge of the mysteries of sex. He seemed to have read a great many books about it, some of which were technical, in the engineering manner. His discussion of girls and women in general drew heavily on his technical knowledge, especially of a part of the female anatomy which he called The Pube. Smiling, gesticulating, speaking with the serious clarity of the Scot, he would harangue me about The Pube through a four-course CPR meal. I had nothing to contribute to the conversation, but that was unimportant; all he needed was an audience. I wonder if he ever found The Girl, and if he did, did he talk to her as he talked to me and the other three men at the dinner table? If he did, I can't imagine that The Girl would have had much time for him. His approach to romance was too technical, too engineering in its bias.

Something about sea travel promotes intimacy. People offer confidences, and are impudently intrusive, in a way that would never pass muster on land. I recall one voyage when, after three days of seasickness, I struggled up to the bar and ordered a glass of ginger ale. It was part of the folk-wisdom that surrounded seasickness that ginger ale was good for it.

As I sat, sipping tentatively, I was approached by an elderly man and his wife. I knew him. Everybody on board knew him, and shrank from him. He was a missionary, a Professional Good Man.

"Young fellow," he said, fixing me with a burning eye, "I'm going to give you some advice. You're killing yourself. Look at you. Pale. Rings under your eyes. No pep. And why? You've got the answer there on the table beside you. Solitary brandy-drinking, that's it. That's what has destroyed the fibre of our Prince of Wales and allowed That Woman to get her hooks into him. Now you give it up, do you hear? Give it up, before you find you *can't* give it up."

Off he marched, followed by his wife, a Good Woman, with a Good Woman's mouth (no visible lips), having done his good deed for the day.

Travel has changed much in my lifetime. For the comparative freedom – combined with instability – of the ship, we now have the confinement, the imprisonment, the shackled misery, of air travel. Air travel in which we breathe recycled air and snuff up everybody else's germs. Air travel where we are instructed before take-off about relying on the cushion of our seat for "flotation" if the plane should dive into the sea. But how do you detach the cushion from your seat when you are hemmed in by a fat man on your left and a woman with a baby on your right? Nobody ever addresses *that* problem.

I have travelled much and have greatly enjoyed some of my experience of foreign lands. But I have not liked the journey. Never. A cliché of the modern travel industry says that "Getting there is half the fun."

Not for me. Getting there is all that is wrong with travel.

# Barbados: The Very Pineapple of Perfection

*If all you want is sleep, go to bed.*
*But if you want to dream, go to Barbados.*

Every day at noon, the Pineapple Woman walks along the shore, crying her wares in front of our hotel.

"Pine–apple! Pine – apple!"

This is almost a song – and it carries up beyond the fences and across the lawns. Five or six of us leave our chairs and, bringing money, cluster in her vicinity.

"Same today as always?" she asks – as if I'd been there all my life.

"Please, missus, yes," I tell her.

Holding the pineapple up by its hank of stubby leaves, she produces a knife and proceeds to peel away the skin with a series of downward cuts that leave the fruit naked and dripping, filling the air with the sweetness of its juices. Then, without pause, she makes a second series of cuts in descending spirals, removing the pineapple's "eyes." All this while she is singing beneath her breath – barely audible.

*Jesus leads me where I wander,*
*Jesus leads me where I go. . . .*

"You want it whole or sliced?" she interrupts her song to ask.

"Sliced," I tell her.

She hands me a clear plastic bag from the woven satchel sitting on the sand by her feet. Inside, besides its load of limes, tomatoes and fresh pineapples, there is also a change purse and a clean white handkerchief. "Hold the bag down under, honey," she says, and lifts the pineapple up where her eye can judge it.

Then, with a series of flashing gestures, she drops the whole thing down in pieces into the plastic bag. I am afraid to look for fear her fingers are in there, too.

"That'll be eight dollars, Bajan, honey. Just put it there in the purse."

Roughly five Canadian dollars. Not bad for pineapple brought right to your doorstep, freshly sliced.

The Pineapple Woman must be in her seventies. Her grey hair is cropped short, most of it hidden beneath a soft wool hat. Her legs are bare and bowed. She wears a cotton dress, one day of white and blue, another day of red and yellow. Sandals on her feet, a crucifix at her throat, and several beaten silver bracelets on her arms. As she walks away along the beach, she hoists the multi-coloured satchel onto her head and, counting her take, moves on to her next encounter.

*Jesus leads me over yonder,*

*This is all I know,* she sings.

She will have walked all day before she finishes and turns for home.

It's not a large island – roughly twenty by thirty kilometres; the natural underground reservoirs in its limestone bedrock hold the purest fresh water in the Caribbean – excellent for drinking or for making the local Banks beer. The island takes its name from the shaggy fig trees that once lined its shores; in Portuguese – the language of an early visitor – they were known as *los barbados*, the bearded ones.

At the southern tip of Barbados, in the parish of Christ Church, there is a stretch of coral sand that is known as St. Lawrence Gap. To the east – with its historic churches, chattel houses, and fish market – the town of Oistins lies in the curve of a wide, green bay. This is where you go when you want to buy fish taken from the sea that morning – or fresh shrimp. Away to the west, beyond the Needham Point Lighthouse, the old city of Bridgetown spreads its narrow streets and alleyways in a maze of charming chaos. Along the roads that run between these towns, there are dozens of hotels and restaurants offering a choice of food and lodging for every taste and pocketbook.

We settle on the Casuarina Beach Club, with its lawns shaded by palm trees, almond trees, and, of course, tall, overgrown casuarinas. Everywhere you look, there are flowerbeds filled with hibiscus, orchids, and oleander. And beyond them, a gorgeous white-sand beach meets the surf.

Every morning, we sit very early on our balcony, overlooking the gardens, pools, restaurants, and tennis courts. We feed breadcrumbs to the birds while we breakfast on tea and pineapple.

Small, grey finches and tiny, hand-sized doves walk on the tiles at our feet. They are chased by Carib grackles – small, black brats with vivid yellow eyes. They have a rude, loud voice and a cocky walk that reminds me of Sammy Davis, Jr. and that famous rolling gait he used when he was playing here come the Judge! There is also a black-hooded hummingbird nesting nearby, and a pair of tiny black-and-yellow sucriers attracted by the sweetness of the cores of our pineapple slices.

For an hour or more we sit and watch – besides the birds – the first arrivals of the hotel staff, the maids and cooks and gardeners who stand and chat with one another on the paths between the flowerbeds before they go their various ways to begin the day's work. This is always a pleasant moment, with laughter rising from the gardens – a pause before the serious business of a holidayer's life takes over; the sunning – the swimming – the snacking – the shopping and the snoozing.

Having opted for a small suite with a kitchen, three or four times a week we pass through the gates and walk down a tree-shaded road past other hotels and houses to do our shopping at the local "99." It is much like a Becker's, but with character instead of sheen. It is also a general meeting place, and the yard – with its trees and fruit stands, its bicyclists and taxi drivers gathered on the steps with cigarettes and Cokes, and its joking, rambunctious kids and sedate, slow-moving elders under their parasols – is a place where a dozen stories could be had for the asking.

All the streets on the island are exceptionally narrow, and many of them have no sidewalks. Taking an evening stroll, you can all too easily find yourself staring down a racing driver as if you had wandered onto the track at Indianapolis. Cars are driven on the left-hand side, as in England, and Canadians and Americans make perfect pedestrian targets because they are always forgetting to walk on the correct side. Raised fists and screams will not help you. Run for the nearest tree.

One of the restaurants we always pass is called T. G. I. Boomer's. Boomer's is more or less exactly what its name implies – a wild ride of music, American food and beer, and hundreds of college students. Every time we go past, I think of an incident that happened before our journey began.

Waiting for our departure call in the restaurant at Pearson, we were seated near two young men who were talking about the holiday before them. From what was being said, it was obvious they were also on their way to Barbados. "All I want," said one of them, who was dressed entirely in black and who wore a silver earring, "is six square feet of sand all day and a seat at Boomer's all night."

"Boomer's?" said the other man, who favoured hot-pink ski clothes and a yellow baseball cap. "What's that?"

"Boomer's," said the Silver Earring, "is this terrific restaurant. Music all night long and women stacked three deep at the bar, wearing nothing but bikinis!"

The Yellow Baseball Cap thought about it. "Three deep, eh?" he said. His face was utterly blank. There was a pause. And then he asked, "Do they have a satellite dish?"

Passing Boomer's in the flesh, I see that, indeed, they do. I hope it made him happy.

Our favourite restaurant turns out to be one called L'Azure. Its Bajan cuisine is enhanced by a delicious touch of the Mediterranean. Its paella is superb. And if you want – as I always do – one meal that will shoot you down in flames, order the *Crevettes Méditerranée*, in which the shrimps are sautéed with chilli peppers, white wine, and lime juice. It makes a glorious fire and awakens the palate for weeks afterwards. Sort of like feeding the palate amphetamines: wake up! wake up and smell the chillies!

But L'Azure is not just about food. It is also one of the loveliest settings we found – set back from the road above the sea and open, in part, to the sky. Waves crash against the rocks and you can watch the moon and the stars while you dine. The proprietor is Monique Hinds, a brightly charming young woman who came to Canada to take her degree in business at the University of Western Ontario. Her father, Cyril Clarke, owns the Rostrevor Hotel, with which the restaurant is associated – and if you are lucky enough to be present some evening when Mister Clarke is dining alone, you may end up, as we did, having some wonderful conversation with him. And any evening, at the waterside tables you can look over the parapet and watch the translucent green of the garfish, as they dart through the waves surging against the breakwater at your feet.

Just down the street, you can have equally interesting dining companions – the little geckos gathered around each pillar light, waiting for the next course of invisible flying insects. They are true acrobats, and often venture upside-down onto the ceiling. No, they never fall. Your soup is safe.

This is Josef's – a white-stuccoed house surrounded by tamarind and almond trees. It is European to its fingertips, and although its owners are Swedish, it's the sort of restaurant you dream about when you imagine dining in the hills above Nice. The wine list is excellent – though the variety of reds is limited, as it seems to be everywhere in Barbados. Nevertheless, we find some very good Merlots and Cabernet Sauvignons. At Josef's you will be glad of these, because they serve, bar none, the best filet mignon I have ever had in my life. Tender and thick, it is superbly prepared and cooked.

From where we sit on one of our visits, we can watch the chef – a young European – through a doorless portal leading to the kitchens. All we can see is his back – but the fascination is in watching him exercise control – with perfect timing – over the simultaneous preparation of what seems a multitude of different dishes. He might be Siva, with a myriad of hands and arms – stirring, lifting, shaking, and spooning each concoction to its plate with panache and artistry.

The service at Josef's is particularly good – and, along with the glorious food, the restaurant attracts an international clientele that will keep you counting languages the way kids count licence plates. One night we hear at least eight different languages in less than an hour. This gives the flavour, to some degree, of one of those restaurants in 1940s movies where the European élite sat out the war while waiting for contraband visas that only Humphrey Bogart could secure. I kept expecting Ingrid Bergman and Paul Henreid to come through the door and sit in the corner. All Josef's lacks is Dooley Wilson and "As Time Goes By." But then, you can always hum it over to yourself.

We quickly learn that the best way to become further acquainted with the local cuisine is to find a restaurant that features a Bajan buffet – such as Brown Sugar, on the road leading down to the Hilton, at the west edge of Bridgetown. Most of what's served comes from the island or the sea nearby, in seafood and meat dishes featuring okra, bananas, curry, or lime. We also learn to avoid something called Neptune Night at one of the ritzier hotels – a gargantuan buffet of repetitious and largely tasteless dishes, followed by an equally tasteless show which, apart from the enjoyment of such ubiquitous Caribbean entertainments as limbo dancing, fire-eating and stilt-dancing, offers endless bottles of cheap rum (and cheap jokes) to the oldest, youngest, most recently married, etc., of its audience.

We learn to deal with the army of beach vendors who constantly interrupt your sunning and snoozing to offer aloe for your sunburn, handmade jewellery and coral souvenirs for your friends back home – or a full range of delights for your nightlife enjoyment. The interruptions aren't always welcome, but the barter – and the banter – is never dull.

While Barbadians can give the impression that life is a laid-back stroll beneath the trees, do not be fooled. The pace of their lives can suddenly shift into high gear.

Yellow buses hurtle through the streets as if their destination were a pit-stop in hell. For a single Barbadian dollar – less than seventy cents, Canadian – you can go just about anywhere on the island. Passengers all sit smiling, rocking back and forth with practised balance, glancing happily at one another – beating time to the endless jumped-up music streaming in the air through the open windows. The streets themselves are twisted and lumpy, carved from the coral in an age when traffic was confined to horse-drawn wagons. The driver pinches his horn at least a dozen times a minute, scattering pedestrians in all directions, the sound of it lilting and disconcertingly Parisian. All the way into town, I have the feeling we've been hijacked by a disaster novel – the kind that always ends with someone saying, Wow, for a moment there, I thought we weren't going to make it! But make it we did – and no crash landing.

You can always find a taxi, if you prefer such a thing – or if it's too late for the buses – and you can rent a car or a light, jeeplike vehicle called a "moke." But for us, by far the best value is the merry-go-round excitement of a bus.

In Bridgetown, we walk through a park beneath some trees and make for the nearby marina. This is the heart of the city, where all the streets converge at the water's edge. On one side is Independence Park and on the other, beyond twin bridges, is Trafalgar Square. We can see the statue of Lord Nelson raised on its pedestal above a mass of green and yellow umbrellas. We call him Horatio at the Bridge.

Everywhere, there is a constant joyous noise. Street vendors cry their wares on every corner; the clock tower, rising over the seventeenth-century public buildings, tolls each quarter of the hour; music rolls and swaggers from the shoulders of hawkers armed with ghetto blasters; small parades of uniformed school-children march across the bridges, calling out one another's names; and, above all this, the buses and the taxis sing out a descant of horns. As noise, it is enthralling; it has an optimistic edge to it – as if some secret happiness you had not yet found were being celebrated.

We head for the Bridge House, overlooking the careenage. This is a shallow inlet where fishing boats were brought in the past to be "careened" – tipped on their sides in order to have their hulls scraped clean of barnacles.

Upstairs in the Bridge House, there is a marvellous restaurant called the Fisherman's Wharf. It has a long, narrow verandah where you can dine looking down at the yachts and launches moored at the dockside, and where you can also enjoy the breezes blowing in from the sea. If you want to sit on the verandah, by the way, say so when you book your table.

The menu at the Wharf is mostly fish and seafood. I particularly enjoy the lobster thermidor and the lobster with lime mayonnaise. My favourite accompaniment to almost anything is the piquant cucumber salad served with chilli peppers and lime juice. There's also Lambie Souse – a Bajan concoction of conch meat tenderized in lime juice – and coconut shrimp, deep-fried in a light, coconut-filled batter. The desserts are among the best on the island, ranging from various kinds of mousse to a wide selection of sherbets and pies. Of course, you can always order a richly refreshing pina colada, and call it dessert.

Mostly, we spend our days reading in the shade and swimming in the sun. The sea on the south coast is a wondrous mixture of Atlantic and Caribbean waters – warm, clear, and multihued. The Atlantic waters are a dark, rich green and the Caribbean waters are turquoise. When they mingle, they produce a frothy, almost milky indigo. The waves can be three to five metres high, and the undertow must be acknowledged. (Over on the east coast, the Atlantic pounds in too spectacularly for swimming unless you know the area very well – while on the west coast, where the more expensive hotels and restaurants can be found, the Caribbean is usually glassy calm.) We swim for half an hour at least three or four times a day, after which we lie on the coral sand in the sun. The sun can be extremely dangerous – and we are justifiably warned by our Bajan hosts to take it seriously. For the first few days we use a #24 sun screen – never less than a #15.

In the evenings, prior to our restaurant forays, we sit with a Banks or a ginger beer on the balcony and watch the sun go down. The air fills with the sounds of birds, and of parents calling their children in from the lawns. It is also heavy with the smells of soap and Noxzema, Nivea cream, and women's perfume – all mingling with the scent of flowers, cut grass, and damp earth.

One day, while looking up the number for one of the restaurants where we wanted to make a reservation, I glance through the rest of the telephone book and discover it to be a mine of information. It even provides medical advice and exercise routines, telling what to do about sunburn, heat prostration, and hurricanes. (Winter visitors miss the hurricane season.) It also reminds us to save enough cash for each of us to pay the departure tax – twenty Barbadian dollars.

The last time we go to the fence to buy our fruit, the Pineapple Woman gives us a dazzling smile and shakes our hands and thanks us.

"Goodbye to you, boys!" she calls, as she walks away. "Good-bye, and journey well!"

We do.

# Night Pictures of Peru

The overhead lights dimmed, then died. My eyes tried to locate the small, dirt-smeared window onto the square, but couldn't: the streetlamps had gone dark, too. We were in a remote town high in the Peruvian Andes, eating unfamiliar food after sundown. Suddenly we couldn't see a thing, and for a few strange moments the noisy restaurant fell silent.

A thin white candle appeared up at the bar. Soon each table in the room had its own small yellow flame. Like everything else we'd seen that had been manufactured in Peru, the candles seemed badly made. They sputtered and threw weak pools of light, not illuminating the room so much as carving a maze of shadows.

We'd been told to be very careful up here on the *altiplano*. By 1980, Peru had become dangerous. In the decade before our visit, tourists had been robbed, beaten, even killed. When we'd first arrived in Lima, we'd remarked on the poverty, the run-down buildings, the urban chaos. Don't leave your coats or bags untended in a public place, not even for half a minute, a guidebook had counselled. Every morning we strapped comfortable money belts onto our skin, went out with more cash than we'd ever carried before, and walked among the poorest people I'd ever seen. How to reconcile our wealth with their beggarhood? In Peru that large historical question lies compressed in rolled-up dollars tied around your waist. The question chafes, but short of shedding your belt and becoming a beggar yourself, there's no quick answer.

That night in the semidarkness we took turns making our way to the dessert cooler. We were lightheaded from the altitude, and physically exhausted from the day's roller-coaster train ride up the steep mountains. From the station, we'd walked a long way with our bags through dusty streets to a hotel. And everywhere we'd gone, people had stared at our fair skin and good clothes. The restaurant was a welcome refuge. I remember feeling pleasantly tired when I came back from the dessert display with my pastry. But even in that thin light I sensed something on the table was wrong.

"Did you move your purse?" I asked.

The purse was gone. A few seconds earlier a man had tapped Fay's shoulder and asked her respectfully for the time. She'd turned for a moment to reply. And in that instant, from the other side, her bag had been snatched by the man's accomplice.

We exchanged pained looks. Our money and papers were strapped around our waists, but in the purse had been her camera with our roll of film from the Amazon: images of giant, magic-realist butterflies floating past psychedelic orchids.

I raged into the street. The sidewalk was a crush of brown faces. I could see them for about six feet around the restaurant doorway; beyond that, darkness drew a curtain. The only lights were the glowing red dots of cigarettes hanging in the air. Around the doorway a few pairs of eyes noted me impassively.

"Foreign aid," I shrugged, when I returned and reported the hopelessness of giving chase. "They need the camera more than we do." But we were both angry about the film.

The altitude, the adrenalin pumped up by a new place, the outrage at being so easily duped all got me going. I decided to do business with the police – an ill-conceived move. In Peru, as in many Latin American countries, there are towns where the line dividing criminals from law enforcers is very fine, and sometimes invisible. But I was emboldened by the waiter in the restaurant. When I complained about the thief on the premises, he said to me in simple, idiot-proof Spanish, "The police, they know who has your camera."

After several wrong turns in the blacked-out streets, I found the police station, an old stone building. I had to bend to get through the tiny doorway. In a corner of the windowless lobby stood a wooden reception booth. There, a single candle fluttered, and a man in a dirty uniform appeared to be sleeping on a stool.

"What do you want?" he growled, his eyes thin slits, his mouth barely moving.

I explained that I wanted to see the *Jefe* about a robbery. This seemed to anger the drowsy guard. He opened his eyes, fired off a volley of splenetic-sounding Spanish that missed me, and waved toward a diminutive doorway covered by a black cloth.

"There?"

"*Si*," he snapped.

I ducked and brushed past the black material. The next room had neither furniture nor candles. I could just make out two other little portals, each draped with the same black curtain. A second policeman passed in the dark and eyed me disapprovingly.

"I want to see the chief," I said, not really believing myself anymore. I didn't like this place, but doubted I could now turn tail. I was a complainant, but in here I felt it would take only a whim to turn me into a detainee.

The second officer led me through two more airless, lightless rooms and left me sitting against a cold stone wall on a bench with several other beleaguered people. A faint wash of light leaked around the curtain hanging in the chief's doorway. I was now deep in the bowels of the ancient station – wondering if and when I'd be getting out. Our photographs of Amazonian butterflies suddenly seemed frivolous. I was thinking more of Amnesty International's reports documenting torture, also about bad period movies with scenes set in watery dungeons.

One by one the people on the bench were ushered out of the dark hallway and into the *Jefe*'s office. The woman beside me sobbed quietly all the time we waited. When she'd gone through the black curtain, I heard her wailing and a male voice shouting back at her. Whatever her problem was, mine couldn't compare.

The *Jefe* sat by an old gas heater. Two candles burned on his battered table, illuminating a sleepy, flaccid, moustachioed face. In the half-darkness, with his hands propped on the table and his ample girth bisected by a row of metal buttons, he looked like a large, upturned beetle – possibly poisonous. His uniform was cleaner, but his demeanour was consistent with that of his subordinates: bored, resentful, suspicious.

I recounted the tale of the theft. At my mention of the word "camera," his eyes flicked open and he shifted to look at me. What restaurant? he asked. I told him.

And how much money is the camera worth?

I tried to explain that it wasn't the camera so much as the film that concerned me.

Yes, but how much is the camera worth?

It had cost us a few hundred dollars, by Peruvian measure a huge sum. He eagerly made a note of this. Then his interest seemed to flag.

"The waiter in the restaurant," I continued, "told us you might be able to help get it back." As I struggled with these words in my deformed Spanish, they didn't come out sounding as innocuous as I'd intended. I stood there semi-paralyzed. Had I just made some sort of fateful accusation?

The chief turned a pair of disgusted eyes on me. *You utterly contemptible foreign scumbag,* said the eyes. *You presumptuous gringo piece of shit.* He considered what I'd said for a few more nasty seconds.

"Perhaps it's not possible," I added, lamely.

"Listen, *señor,*" he declaimed at last, addressing the dark air in the pompous tones of Peruvian officialdom. "It's a very difficult problem. Very difficult. To repossess your camera, you must go to the restaurant and speak again with your waiter. Your waiter knows who has your camera."

I walked back to the hotel, the black-out broken now by a star-lit Andean sky. I was the only fair-skinned man in the streets, and the only pedestrian over five-foot-nine. It occurred to me that perhaps everyone here knew where our camera was, everyone but us. The police chief had instructed me to be sure to return in the morning to file a formal statement. But we decided to catch a bus to Ayacucho.

The thieves of Huancayo, were they simply petty criminals? Or proud avengers of the local culture that had been ravaged for more than 450 years by the Conquistadors and their descendants?

Or are those even the right questions? Later we learned something new. As we continued overland towards Cuzco, the old Incan capital, other travellers told us that an unknown Maoist guerrilla group had claimed responsibility for blowing up a hydro tower near Huancayo, disrupting power transmission for miles around. It was their first act of massive violence.

Later still I learned that the guerrillas called themselves the

Shining Path. Whenever I see their name in the press, where it has often appeared since, I think of that powerless night, the white candles, the black curtains, our never-developed blue-butterfly film, and all the eyes staring as we walked in and out of the town.

GRAEME GIBSON

# Notes from a Cuban Journal

## Sunday, April 5, 1987

After a crazed seven-hour drive westward from Santiago de Cuba
(the last three of them in darkness on an unfinished road), I'm
writing this in a reassuringly commonplace seaside resort called
Marea de Portillo. It was built, in partnership with Canadians, for
tourists who fly into Manzanillo; as a result my generic room (with
about as much character as transnational lite beer) could be in
Brisbane, or Mobile, Alabama – or Algonquin Park. Dinner was
surprisingly good, but the greyish beach at dusk looks narrow.

The Sierra Maestre, which sheltered the young Fidel and his
followers, rises like a jagged black wall behind us. Much of the
staff is clustered around various televisions, watching an older *El
Jefe* deliver a speech at some Congress in Havana. One or other of
them periodically trots out with drinks for the tourists, who are
boisterously shouting and laughing by a huge bonfire on the
beach. This has been going on for some time. Fidel's still a striking
man, but the grainy, black-and-white images make him look
washed-out and tired. None of us, however, is getting any
younger.

I am here, where the Revolution began, with the hope of finding enough spots for a series of birding trips to complement those I've been running to Zapata, by the Bay of Pigs. Or at least that's the excuse, the justification.

Three Cuban scientists are travelling with me. Orlando Garrido, whom I've known for several years, is a complex man and an indefatigable, quite remarkable ornithologist. An athletic sixty year old, he was a member of Cuba's Davis Cup team before the Revolution and runner-up, in the Canadian Open, to his brother – who is now a golf pro in Florida. Although I've seldom met a man so dedicated to his country and the work to be done, Garrido seems to have little, if any, political interest.

Dr. Gilberto Silva, an authority on bats and Director of Research at the newly established Cuban Museum of Natural Sciences in Havana, is clearly our leader. A very bright, engaging man, he's a fellow cigar lover – who enjoys a dram or two from my bottle of duty-free Famous Grouse. Clearly a fine companion.

Luis is a younger, brasher fellow. I haven't yet figured out what he does, but his cool and shadowed little house (in Santiago de Cuba) is cluttered with dusty pinned and mounted butterflies, with glassy-eyed stuffed birds and reptiles. Finally there's Pablo, our driver. Strong and paunchy, with formidably hairy forearms, he combs his hair a lot. Moreover he has a vaguely hysterical giggle and drives badly.

Because I'm on tourist business, we were assigned a "protocol" host in Santiago de Cuba. His name is Calvo, and both breast pockets of his immaculate blue shirt were filled with pens which glinted in the sun like decorations, like medals.

Clearly he had no idea of who I was and what a picayune enterprise I run, because he behaved as if I had authority or money. As if I were a potential investor. His task was to introduce me, with his persistent gravelly voice, to the wonders of Bacanao, La

Riviera del Caribe. This impressive development, of eighty thousand hectares, sprawls just outside the city of Santiago. As a result we didn't escape until late afternoon. Still, Plan Bacanao is undoubtedly paying for much of this trip. So fair, I suppose, is fair.

Quick as my visit was to the city itself, I warmed to Santiago. Wooden houses with balconies and fine, lacy grilles. An impression of liveliness in the streets. A handsome cathedral and the celebrated Moncado barracks (now a school), where Fidel and his rebels made their first, abortive assault.

The city also celebrates Cuba's finest carnival. Despite the Revolution's organized seriousness, the locals have apparently managed to hang onto the spirit of chaos that properly underlies all the best carnivals. Such independence may help explain why most Cuban revolutions have found their earliest support here . . .

Although not so widespread as in Havana, there's a helluva lot of people in the streets wearing T-shirts that advertise Capitalist Wonders from abroad. BMW, Adidas, Firestone, UCLA, European Soccer Final. It's weird the way clothing has been substituted for the actual objects. It happens at home, of course; we're all subject to the hunger for objects. But in Cuba there's no chance of owning most of what is being advertised.

Our big white American van (made in Mexico!) attracts much attention. Staring as we pass, certain men (most of them young) absently pick at their crotches. I've noticed a tendency to do this, unthinkingly, as a kind of macho gesture. It isn't clear, however, whether it is a sign of vulnerability or aggression. Perhaps both?

Finally escaping Calvo, we drove westward along the coast towards the sun. Clint Eastwood cowboys (without the guns) herded cattle among bare, thorny bushes on the flat lands between us and the mountains. Few cars, but many horseback riders on the road; some were women in straw hats and bright kerchiefs, who cantered past us with a seductive abandon. It strikes me, once again, that women here dress well, stylishly, with very limited resources.

Beyond gravel beaches slipping by to our left, the sea was a sombre oily blue. Sprawling arid streambeds were filled with dry stones. Fewer buses in Oriente, and those we've encountered are ram-jam full, so people walk long distances in the sun, often with heavy loads. Men and women wander in the shade of umbrellas, and there are lots of school kids in maroon or mustard-coloured shorts or skirts. Striking billboards encourage, cajole (demand?) – with all the optimism this beleaguered country can muster – the Power of Positive Thinking. THE BLOOD OF HER SONS FOUNDED THE SOCIALIST STATE, and so forth. USE YOUR TIME CONSTRUC-TIVELY, and VOLUNTARY WORK IS A SCHOOL FOR TRAINING THE CONSCIENCE. Then a series of five signs about fifty yards apart – like the old Burma Shave ads in the States:

THE REVOLUTION IS NOT ONLY IN YOUR HEART,

AND IN THE LIVES AND FUTURE OF YOUR CHILDREN,

IT IS IN YOUR ARMS AND HANDS,

AND IN YOUR VALLEYS AND CAVES;

AND IN ALL OF AMERICA.

My companions all talked at once, and loudly. After months establishing the new museum, doing administrative and theoreti-cal work, they're thrilled to be in the field. Both Silva and Garrido were among a group of natural scientists who resigned from the Academy of Sciences in protest at what they believed to be a damaging lack of support for their disciplines. As a consequence (and for other reasons), there was a long stretch of time when neither man could make field trips. Or, indeed, do any "official" scientific work. The fact they are here, as senior members of the newly established museum, is a clear sign of the improvements taking place in Cuba's intellectual life.

Lenore Atwood

Garrido, in particular, was high and urgent with talk, with excitement. Waving his hands and staring straight ahead, he got louder and louder, repeating phrases, almost shouting. I gather he was speculating about relationships among various species and sub-species of local reptiles. In particular, there's one that lives in the grass which might be a new species.

Eastern Cuba has been little explored scientifically. These mountains are dramatic as hell. Very dry, at the moment, they're piled close to the shore, and rise one behind the other as they progress inland. Wild and largely uninhabited, they are shot full of isolated valleys. Such terrain, like islands, can be a rich source of endemic plants and animals.

Because of the coffee and beer consumed at Bacanao, we stopped to pee. The driver did so with a macho flourish, as if putting out a four-alarm fire. After this spectacle Silva crossed the road to sit and smoke by the shore, and Garrido searched for reptiles. Rooting among logs and stones, Luis was after insects. Meanwhile I poked happily about with my binoculars in desiccated scrub bush and wonderful cacti, hoping for the Cuban gnatcatcher, or Oriente warbler, endemic species that don't occur in Western Cuba. The silence was abruptly broken by exultant shouts from Garrido. Jumping up and down, waving his arms, he appeared to be hurling rocks into an almeciga, a lovely reddish tree that reminds me of the arbutus in B.C. "Gibson!" he shouted. "Quick . . . Gibson, quick!" By the time I lumbered up he'd lost sight of what would turn out to be a very handsome giant lizard. Circling the tree, staring excitedly into the foliage, Garrido had a fist-sized stone in either hand. When he briefly caught sight of it again, with another series of shouts, he fiercely hurled his rocks, one after the other, dodging away as one rebounded almost to his feet.

I know the rationale for scientific collecting. Garrido is an indefatigable student of Cuban fauna. A legendary ornithologist, he's also discovered hitherto unknown lizards, mammals, and fish. Obviously, in order to be certain he'd found a new species, and in order to describe it adequately, he'd have to have the wretched creature in hand. On top of this, as a Cuban, often working on his own, Garrido would not have been believed without well-documented specimens. Still, I find myself troubled by the way these men must kill like small boys.

From where I stood I could see the extraordinary beast poised with heaving sides in the crotch of a bare limb. Maybe ten inches long, and chunky, it was an exquisite green, with a brilliant yellow band along the side. After a few heartbeats it crept from sight, and I should have told Garrido where it had gone, when I had the chance, but I didn't.

All that was left of the sun, when we stopped for supper in a tiny village by the sea, was a blood-red band along the horizon.

Men wearing sombreros were clustered laughing and smoking in darkness beneath a pale ceiba – that great tree which the Mayans venerated because it best understood human sorrow. Unbelievably loud and terribly distorted dance music blared from a pole behind us as we filed into the restaurant, which was crowded with others watching a ball game on television. Cubans are crazy about baseball. League games are free, by the way. Whenever there's a game, men crowd intently around public televisions, and the commentary can be heard everywhere in the streets. There's almost as much interest as I found in St. Vincent, when the West Indies hosted an International Test in cricket . . .

No choice for dinner: beef ribs, black rice, and an odd mushed banana as vegetable. Then mango marmalade and cream cheese for dessert. The beer and coffee were both welcome and good. But the noise was appalling.

Emerging, we discovered the van's battery was dead. However, since we'd parked on an incline, we managed to get going with a rolling start.

## *Tuesday, April 7, 1987*

6:15 A.M.: A fresh but already warm breeze is blowing off the sea, and a sleepy waiter has just given me an orange, a curious sweet bun, and a demitasse of very strong coffee – which is syrupy with sugar. I'm waiting for the others before our six-and-a-half-hour drive back to Santiago de Cuba. Then it's on to Guantanamo.

My growing suspicion that this first part of the trip will prove useless, so far as birding trips are concerned, is being confirmed. We're obviously here so my companions can collect specimens for the museum. Yesterday we drove for several hours, to a village with a fine old lighthouse and a straggle of shacks along the shore. Each with a wooden privy on rickety stilts over the water. In front of one house, an ancient woman was methodically sweeping her dirt yard, with a homemade broom. Chickens and a tawdry rooster followed stupidly in her wake. Although a common-enough sight throughout Latin America and the Caribbean, there was a difference – this old soul was wearing a pair of shiny new, government-issue spectacles.

No birds to speak of, but my companions scampered happily off in search of whatever. Mostly they were hoping for slender, elegant-looking lizards called anoles. These are delicate little creatures with – depending on the species – different coloured dewlaps, or loose folds of skin, at the throat, which can be expanded when they want to show off. There have been more than twenty species of anole identified in Cuba, and Garrido is convinced there are more.

Garrido and Luis catch many of the animals by stunning them with rubber bands, expertly shot from the tip of their thumbs as kids do, then store them in carefully marked plastic bags.

I wish the tiny corpses didn't continue to bother me . . .

Although troubled and frustrated by the relative shortage of birds, I'm delighted by the landscape. Especially by the trees. The almacigo with its graceful, often twisting cinnamon trunk and bark peeling like coloured paper. The Mayans' ceiba, a large pale creature filled with air plants that look like enormous dream porcupines. And a myriad others that I don't know. Some with heavy, elegant canopies – at a distance they resemble green mushrooms. And pine trees in the hills. With my eyes closed, hearing the wind in their branches, I could be in northern Ontario; however, when I look I see palm trees among the evergreens, and cacti among spiky scrub bush that is totally unrecognizable. The overall effect is prehistoric.

*Mid-afternoon, Santiago de Cuba*: In the restaurant of the Hotel de las Americas. Dark wood panelling, big windows that open, worn white tablecloths, and a ceiling fan. There's no beer, but a wizened fellow in a shiny, dark (probably pre-Revolutionary) suit is playing Nat King Cole songs on the piano. He's good, too, although lunch was mediocre. Despite the shortages and generally run-down atmosphere, I like these older hotels. If only because they're frequented by Cubans. The Havana Libre and the Riviera (Meyer Lansky's old money-maker on the Malecón) service organized tourists and businessfolk who fume in lines by the erratic pay telephones. Most of the others, the big official ones, places like the Triton or the Commodoro, in Havana, have their lobbies and elevators filled with stolid Russians or Poles, with athletes from Nicaragua or Mozambique, and all sorts of "officials" from Cuba, and God knows where else, stocking up on consumer goods in "tourist" shops. In none of them can an "ordinary" Cuban venture above the ground floor.

Still, even these hotels have their charms. I once watched a group of Russian men wrapping their companions in toilet paper on the dance floor after dinner. The women stood absolutely still, like vertical mummies, while the band played a gallumphing, repetitive melody and the men pranced about them unrolling the toilet paper. There didn't seem to be a winner, or any losers, although some did a much better job of it than others.

Nothing like that here, though. Lunch is over and most of the other patrons have left. We're waiting for the van to be returned from "an electrical specialist" because it failed us once again. We'd stopped where another ceiba burst evocatively above weedy brush. There I was delighted to find, among a mixed flock of migrants between the sea and the road, my two Oriente endemics, the Cuban gnatcatcher and the Oriente warbler. When the time came to leave, however, the van was dead. Forty-five minutes later a passing military jeep, carrying a pair of Czech geologists, gave us a boost. It turned out to be a fortuitous delay, because Garrido found only the third nesting colony of tropic birds in Cuba . . .

Still, it's a drag.

*Evening, Hotel Guantanamo*: More drama with the van. After we'd waited three hours, first in the hotel, then at the protocol office, it finally appeared and we set off for Guantanamo. About thirty kilometres along the road, Luis discovered that he'd forgotten his briefcase. Much consternation and elaborate talk, until Garrido and I got out to explore while the others returned to fetch it.

We were wandering past some casuarinas (an extraordinary Australian tree that seems bent on world conquest), with a motley collection of wood warblers, indigo buntings, and local green and red-bellied woodpeckers flitting about, when Garrido suddenly bellowed and dropped to his knees. Staring as he shouted – while furiously bashing his palms against the earth – it occurred to me that he'd gone mad, or taken a fit. But it was the lizards, his grass anoles. He'd seen one, no doubt about it, and there were others. Crawling on my knees beside him, I also saw quick, dainty little forms, but we couldn't catch any. Eventually, because the others would soon be returning, I left him creeping about and returned to the road.

Waiting for the van, I smoked a cigar with my back against a post. Obviously this is not a part of the country that sees many tourists. Worn, hard-looking little men and women in faded clothing slowed down, then paused just up the road to get another look. Others peered suspiciously from nearby houses, wondering what the big gringo was doing. I remembered, with some unease, my arrest in Havana. This happened in 1984, during my first visit to Cuba. Poking about the suburbs, again with my binoculars, I apparently circled close to one of Fidel's safe houses. As a result some local worthy, a gardener I think, collared me with a "citizen's arrest." It was five hours before I was released from a large and busy police station. How long would it take down here?

Garrido finally joined me with three small, limp bodies. No longer quick and graceful, they were deflated, nondescript. He was hugely excited. And oddly tender. Picking at them, extending a leg, the tail, staring at the adhesive pads on their delicate feet, he decided they were almost certainly new to science.

It was more than two hours before Silva and Luis returned, this time in a small Alfa Romeo with a new driver. It wasn't their tales of a broken distributor and the van bursting into flames, but Garrido's discovery that preoccupied them as we sped off at breakneck speed.

## Wednesday, April 8, 1987

At Rio Yumuri in the mountains between Guantanamo and Baracoa, after a dramatic drive up a good, steeply curving road among red hills shot through with green basalt. The gang is off, once again, searching for insects and reptiles. They're well pleased with the trip so far, and seem to be making a good haul – which they keep on ice in the trunk.

In the first town where we stopped for lunch, back down there on the plain, there wasn't a restaurant. In the second there was, but it didn't open until 12:30. At the third, half an hour further on, we were presented with a choice of tinned fish, or eggs, and rice, bean soup, and the ubiquitous marmalade with cheese. No beer or soft drinks, and no ice . . .

Although I've searched, there are few birds, and time runs on. No cars pass on the road, and only a couple of trucks have laboured by. A worried hen tries to supervise her insanely peeping chicks behind me, and a plump turkey revels in its dust bath to my right. There's a breeze up here, but the sun is extremely hot and I'm surrounded (but ignored) by brown-eyed, slow moving men. All of them very short.

I wish I could relax and enjoy myself. It's an intriguing, complex, and lovely country. My companions are terrific. But the dreaded "business" meeting with the director of Plan Bacanao at the end of the week preys on my mind. Unless we're surprised by something very good, it will be difficult, if not impossible, to put a positive face on our "business" discussions. What can I say to justify his investment?

Moreover the van seems gone for good. Kaput. The Alfa Romeo is too small to be comfortable, too close to the ground, and much too old for rough roads. So we've had to abandon what might have been a rewarding side trip.

*Baracoa, late afternoon*: Baracoa, which was Cuba's capital from 1512 to 1515, is lusher, much more tropical, more "Caribbean" than the rest of the country. A punishing sun, and great humidity, but here on a hill overlooking the glistening town, with its red-tiled roofs and masses of flowering trees and shrubs, there's a fine breeze.

On October 27, 1492, Columbus first landed, in Cuba, on the unprepossessing crescent of sand that curves just below our hotel. This was, he said, "the most beautiful land ever seen." Even now it is hard to disagree. Only twenty years after Columbus, a certain Diego Velázquez arrived with three hundred conquistadores and orders from Spain to conquer the island. Among his company were Hernando Cortés, and the remarkable priest – known as the "Apostle of the Indians" – Bartolomé de las Casas. On the other side was Hatuey, an heroic but doomed leader of the resistance, who managed to pin the Spaniards down for three months before being captured, then burned at the stake. The rest, as they say, is history.

There's a predictably good Cuban beer called Hatuey.

It is now raining gently. A radio plays rhumbas in one of the public rooms to my left. I'm drinking a glass of Cuba's great seven-year-old dark rum while smoking a cigar under the sheltered walk-way facing a garden full of brilliant flowers and small coconut palms. At its far end there's a living fence, which was made (according to Silva, who just left me to shower before dinner) by planting lengths of *piñon flordito*, close together, in the earth. The sticks soon take root and grow interlocking branches, thus providing an almost impenetrable wall.

Beyond the fence rises a massive hill called El Yunque, or Sleeping Beauty, and behind it another forbidding range of mountains. Dispossessed Indians, runaway slaves, along with all sorts of rebels and renegades, have, for centuries, sought and found sanctuary in those hills. For all I know there are fugitives up there now.

I've really taken to Gilberto Silva. He's elegant, smart, humorous, very experienced, and sad. Wonderful talks about Cuban history, and what the Revolution has meant for this country. The profound gains it has made. Silva was here in Baracoa before the Revolution. There were no roads over the mountains then; he had to come in by boat. It was poor, he said. Terribly poor and without schools. Because the people were so exploited by the landowners, they took to the Revolution right away.

I have been told (although not by him) that Silva was invited to a conference in the States in the early sixties. The American authorities immediately seized him. After being interned for several months, in Florida, he was deported as an "undesirable alien."

Back in Cuba it was decided, because he'd been locked up by the CIA and FBI, that he must have been "turned around." So he was sent to prison on the Isle of Youth.

Great stuff, too, about Cuban natural history. Especially the bats – one of which catches fish at night. It has developed a sonar that adjusts to the distortion created by water. And the extraordinary caves found in Cuba. Both the longest and the second deepest caves in Latin America are here.

In my half-a-dozen visits during the past three years, I've encountered others who have suffered within Cuba's defensive, ideological, and often arbitrary political culture. Most have been punished with "under-employment" and/or a loss of privileges. Some have been imprisoned. Despite this, the majority I know remains committed to the ideals of the Revolution. To the best that it has accomplished. Whatever it is they want for the country's future, it's not a return to the status of a de facto, neo-liberal American colony. They retain real affection for Fidel. And a puzzled, spine-stiffening resentment at the intensity of American opposition – the prospect of what Washington seems to want for their country.

I guess our equivalent would be Joe Clark's remarkably sustained loyalty to the Conservatives, his willingness to beaver away on the party's behalf after its cruel treatment of him. Which says something about faith, I suppose, and conviction.

## Thursday, April 9, 1987

I'm sitting on an orange, fifties-style, free-form chair in the lobby. Garrido and Silva talk energetically, a telephone rings unanswered, a woman is calling for someone loudly, and there's a radio playing around the corner.

I'm intrigued by the way Cubans repeat themselves in free-flowing conversations. Instead of "yes," it's "yes-yes-yes," and they come back to phrases. Someone's name, for example: "Roberto, yes-yes-yes, Roberto Sendina. From Havana. Sendina . . . I remember him. Roberto Sendina."

Wonderful visit with Anfiloquio Suarez Castillanos; an older man (seventy-two, or something) who was having a bit of trouble with his false teeth. Known as *El Rubio*, he's a farmer. Also an amateur but expert naturalist who started Baracoa's zoo – donating many animals from his own collection. Professionals in Havana, people like Silva and Garrido, have long depended on him for information about the region – as well as for useful specimens, of course. At the same time, he's a fierce conservationist, one who has evidently converted many of the local kids. Returning from a guided tour of his property, we encountered a trio of ten-year-old boys, who were studiously watching a small pink constrictor – a rubber boa – entwining itself around a fence rail. Few snakes are fortunate enough to survive such encounters with young human males . . .

Robust and genial, *El Rubio* is a fascinating guy. Although a landowner, he was quick to join the revolutionaries, whereupon Batista's forces razed his home and farm. A deadly shot, he distinguished himself, and after the triumph of the Revolution he returned to rebuild everything. Not long after, discovering the revolution had turned Communist, he dashed back into the hills to join the fight against his former comrades. The rebels were eventually captured. *El Rubio* spent a number of years in jail, then returned to his farm. There's a prominent, most engaging picture of Fidel on his sheltered verandah; an equally large painting of the Virgin is displayed just inside the living room door.

# Friday, April 10, 1987

*Santiago de Cuba*: Last night, after some delay, we flew back here in a Russian Yak 40, which carries maybe forty-five passengers.

This evening I return to Havana. In the morning it's back to Toronto.

The dreaded meeting with the Director General of Plan Bacanao, which was scheduled for last night at nine o'clock, didn't start until he arrived, from another meeting, just after ten. A strong-looking, tough-looking man with a palpable air of authority, he put me very much on guard at first. Poor, worried Calvo and a small-moustached, expressionless middle-level bureaucrat hovered about while we trudged through the preliminary talk. We explained that we hadn't found an effective focus for my trips. He said there were lots of birds. We said the reserve at Zapata (where my other trips go) had been thoroughly studied and explored, but there hadn't been enough work done here to find the "hot spots." The mood got a bit dicey, a bit sharp and persistent. Meetings with Cubans often begin like this, especially when you're dealing with those in authority. At first there's an obligatory formality, all masks and ceremonious talk, but with many people that soon collapses and the individual reveals himself. It's almost as if Cubans are too gregarious, too curious, to maintain the bureaucratic pose – although, God knows, I've met some who revelled in their abstract power!

In any event, while we were sipping our second glass of rum and nibbling small canapés prepared by Calvo, the Director General abruptly, and quite wistfully, confessed the delight he finds in nature. He'd love to go birding with us, to wander and learn from people like Silva, he said. But his boss didn't understand anything except work and more work. It seemed a wonderful, disarming gesture, and it won us all over. I have begun to sense there's a whole bunch of upper-middle bureaucrats in Cuba who work compulsively, trying to carry the country on their backs. In their late forties or early fifties, they look a decade older. Below them, it often seems, there's inertia; above them an entrenched official-ism. In Havana I was told by a serious man that it's not the Party that runs Cuba, but the bureaucracy. The Party, he said, is the opposition . . .

The Director General is also a problem-solver. As a result we came away with a perfectly respectable proposal for a series of nature cruises, in a good-sized yacht they own. Although it may or may not work out, it's a terrific idea. In the event, we'll see.

A touching moment at dinner, just before we left Baracoa last night. Casually but studiously, Garrido and Silva told me that, should the little grass anole prove to be a new species, they were going to name it after me. *Anolis gibsoni*, or whatever the Latin might be. I was utterly taken aback. We've travelled a long way together, and I've come to admire and love these men. And their country. Perhaps as a result, I was surprisingly moved by their gift. And secretly embarrassed by my unspoken and sentimental diffi-culties with the collecting of animal specimens. Even now, remembering three little corpses in Garrido's hand, I find it ironic, curious to say the least, that these lizards (and their kind) might carry my name. The trio, which are somewhere still on ice, will have paid heavily for that unlikely honour.

PETER GZOWSKI

# Up the Liard by Magic Carpet

High on one of the canyoned walls where the Liard River mean-ders from the Yukon's Pelly Mountains toward the boundary of B.C. is a plaque that salutes the memory of George Mercer Daw-son, the geologist and botanist who mapped much of the area a century ago. As a tourist attraction, the plaque is unprepossessing: a few words, and Dawson's dates (1849-1901). But the surround-ing panorama of rock and river, of spruce and poplar and jack pine – of untrammelled wilderness and the history it holds – is worth both the journey and a moment or two of reflection.

There are a number of ways to get there. You can hike cross-country if you want, cutting in off the Alaska Highway. You can canoe up from B.C. and peer at the plaque from the river. Or you can do what I did, which is to start a golf tournament a couple of thousand miles away, and, eventually, someone will show up in a helicopter and ask if you'd care for a ride.

My trip to the Liard took six years. It began in Ontario, at the Briars, on Lake Simcoe, where I had learned (more or less) to play golf as a boy, and to which, having settled into a job of hosting daily radio from Toronto, I'd returned. In the summer of 1986, I gathered a few friends to play a little game, and to raise, if we could, a little money for literacy. Since we knew no better – few of us had ever played in a formal event before, let alone trying to run one – our tournament had a few departures from the norm: music on the first tee, for example, and a "poet laureate" (we invited Dennis Lee) who wrapped things up with a verse. Somewhat to our surprise, our idea caught on, and before you could say George Knudson, who played his last Canadian tournament with us, there were PGIs, as we came to call them (for Peter Gzowski's Invitationals), all over the Canadian map, from Victoria in the lower left-hand corner to Baffin Island, where we played on the ice off Pond Inlet, in the upper right.

In 1992, though, there was still a blank in the upper left: the Yukon. So even though it would be difficult for us to get there – our most generous national sponsor, Air Canada, no longer flew to Whitehorse – and even though the people who had formed the local committee seemed to us more ambitious than would be practical – they wanted to stage a tournament not only in the capital of Whitehorse but also in the tiny community of Watson Lake, some two hundred miles to the east – we signed on. A few of us scrounged the air fares as best we could and made our way up from the south. And, one August afternoon, there we were, finishing our first tour of Greenway's Greens, just outside Watson Lake, when the helicopter showed up, fluttering out of the sky and settling into a clearing just off the ninth fairway.

Greenway's Greens, I should make clear, is no ordinary golf course. It's the work of one man, Bob Greenway, a one-time trapper and ex-construction superintendent who, having grown tired of taking one golf holiday a year in North Carolina and leaving his clubs in storage the rest of the time, took a bulldozer to the wilderness and carved himself nine tailored holes, a couple of whose fairways, just so you wouldn't think you were at Pinehurst, crisscrossed en route to their greens.

The man in the chopper, it turned out, was no ordinary pilot either. His name was Ken Birss. He came, originally, from my own old home town of Galt, Ontario. For more than twenty years he'd been hopping about the north, flying freelance mostly – he'd been to the Pole four times. But his avocation was sculpture. In winters, in recent years, he and his family had hunkered down in the Queen Charlottes, where he could work on his powerful, lifesize carvings. When I met him, his works were selling for as much as $30,000. But the daunting cost of his raw materials – his current project started as more than a ton of hardwood, for which he'd paid some $5,000 – and the fact that each carving took him a year or so to complete, meant that in summers he still kept his hand in at flying the bush. When the Watson Lake PGI committee, knowing only that he did a little carving in his spare time, approached him to see if he might donate a sample as a golf prize, he'd said, sheepishly, that that might be a bit more than he could afford, but that he'd be happy to take some of the visitors for a spin.

We climbed aboard. As we clattered into the air – a raucous magic carpet – a raven swooped below us. Beside me in the back seat, our Yukon poet laureate, P. J. Johnson, the Raven Lady as she's known, gestured in acknowledgement.

We left raven altitude and rose to the eagles'. Below us, to our left, a cleared line through the scrubby bush marked the border with B.C., but as Ken swung north and west, heading for the Liard, all signs of civilization disappeared. Less than half an hour after I'd crouched over a four-foot putt – I missed it, if that matters – I was aloft over the endless landscape.

We descended to follow the river. In the canyon, we hovered over Dawson's monument long enough to read the inscription, and rose again to head for Watson Lake.

"You know," said Ken Birss over the clamour of the engine, "if I overflew the golf course we could go five hundred miles before we'd see the mark of another human. People in the south think we're running out of land. I guess they're right – down there.

"But up here it goes on forever."

# Il Porcellino

October, 1992. I hadn't been home from Australia a week when I received two calls from Sydney, not half an hour apart. The first was from a fellow who'd heard me on an ABC radio talk show. He'd called the station, he said, and the station had given him the telephone number of my Sydney hotel; the hotel had given him my publisher's number in Brisbane; my publisher had given him my home number in Canada. Listen, he said. Hearing my interview had given him this great idea, it might be too crazy to consider but he thought there was no harm in trying it out. I'd seemed like such a friendly bloke on the air.

He and his mates were a group of solicitors and dentists in Sydney and other cities around New South Wales, he explained. Once in a while they got together for a party, to escape the city for a few days. "Sometimes we go up behind Bourke to shoot rabbits and feral cats. Sometimes down the Murrumbidgee to shoot 'roos, sometimes we bring down one or two wild pigs."

He thought I might like to come along, he said, next time I was in Oz. Sometimes these parties lasted just a couple of days, sometimes longer. In fact, he said, if I could manage to arrive in January I could be part of his "bucks" party. He was getting married, and his party would last nine days, crossing the entire state of New South Wales and arriving in Adelaide the day before the wedding. Usually, they would shoot and drink until midnight, play poker till dawn and then, after a short nap, move on.

He was a filmmaker, he eventually said, as though he'd just remembered this. He would be interested in filming the party, if I agreed. "Especially if there's a Canadian equivalent to the ABC that would like to be in on it. We could call it 'Jack in Australia.'"

Playing poker till dawn? Shooting animals all over the Australian landscape? I supposed I could fake the shooting if I had to. I'd been on plenty of hunting trips as a boy. When my father tried to teach me to shoot, however, I had killed the first breathing thing I aimed at. A tiny snipe flew up out of the swamp and dropped abruptly to the ground. At a hundred feet I'd drilled a hole through his head, though his head was the size of my thumbnail. If killing things was going to be this easy for me, I'd better not even start. I'd not carry a gun again.

What on earth had I said in that interview to earn this invitation? Possibly, I'd mentioned the man on the little propeller plane that would take me across the Strait to the Vancouver International. We hadn't even left the Victoria runway when he leaned across the aisle and said, "I noticed when we checked in that you're flying to Australia. Why?"

I might simply have told him I'd fallen in love with the place on my first visit – this was to be my third. I might have told him I'd had a privileged trip through the outback on the second visit, with an Australian novelist friend, and that I'd written a book about that trip which I was going back to publicize. But instead I told him that once, during my last visit, when we were pulling away from a sheep-shearing shed where he'd been interviewing the shearers, my friend mentioned that we'd been invited to stay the night if we wanted – the boys were going on a wild boar hunt after supper and we could come along. "But I told them we had to get on to our campsite before dark." What? What? I had protested. He'd turned down a chance to go on a wild boar hunt? "Just think about it, Jack," he said. "You saw them. They'll be all tanked up on grog, they'll be reeling around in the dark with loaded guns, chasing boars that could easily turn and charge. Do you really want to be with them?"

I guessed not, though my novelist's heart felt cheated out of something it might one day need. Now, two and a half years later, I was going back, I told this fellow on the plane, because now my novelist's heart felt cheated out of something it *knew* it would need. "I'm going back to see if I can get myself invited on a wild boar hunt. Or talk to people who have."

"Well," said the gentleman across the aisle, grasping his tidy umbrella tight in his lap, "am I ever going to save you a lot of money! You can turn around in Vancouver and go back home, because I've been on a wild boar hunt in Australia and can tell you all about it."

By the time we landed in Vancouver, he had kept his promise. A few years ago, he said, he'd read about the man who'd inspired the movie character Crocodile Dundee. He wrote to this famous hunter, and arranged to visit and to accompany him on his excursions – "before he started doing this sort of thing commercially." He and the man had set off across the plain in a topless Land Rover, he said, with two trained dogs wearing suits of armour. When the dogs caught the scent of wild pig, the hair on the backs of their necks stood up, and they began to bark madly, straining at their leashes. Released, they jumped out and raced off across the dust. The two men followed in the four-by-four. "When the dogs caught up to the pig they cornered it and kept it in place until we arrived." He'd been surprised at what a long-legged animal it was, he said, strangely truncated – too short – with a hairy hide of a sort of blackish-brownish colour. "Anyway, I stayed in the truck, but he got out and moved in with a long spear until he was up as near as the dogs. Then he drove the spear down through the back of the animal's neck and into its heart."

Two weeks later, in north central Queensland, when I related this man's tale at the supper table on Lorraine Station, the grazier and his son both had laughed derisively at the account. "Nobody kills them like that, Jack, not with spears! And what's this 'suit of armour' business? – nothing but spiked collars on the dogs. He was havin' you on, mate. You believe everything you hear?"

"You may be right," I confessed. "It turned out he was flying home to Hollywood. Probably a scriptwriter – too much imagination."

Yet when supper had broken up and everyone was heading back

to the separate sleeping quarters, Karen – the woman who had cooked our meal – took me aside where the others couldn't hear. David and Tony could be mistaken, she said. Once, when she'd lived in the Northern Territory, she'd known the woman who'd later married the original Crocodile Dundee. He was, she said, the kind of man who would naturally imitate the hunting techniques of the Aborigines. "That man's story could very well be true. Certainly not as far-fetched as those two seem to think."

But this was not until after I'd been at Lorraine Station for a few days. By the time I'd driven there – eighteen hours from Brisbane, north of the Tropic of Capricorn and west of Longreach – I no longer hoped to get in on anybody's wild boar hunt. I was content to accompany the son, Tony, who ran the wool-growing end of the family business, on his daily round of chores.

Lorraine Station is a sheep grazing property of 31,000 hectares, with 23,000 sheep. Between the towns of Longreach and Winton, it is only a half-day's drive from the site of a dinosaur stampede. A goanna named George – possibly a descendant of those dinosaurs – runs out from under the canteen building to attack your ankles. Gallahs fly up from the trees in squawking pink clouds. The Robinson family takes in guests, in these days of falling wool prices, to keep the farm out of the hands of the bank. Visitors are invited to relax if they wish or help the family with chores. I wanted to learn as much as I could about how a large property works.

It was thirty-eight degrees Celsius, the beginning of spring.

One afternoon, Tony and I visited half of the several water holes on the property: "dams" and "turkey nests" and troughs, fed from an artesian well through forty kilometres of pipe. We checked fences, examined troughs, unplugged pipes. Nearly every grove of trees on this hot flat dusty plain harboured kangaroos in its shade – usually big reds – who looked up and twitched their ears as we passed. Tony pointed them out with considerable pleasure. Yet at dusk, at the last water hole before we started home for supper, when two kangaroos stood up and looked at us, Tony reached under his seat and pulled out a rather plain-looking shiny pistol. He loaded it with bullets and shot, first one, and then the other kangaroo.

They hopped away. One faltered; the other took off across the paddock and into the falling dark. The first dropped from a second bullet. Then it flipped over onto its back and set all four limbs racing across the sky. We went after the other in the truck, and came upon it still twitching, one front paw continually swatting against its ear. Tony put the gun to the back of its head and finished it off.

Perhaps seeing my surprise, or sensing distaste, Tony explained that he liked to see kangaroos on the farm: "After all, they were here before we brought in sheep and cattle." But the station's water supply attracted far more than the land could sustain, so they had to be culled. He had a licence to kill five hundred a year. The previous year, he shot the whole five hundred in one paddock in a single month – "Without having to shoot a single one under six feet."

The next afternoon we set out for several hours to tour the other half of the property. At one of the water holes, sheep had broken through the fence. Fifteen ewes were mired in the mud around the water's edge, up to their necks and bleating. With a rope around their necks, Tony hauled them out, then set them on their feet. When they fell, he set them on their feet again and gave them a gentle push to get them moving. Patiently, affectionately. Kangaroos had died so that these thick animals might live a better life.

A wedge-tailed eagle flew out from its nest in a gum tree – a nest built like a beaver dam out of sticks, and as big. Below, we

poked through the spilled-out debris. Hair balls. Bones pushed from the nest. A cockatoo's skull. A bit of black pig's hair on a bony joint.

Something in this alerted Tony. We drove farther along the track and approached a dry channel that meandered through the property, populated with a wandering line of eucalyptus. The radio was on – afternoon news. Police were trying to discover the identity of a man found murdered in Adelaide. "There! A pig!" In the shade of one of those trees lay a large, dark figure, looking the other way. "They follow the channels up, knowing they'll come to water and sheep eventually." We stopped, and this time Tony reached for the rifle that rested by the gearshift between us.

At the first shot, the pig leapt to his feet and ran, though limping. Tony ran after him, and shot again. The pig tripped, and wheeled, and tried to run some more. Tony took out his pistol and shot again. The pig turned, and lowered his head. We were moving in closer to him – down into the channel sand and up the other side. Would he charge? If this were a movie, he would not go down without making an attempt to drive his tusks into us both.

"You want a shot?" Tony said, offering me his pistol.

"Naw. Go ahead. I'd probably miss."

I probably wouldn't. I remembered that tiny snipe – one bullet in the head.

He shot again, and the pig dropped. Then, like the kangaroo, it flipped over onto its back and tried desperately to run away, its four sharp hooves flailing wildly in the air.

It was not an easy thing to die, I thought. The first kangaroo had also tried to run away from death with nothing but air for purchase. The second had slapped at its ear as though death were a persistent fly. The truck radio could be heard from across the channel: "The murder victim's clothing included dark blue trousers and red boxer shorts with white dots." Undignified as well.

Tony found a short tree limb and we approached the pig, which lay motionless on its side. It was dead, bleeding from its shoulder. The hide was indeed hairy, as the man on the plane had claimed. Whiskery, in fact. The black skin was mottled with yellowish spots. The scent, which I had begun to smell from the far side of the channel, was a sharp, foul, feral assault on the nostrils. Tony pried open the mouth with the tree limb to show me the tusks and the sharp bottom teeth. "Between them, they can rip a sheep wide open." This particular boar, he told me, was capable of eating fifteen lambs a day. His death apparently deserved none of the sympathetic justification the kangaroos' deaths had provoked. It was a matter of protecting the stock.

"Could he be eaten?" I said.

He made a face. "If you saw the contents of his stomach you wouldn't ask. Sheep and cattle and chickens eat grain. But the

wild pig eats carrion." We started back towards the Land Cruiser. "Of course the Germans, now – *they* import them! They reckon they're a delicacy." He chuckled, thinking about those Germans exclaiming over the taste of this foul-smelling eater of carrion.

But this one had become carrion himself. Something else would clean him up. Then sun would bake him, dry him, mummify whatever was left.

On the way back, we stopped by some buildings near the sprawling family home but did not get out. Two, three, five large pigs came grunting excitedly out to meet us, accompanied by several dozen squealing piglets. We sat in the Land Cruiser while they surrounded us – looking up with curiosity, excitement, expectation. Tony laughed, and shook his head. "They've got a lot more personality than sheep, I'll tell you. Smarter, too." Then, still grinning, he started the engine so that we could move on down to the canteen in time for supper. He didn't have to tell me why we had stopped.

A week later, in Sydney, I came up from the subway at Martin Place and found myself uncertain of directions. Here, where the sun was in the north and went the wrong way across the sky, my sense of direction consistently failed me. I wandered uphill thinking I was heading west, but learned a few blocks later that I was heading east. Directly ahead was a hospital. Across the street stood the large statue of a boar, watching me.

Actually, he wasn't standing. His hind quarters rested sidesaddle on the pedestal, which contained a small pool and fountain. His two front legs were straight and spread wide, lifting his chest and neck and massive head to survey the passing traffic. He seemed to be a wise, dignified, and curious creature – part fairytale monster, part figure of legend, part portrait of some grazier's nemesis. Something had disturbed him at his rest. He seemed alert but not alarmed. "*Il Porcellino*," said the brass plate mounted at the edge of the footpath. "If coins are dropped into the fountain or donations put into the box, legend says that if you rub the nose of the boar you will be endowed with good fortune. All donations will care for the sick in Sydney Hospital." Bright sunlight glanced off his forehead. His long dark ears were erect, his hide the blue-black of some river pebbles. He might have been a boar beneath a coolibah tree on some outback station watching the approach of a Toyota Land Cruiser, but he had been removed to the centre of Sydney and human hands had rubbed his snout to a pink as tame and appealing as that of a barnyard pig. He was safer here.

Then there was the second phone call when I'd been home for only a few days – not a half hour after the first.

"Mr. Hodgins?"

"Yes."

"My name is Herb Drummond, of Hertz in Australia?"

"Yes?"

"You hired one of our cars?"

"I did. Put six thousand kilometres on it, too, I think."

"Good onya! Saw some beaut country, too, I reckon."

"Sure did. I drove out from Brisbane to Charleville for a while, and then all the way up beyond Longreach to stay on a station up there."

"Well, Mr., uh, Hodgins, about the car, could you tell me – where did you leave it?"

Surely this was a joke? "You're pulling my leg." The entire map of Australia rose before me, a huge island-continent, mostly flat, red, dusty plains. I couldn't remember where I'd left the car. I imagined this man looking at the same map and wondering where in all that desolation I might have abandoned his little blue two-door sedan. I thought of the numerous automobiles I'd seen at the side of the outback roads, stripped of every accessory, sometimes the only feature on the landscape except for a eucalyptus or two. Did this sort of thing happen to Hertz of Australia often?

But he wasn't pulling my leg. It turned out that a computer in Brisbane had not informed a computer in Sydney that I was leaving the "hire car" in Armidale, somewhere in between. How quickly the Australia I'd just days ago encountered in sharp, specific detail had receded to the vast, blurry, distant outline of a dusty map. In a single afternoon it had become a drawing in a geography book, littered with the mummified corpses of kangaroos and wild boars, the bodies of forgotten cars, and the trail of beer cans and rifle shells discarded by my Sydney admirer's mates.

# ISABEL HUGGAN

## Notes from the Philippines

The cat and I hate it here. We convey this heresy to each other by the merest flicker of our lids, me stretched out on the couch, him lying on the tile floor at my feet. It is too hot to move, too hot and sticky for him to lie on my lap and be petted. We're thrown off a routine we've known for nearly a decade. He sprawls on his back and flicks his tail as he watches a skinny gecko hot-foot it across the ceiling, but he knows better than to get all excited. He'll never get the gecko. It's too damn hot to try, anyway.

The truth is, this humid heat doesn't suit us, not the cat nor the rest of us in this family. We were made for a more northerly clime. Even after half a year, we are still defeated by the heat and humidity of the lowlands where we live in southern Luzon.

Yes, of course it is also lushly beautiful, in an extravagant, breathless, tropical sort of way, and I am not immune to orchids, nor to sunlight sliding off banana leaves in the garden like melted butter. Nevertheless, my homesick heart is stubborn, and night after night I dream of snow.

We decide to go up into the mountains of northern Luzon during the Christmas holidays, knowing we won't find snow but in search of cooler weather. We're hillwalkers, highland people at heart; during our seven years in Ottawa we always headed down to the Adirondacks whenever we had a long weekend. In the seven years since then we've lived on Nairobi's high plateau in Kenya, and in France we were only an hour away from hiking in the Cevennes.

We're also going north to see the ancient Ifugao rice terraces of Banaue. Even before arriving in the Philippines we'd heard about these terraces, billed as the eighth wonder of the world, and although I am prepared to be disappointed – I find reality almost never lives up to its advance notices – I am delighted to be leaving Los Banos, the small university town south of Manila where we live in the staff compound of the International Rice Research Institute.

We set off well before five A.M., in order to get through Manila before the traffic jams up as it does each day by six. Even as we are driving through the city the highway is thickening with jeepneys and trucks, and on the shoulders hundreds, thousands of people are walking or running to catch buses. Sun not yet up, the daily nightmare of this grotesquely overcrowded city has already started.

The distance to Banaue is only around four hundred kilometres, but it will take us ten hours to get there, slowed not only by heavy urban traffic but by the road itself, its surface eroded and pitted by torrential rains and huge transport trucks. (As we go further north, we encounter damage from the killer earthquake of 1991 – at one point the old road simply disappears into a riverbed, and rough detours now seem a permanent fixture. Further still, when we are into the mountains, we skirt by fallen boulders big as houses and edge around great slides of dark red mud, some of it alarmingly fresh.)

As darkness gives way to a silvery drizzle which accompanies us all day, it's possible to see geographical features altering. With the changes, excitement is stirring my blood; I can feel the mountains coming. By the time lowland rice paddies have transformed themselves into broad plains, coconut palms have long disappeared. Brown fields of rice stubble stretch off to meet old blown-out blue volcanoes in the distance. Another terrain, another type of rice, another cropping system – as head of information for IRRI my husband has these details at hand. What is evident even to the uneducated is that rice dominates the landscape. There is always rice.

We pass over wide riverbeds only recently charged with wild flood water during typhoon season but already drying up; in places the water is only a trickle through pale gravel and rocks. The only bits of colour in this grim stonescape are peasants crouched beside the silty water, washing clothes, laying them out flat to dry on the stones even in the rain – where else is there to put them? Sooner or later the sun will come out. It is this kind of cheery accommodation to climate I tell myself I must make too. Sooner or later.

The Cordillera range hikes itself up quickly out of the plains, there's no long drift of foothills before you find yourself climbing steep and winding roads. The average height of the mountains running like a triplicate spine down the centre of north Luzon is 1,800 metres, and several peaks are around 2,800 metres. Tree-covered where illegal logging hasn't stripped the hillsides of hardwood forest, the high ridges are supported by long buttresses covered in narra (Philippine mahogany), pine, palms, and thick tropical undergrowth which always makes me think of monster houseplants on holiday.

By the time we got to Banaue, night is nearly upon us. The valley is stuffed with fog and it is impossible to see the terracing. We can only make out the immediate town itself: a jostle of corrugated metal shacks sat on concrete stilts on the hillside, other more substantial cement block buildings – a church, a clinic, a school – forming a core at the bottom of the hill. In the rain the overall effect is depressing, and the impoverishment a nasty contract to the fancy tourist hotel on the edge of town.

We elect to stay in a small pension called the Spring Village Inn – indeed, the spring splashes noisily outside our bedroom window. The wood-panelled room is small and smells like linseed oil; the single ceiling-light is dim but enough for my husband to begin reading his Christmas present, *Johnson and Boswell in Scotland*. We have brought extra pillows, fruit cake, and a bottle of Grants, and consider holing up in the room until our books are read or our supplies have run out.

But curiosity propels us out into the dark, muddy streets, where we get soaking wet but dine well on rice and curried vegetables at a café which is not much more than a concrete hall halfway down the hill. There are a few other travellers, all of them young and most looking hearty the way trekkers do, but mainly the place is full of local families with kids and groups of giddy teenage boys. We remark on something we notice over the next few days: Filipinos here – the Ifugao – are smaller, more compact than their brothers to the south. These are mountain people, shorter, darker, their faces bringing to mind their counterparts in Nepal or Guatemala.

Walking down the one main street in town, we poke into tiny shops selling woodcarvings, baskets and weaving; handicrafts for which Banaue is famous. We stop at one visibly different from the others – the merchandise is arranged artfully on shelves, the objects have been chosen from various places in the Philippines. We strike up an easy conversation with a sweet-faced man working at a sewing machine at the back of the shop. He is a tailor and his name is Moises. The shop is named for the organization it supports, he says: the Ilob Foundation. What is that, we ask . . .

And so we take the first step, which is to learn about Antoine

Overlooking the Ifugao village of Banga-an

Zenner, who created the Ilob Foundation in 1989 as a means of legalizing his project – caring for a "family" of twenty-five Filipino children, two of whom he has adopted as his own. And then we take the second step, which is to say we'd like to meet Antoine Zenner tomorrow.

The next morning dawns as inclement as the one before, and we don rainproof gear before going out. However, in daylight it is possible to peer through the mist and see the slopes around and above Banaue – we are suitably impressed, awed by the vastness of the endeavour. I admit to my husband that in this rare instance the actual view is better than the glossy photos of the travel brochures.

These rice terraces, although the most famous, comprise only a portion of those in the surrounding hills and mountains, which, my guidebook assures me, if laid end to end (I adore statistics of this kind and never question why anyone would want to do such a stupid thing) would measure fourteen thousand kilometres, or nearly half the circumference of the earth.

There is some argument about the age of the terracing, two schools of thought at opposite ends of a spectrum which runs from two thousand years old to a mere four hundred, the latter position supported by lack of evidence – no mention made by early Spanish invaders who came in search of gold. I tend towards the other, possibly romantic, view, for there seems something timeless in the way the wild mountains have been tamed into a giant garden. Each individual terrace fits itself to the incline and the contour, as well as to those above and below, and the resulting whole is harmonic, graceful, satisfying.

Unlike grand monuments, the rice terraces of Banaue are not the brainchild of one genius, or two, or even a committee. These layered slopes are the ultimate in co-operative creativity. Here's what I like: You don't have to feel sad here as you do for the poor souls who under the lash built the pyramids or, for that matter, York Minster.

Although the terraces are not about conventional power – religious or royal or political – they testify to the power of rice in Asia. The scene is ripe with irony, for although it appears that man has utterly taken over the mountains and controlled nature, it is clear where the real power lies – not with the Ifugao but with the grain they put in their stomachs. Their entire existence is regulated by it, tied to it, springs from it – their gods, their calendar, their social system.

The scene before us is so tranquil it is hard to believe that until the early part of this century the Ifugao were headhunters, settling

most disputes by taking the losers' heads. Like hillbillies everywhere, they seem to have been a cranky lot, fiercely territorial and
protective of their terraces, which, in every sense, were their
wealth. A man's status in the community was – and is – reckoned
by the number of rice fields he and his immediate family possess.

Even now, if there is an Ifugao quarrel ending in violence, it is
more likely to terminate in beheading than in shooting or stab-
bing. Today, however, heads no longer get buried in the front
yard until the skulls are cleaned of flesh so they can be hung as
trophies – of prowess, or retribution, or as a gift for the gods – by
the door-post.

I am unsettled, thinking about this bloody business. It isn't
only that headhunting strikes a placid Canadian like me as, well,
bizarre, but that such domestic people, whose existence was dedicated to food production, could also have been so bloody minded?
How is it, I wonder, that bland rice can fire up men to hack off
each other's heads? There's no sense to it, really.

But then if six months in the Philippines has taught me anything it's that not very much makes sense here. This is a country
of such juxtapositions and contrasts, the only thing you ever
know for certain is that logic is not the tool with which to dig out
meaning.

This morning, for example, I pick up the *Philippine Daily Inquirer*,
which I am in the habit of scanning to start my day. There's the
usual melange of rape-slay and tax-scam stories playing second fid-
dle to the top headline report of the first typhoon in the new year.
Only eight dead so far. Not so bad, really. There were four hundred last month. I check the bottom of the page and discover a
fascinating piece about a recent increase in Marian visitations.

Turns out there was an avalanche of miracles in 1993 as the
Mother of God appeared all over the country, healing the faithful,

warning the godless, doing her thing. In one place she drove the sun into a frenzied dance across the sky; in another she transformed the communion host in a young boy's mouth to flesh and blood.

Bleeding statues, hovering visions, weeping trees – miracles here are common as dirt, common as grass, fodder for the media, food for the masses. There's a hunger, a lust for the miraculous – people turn out in the hundreds of thousands to wait for apparitions in a farmer's field in Agoo. It's partly New Age stuff, which is wildly popular in the trend-vulnerable Philippines, and partly that peculiarly upbeat hybrid of animist and Catholic superstition, which stems from the certainty that anything, anything can happen here. And you are never safe.

Sometimes the earthquakes and volcanoes and typhoons work together in a kind of hellish partnership that defies belief – the floods following a storm set in motion mudslides in mountains shaken up by a recent earthquake . . . or, in another ghastly variation, rain washes volcanic ash down the sides of Mt. Pinatubo and turns it to lahar, deadly grey mud that flows across sugarcane fields, burying whole villages in its wake. (On the way home we passed through devastated territory near Pinatubo, its peak cloud-covered as if hiding itself, ashamed of all the damage it had done. For half an hour we drove through desert, the dry ash blowing up around us like sand, the outstretched empty cans of dispossessed beggars coming up against the car window whenever we slowed down.)

In a country where calamity knows every trick in the book and nature loves to play dirty, maybe miracles provide a kind of heavenly balance. Anything can happen, and does. It's that simple and that complicated.

That next day Moises guides us to Ilob, an area on the edge of Banaue where Antoine Zenner owns four thousand square metres of land on which there are metal-roofed houses in native style – dormitories and a kitchen – and his own house, which is a fine old Ifugao thatched house (a *bale*) standing on high wooden stilts. Dismantled and removed from a village forty kilometres away and rebuilt here, it houses Antoine and his adopted children – Melchior (two) and Sarah (four) – with only minor concessions to modern life: electricity and two window openings in the high cone-shaped roof.

He is a tall, gaunt man wearing a shabby brown pullover. We find him in a small wooden hut, where he's boiling water over an open fire: later, he offers us tea which we drink in glasses. We are urged to sit down – we talk first in French but lapse into English – and soon have his children and their kittens in our laps.

He answers questions with the calm air of a man resigned to doling out the details of his life. Born in Basel thirty-seven years ago but raised in Biarritz, he began travelling the world when he was twenty, and although he once returned to school soon left again (and now is studying law by himself here in Banaue). Travel and work in South America, then in India where he spent two years in Calcutta with Mother Theresa . . . these events and experiences shaping him, creating a person who, in the mid-eighties, found himself in the Philippines.

Although his work had been mainly with the elderly and the ill, he now took an interest in the street children of Manila. After visiting Banaue, and spending a month here being taught how to sew by our Moises, he took all the money he had to buy this land, to create a refuge. As he goes through the tale of his life, he smokes cigarettes which need constant relighting – it is a wet day, the dampness all-pervasive. I wish I had a fresh dry pack of Gitanes for him.

In his first Banaue summer seven years ago, he brought 150 street children up from Manila in groups of thirty to spend time in the cool fresh air. Predictably, many were restless, anxious to get back to the slum haunts they knew – but the idea of giving children a better chance took hold. Soon he had made arrangements to provide a home for twenty-five children, of varying ages, all from desperately poor families in these hills.

"But how did you accomplish this?" I ask, imagining all kinds of logistical problems.

"I just made myself available," he says. And then, with a smile indicating it is a phrase he often uses, he adds, "If your desire is deeply rooted in your heart, everything is possible."

He raised funds by writing to one hundred friends asking for money. Miraculously, most of his letters were answered and, miraculously, most people sent assistance of one kind or another, and have continued to do so. At the beginning, a Québécoise named Isabelle helped him at the home for a year, followed by other young women, Danish and French. It is necessary, he admits, to have a feminine sensibility in the home when raising teenage girls.

With a large beaky nose and a ragged moustache, Antoine is not a handsome man, but he has a magnetic presence which commands attention. I keep trying to pull back from my intense involvement with what he's saying so I can analyze him. What is it: his smile? his skeletal, ascetic presence? His eyes? They're warm, brown eyes, shining with intelligence, and kindness. And something else – what? Devotion? Conviction? He seems more like a priest, a monk, than a father of two rollicking Filipino infants.

"Is this a spiritual journey?" I ask, embarrassed to death by the baldness of my question. He's nonplussed, even expands his answer to include his slow departure from the Catholic church into which he was born, and his increasing interest in the Orthodox – he is hoping to retreat to a Mt. Athos monastery in the summer.

We stay for several hours; it is too wet outside to walk, and this conversation goes down many avenues. We hear how one of his children, a young boy, died suddenly three years ago, and how the boy's mother, then pregnant for the fourteenth time, gave her baby to Zenner when he was born to make up for the loss. Besides adopting Melchior in memory of his dead brother, Zenner also undertook to rebuild and improve the clinic in Banaue to keep others from the same fate. And then health care led him to child care – a small preschool has been established – and to economic welfare for his children: besides the shop, a tricycle business and a new furniture-making project are under way.

His presence is indeed a kind of miracle in this place, I think.

"What do the people in Banaue think of you?" I ask, and he laughs and says I should ask them. I do so, later, and the answer is always the same: "He is a missionary," they say, and they do not mean he is converting the children but that he is a saintly man.

The next day, in spite of the cloud and rain, we hire a jeepney to go out into the neighbouring valleys where the terraces are said to be even more beautiful and where life in the remote villages is essentially unchanged from past generations. The road is horribly rough – my head bangs frequently against the roof as we bounce over rocks and into potholes – but worse than bone-rattling it is narrow; there are times where there's not much more than a grass blade between our wheels and a drop of hundreds of feet. These mountains are, at heart, deeply hostile; the civilized look of the terracing is a poor disguise.

I'm hard pressed to imagine why the Ifugao chose to stay on here in the first place – surely there are friendlier, easier places to grow rice, surely there are lots of other things to eat besides rice. Actually, the tribes used the rough, rocky landscape to their advantage, taking stones and rocks to make the thick walls which separate the rice paddies from each other. The walls curve around the mountains in a sinuous fashion; the design is both elaborate and simple – fluid lines curling and swirling out into little curls and then back again.

From a distance, all you see is agricultural order imposed on the landscape – not in the way of liner vineyard rows along the Rhine, however. In Banaue there are no straight lines.

The jeepney driver is nonchalant about the wicked road conditions, he's been driving this route for eleven years, he says, no problem. He suggests, because of the weather, we attempt only a short walk of an hour or two down into the tiny village of Banga-an. We stop at a small family hotel overlooking the valley, and as we can see almost nothing through the rain we order up pots of tea and bowls of rice and talk to the proprietor, an elfin woman named Conchita.

An Ifugao, she was born in this place and has erected on her property her father's granary, a house on stilts called an *alang*. She invites us up inside it and shows us how the bright gold bundles of grain are stored up in the dark rafters. She explains how she's making *bayah*, fermented rice wine made by mixing roasted grain and yeast and letting the mash drip through a "filter" of leaves into a pot. Ready to drink in less than a week but even better and stronger if left for another two, she says.

Eventually the sky clears and we start down into Banga-an, a sensation not unlike entering an enormous green bowl. The walls of the valley swirl like a repetitive melody – this is the geographic equivalent of Ravel's *Bolero*, say, or Pachebel's *Canon*.

However, being *in* the terraces is quite different than viewing them from afar: the trail is steep and slippery, and the footing is precarious along the tops of the stone walls. I felt gigantic sitting next to Conchita on the floor of the *alang*, and here again I feel enormous – these narrow walkways are meant for the small nimble feet of the Ifugao, not for my size 11's.

As we start down the steep hillside, we watch a woman planting seedlings in a rice paddy near the village of Banga-an itself. (We guess the bent figure is a woman and as we draw nearer we see we are right. In this village, as in so many others in the region, men are working to make money elsewhere, and only the women, children, and elderly are left.) She's wearing a red sweater and has red plastic tied over her bamboo coolie hat, and she never straightens as she works to a steady rhythm – taking a single seedling from the bright green bunch she grasps in one hand and sticking it firmly down into the watery mud with the other.

Later, in the village (miserable, filthy, and impoverished, nothing like the dreamy little picture postcard place it appears to be from Conchita's verandah), as we are sitting on a log bench to take photographs, the woman looks over at us and gives us a vermilion, betel-nut-stained smile – her thin face is wrinkled with sun and age, and she looks far too old to be working as hard as she is. We realize when we have climbed back up to the top of the terraces – perhaps three hours have passed – that she has not stopped in all that time.

The mountains of Banaue fade like Brigadoon once we are home in the heat, and I can hardly remember the delicious sensation of being cold and wet. Again I complain to the cat, and, again, I dream of snow. But also in my dreams is the bent figure of the old woman planting seedlings in the paddy, working without pausing. It becomes clear to me, in the way things become perfectly obvious in dreams, that she alone is responsible for the terraces – she has built them and now farms them entirely on her own. Like the little red hen, she has done it – miraculously – all herself.

Which, in a sense, she has.

And it occurs to me that in Banaue I witnessed another kind of miracle from the supernatural variety so beloved in the Philippines. No flashing lights or shimmering visions of Mary, no surprising shocks out of the blue. In fact, perhaps it stretches the O.E.D. definition of miracle to use it in the way I do, but how else to express the extraordinariness of the sculpted hillsides, which seem to have been executed by one divine, artistic intelligence? The miracle is not only that a primitive people has shown such incredible ingenuity and engineering skill, but that individuals, each working separately – and working simply in order to eat – created a landscape of such beauty.

And I think of Antoine Zenner. No wonder he has chosen Banaue to work his own small-scale miracle of generosity and compassion. Surrounded by the terraces, it is easier to believe that one individual can make a difference, that not only can anything happen but that everything is possible.

# Kiev, November 1993

You do not simply pick up and go. You pick up, and pick up, till your arms become so full it seems you'll never manage even one step towards that place your family fled more than fifty years ago, that you have heard about through all the stories of your child-hood. What has been a rich, private fold in your imagination has suddenly been shaken out, become a country you can travel to like any other – and you are afraid, there is no other word for it. Afraid to be on the verge, exchanging all that wealth of stories for currency that may turn out to be worse than valueless.

You pick up, and put down, and put off. It is difficult to get a map of the country – and as for the city itself, impossible. You can't set off as if it were any of the European countries you have visited; nor can you go as if you were a total stranger, having no connection to the place. You seek out people in Toronto who know Kiev, who have contacts there who can show you around. It is still a place, they say, where strangers mustn't wander freely, strangers who don't know the language of what is safe and where is dangerous, and whom you have to keep away from. You are ask-ing for information, but most often they tell you stories: *The coun-try's in a mess; there's no fuel for cars, never mind planes; bands of thugs attack the trains; rape isn't considered a crime; there's no food to eat; everyone's desperate to get out and come here, so why would you even want to visit there?* A few are more sanguine, they've been many times – it's no more dangerous than Toronto, they say, though cautioning, *Take toilet paper, take Kleenex, don't go out on your own, you have to be able to speak the language – even if you can, you should still have a guide with you at all times.*

Two weeks before I'm due to leave, I go to Toronto to pick up my visa; it still isn't ready, long after they've promised it, and I have to pry and bully it out of the consul. I pick up the gifts I've been advised to take: instant coffee, tea, fruitcake my mother has baked, nylon stockings, pens with CANADA printed on them, and, most importantly, packets of American one-dollar bills. I pick up forms and letters faxed me by the friends who have already been, and who have organized the contacts, the lodgings, the guides without whom I could not go. I pick up my passport and tickets and suitcase and, even when I'm flying over Labrador, tell the person sitting next to me that I'm on my way to Germany, to a conference, with a short stopover in Kiev. My neighbour tells me that his landlady, when he first came to Canada, was a Ukrainian: she had told him how, during the war, she and her husband had done forced labour in a camp in Germany; how she had seen her husband die each day before her eyes – a tall, robust man, six feet tall, become a skeleton in six months' time.

So that even as I journey back to this place I've never been, I am still picking up stories. I add this new one, so randomly acquired, to the others in my arms, then try to blank out everything but the fact that in two hours' time we will land in Frankfurt, where I will board another plane, to Kiev. I adjust my eyeshade, souvenir of a flight to a safer destination, a place to which I have no obligations, no family ties, no imaginary or physical debts to pay. For Kiev, capital of a country that is larger than

France and with twice the population of Canada, is not just a thousand-year-old city, but a part of how I have defined myself, part of the slash or hyphen between the two parts of my identity: Ukrainian-Canadian. This is why I catch myself saying *I am going back to Kiev*, why I think of this journey as a return, for all that I go there as a foreigner, a stranger. A genetic prodigal.

The Kiev of my Saturday-morning Ukrainian school is a legendary kingdom, Kievan Rus'. In the basement of the cathedral on Bathurst Street, against the rattling of the water pipes in the poison-green walls, we learn of the founding of Kiev by three brothers and their sister, heads of the Polianian tribe; of fierce battles against the invading Varangians and Khazars, and of how, in 862, Oleh, regent of the king of Novgorod, seized control of this walled city on the great river Dnipro, down which gold and furs, honey and slaves were shipped to the Black Sea, and beyond to Byzantium and Islam. Seized control by a ruse, luring the city's commanders outside the gates, and murdering them. Oleh, Ihor, Sviatoslav, and Yaroslav the Wise, all the legendary rulers of Kievan Rus' – they were full of greatness and cunning, and I learn their various reforms and revenges by heart, as they are told to me by my teachers: stories straight out of *The Chronicle of Bygone Years*, written by an eleventh-century Kievan monk, living in a cave hollowed under the great-walled and golden-domed city.

I memorize the tributaries of the Dnipro River long before I have even heard of the Mackenzie, the Red, the Fraser. I act in plays about the bringing of Christianity to tenth-century Kiev by Princess Olha, she who avenged the murder of her husband by inviting the warriors who'd slain him to a great feast, locking them in the bath house where they'd been invited to refresh themselves after the long journey, and then setting fire to it. I learn, sight unseen, the glories of St. Sophia's Cathedral with its fabulously rich mosaics and marble sarcophagi, in which, by some miracle, lie the real bodies of the legendary rulers of ancient Rus'.

I am taught all these legends as if they were historical truths; I seize on them because they are all there is to hold of a country that has vanished, that I cannot point to on a map, saying, my family comes from here. On most maps of the world, there is only Russia, with Ukraine marked as Malorus – little Russia – to the south of it, or as the Ukrainian Soviet Socialist Republic, a country that has nothing to do with ancient Kiev, a country that is busy turning all Ukrainians into Russians, my teachers tell me – killing off our language, our history, everything but a folk culture standardized, controlled by Central Command in Moscow.

Once, after a rehearsal for our play, I steal the headdress of the Princess Olha. It is not just gold-foil wrapping paper and egg-shaped beads painted to look like pearls. As I fit the crown on my head, I am putting on her power and her cunning, I am plotting an immortal revenge against the Derevlianian traitors. Revenge for a monk to set down two centuries after my death, inscribing my praises in ink that burns, sweet as incense, on the page.

The instant I walk off the plane, all my airborne expectations crash; this is not an airport like any other I have passed through – Heathrow, Charles de Gaulle, Frankfurt, Rome. Through the milky, November air, a flight control tower looms as if from the set of a fifties science-fiction film; the two old women walking towards us – women in head scarves and shapeless skirts and men's padded jackets – have come to clean the plane we have just left. They carry galvanized tin pails, and in their hands are long straw whisks, the closest thing to a sheaf of wheat I will come across during my stay in Kiev.

I have never been to Africa, to Indonesia or India. My travelling, up till now, has all been European, North American. But this is not Europe; this airport inhabits a zone that no longer exists, but whose material existence stubbornly persists. Not stubbornly – hopelessly. The hammer and sickle stencilled on the glass doors leading into the terminal will remain until sleet and rain erase everything but a thick blue shadow; blue, not red, to show that we are in Ukraine, not Russia. But the men dumping our baggage on a floor that may never in its entire lifetime have been washed speak Russian, though I find an English version of the form I have to sign, swearing that I am not importing gold or icons or raw foodstuffs of animal origin and slaughtered fowl. It is printed on paper so rough and thin I'm terrified it will split at each touch of my pen. The small print warns me to keep this form with my passport, that I cannot leave the country without it, and that it is *not renewable in case of loss*. I have not been in this country for half an hour, and already I am panicking about not being able to get out again.

You are what and how you speak. Even before we get to the city, driving past miles of pine and beech and birch woods, it is clear that, linguistically, I am what the French call a *mutilé de guerre*: I see my tongue a stump, swathed in clumsy bandages, like the legless beggars in Brueghel paintings. It is not just that I forget which ending to put on which noun or verb – a calamity in a language as highly inflected as Ukrainian, its grammar as byzantine as its churches. The little language I have is, by and large, archaic or comprehensible only to someone from western Ukraine; the people I meet here speak a Ukrainian that has been highly Russified, and that has borrowed all kinds of words from English or German or French. (Later I will find out that I have bewildered

Maryna, my guide, by asking for the *lazynka* when I should have said *tu-a-let* – coded, here, not by the silhouettes of a woman in a dress and a man in trousers, but by drawings of a high-heeled shoe and a bowler hat.)

That we are driving at all is a miracle of the sort Kievans are used to, by now. If you have money – American dollars or *valiuta* – you can get anything; even a small, rusting Lada, with seat belts that don't fasten, and a tank full of what they call benzine, which, in terms of what they've had to pay for it, might as well be cognac. Maryna, it turns out, studied English at high school, but understands better than she speaks – and she speaks a few correct, memorized phrases, the equivalent of what I've learned in Ukrainian for this trip.

Still, somehow we make ourselves understood. *Zoloti Kupoly* I catch from the words addressed to me when we have entered the outskirts of Kiev. And I turn and see, out the window, a splurge of gold. Yet opposite the gleaming, onion-shaped domes, pushing up above the leafless trees is something I cannot identify at all, something monumental and terrible, the aesthetic equivalent of a bomb going off behind your eyes. A Soviet memorial to the Great Patriotic War, they tell me, and it's hard to gauge the irony, or lack of it, in their tone. It's hard, too, to know how they expect me to respond. Imagine a structure as prominent as the CN tower, but shaped like a tubby version of the goddess in the logo for Columbia Pictures. Imagine this goddess fashioned from a substance like asbestos. She is even more monstrously tall than she need be, because she is holding a curiously blunt sword, high over her head. As we drive by, I see that the base of the statue is made up of concrete cubes: later, when I see the enormous mosaic of the Mother of God in the gilded apse of St. Sophia, I wonder if this prefab war goddess was meant to recall that miraculous image, dark, dark blue against the deep and flickering gold of the tiles. The

Myself, in a playground in Kiev, near the apartment I stayed in

mosaic has survived since the eleventh century; this statue, with any luck, will be torn down before this century's done – imploded, the way they do to obsolete hotels in places like Las Vegas.

I had been warned, before I left, that the men here will kiss your hand; they do. The official sent to greet me at the airport accompanies us into the apartment building where I will sleep the five nights of my stay in Kiev: shows me the gas stove, the bathroom and toilet, the piles of neatly folded linen on the fold-out bed. Shows me how to get CNN on the TV which I have already decided I will never watch. Makes a little joke about how I even have my own private balcony – and I do; a glassed-in plywood alley running the length of the two rooms that make up the apartment. The balcony windows look onto the spire tips of the Catholic cathedral and the cubelike tower of the SPORT hotel, just visible behind the clutch of other apartment buildings facing mine. Almost all have laundry festooning their verandahs, glassed in or not, even though I cannot see how, in this permanently damp, milky air, anything can dry at all.

After he shows me how to double-lock the door, the official wishes me a happy stay in Kiev and kisses my hand. Yet the only thing going through my head as I assure him how perfectly comfortable and convenient I find the apartment is *I will never be able to fall asleep here. I will never be able to survive more than fifteen minutes on my own in this prison.* For the moment I won't have to. Maryna asks if I would like to rest after my long journey, and I say, too quickly, no. And so we set off, taking the stairs this time instead of the tomblike elevator, and following a maze of deserted paths down to the street which joins Red Army boulevard.

Apartment blocks, cinemas, repair shops; all the signs in Cyrillic, that hidden alphabet of my childhood. No cafés, though, or at least, no picture-window restaurants in which you can look out at the people strolling by. This is not a café but a kiosk culture: clustered every hundred yards or so, they look like abbreviated trailers, mobile homes with one great window showing off not flowers, and only rarely newspapers, but most often shampoo and lipstick (French), fruit juice (German), Campbell's soup, and rows of Johnnie Walker, Cinzano, Jack Daniel's, Martini and Rossi. The kiosks are on every major street: fluorescent-lit, functional, wholly unbeautiful. The desire they contain is condensed, oversweetened like Carnation milk. I see only a few people stopping at the windows – are these traps only for tourists desperate for a quick fix of normality, the kind a brand name assures?

One of the huge shopwindows we walk past on Kiev's main boulevard, the Khreshchatyk, is filled with only one item: a giant reproduction of a Tampax box – Tampax, like toothpaste, a status symbol only tourists or the very wealthy can afford. Worse than all of this is the way that food itself has become a marker of class and privilege. Maryna takes me, at my request, to the Bessarabian market, a turn-of-the-century building, one of the few that survived the explosion on the Khreshchatyk, set off by the retreating Soviet army, in 1941. It's like a giant greenhouse, with a children's picture-book frieze going all the way around the wrought-iron walls: pictures of cows, lambs, pigs, fish, every kind of fruit. Yet on the counters themselves, there is no abundance: a few walnuts arranged in an enamelled pan, one pomegranate, a small basket of mushrooms. Maryna says, "Only rich people come here to shop." I can't quite read her tone of voice: disapproval rather than envy? A slight measure of disgust? As we leave the building and turn a corner, we see an old peasant woman from one of the villages on the city's outskirts; she is sitting on a piece of cardboard, a kerchief spread out before her, bearing eight or ten bruised apples. They look like little yellow globes, each spotted with a hundred continents. Perhaps that's why people buy them – for the feeling that they hold a little world, however blemished, in the safety of their pocket.

We walk on, from souvenir shop to souvenir shop, until we've found what seems to be the right place to change a few of the American dollars I have brought to Kiev. Maryna counts out the bushel of coupons – *karbovantsi* – I've been given in exchange, making sure the amount's correct. I don't know how or where to carry all this paper. I will not be able to spend it all, the twenty dollars' worth I exchange my first night in Kiev. When the vultures come up, as they do to anyone at a currency exchange booth, Maryna gives them a glance that's the equivalent of an elbow in the eye. Then she takes my arm and leads me out from the hot, stuffy brightness of the shop, into the abrupt darkness of the city.

The city is dark because there is a shortage not just of energy but of lightbulbs, too: people unscrew them from apartment corridors and elevators and outer walls – perhaps they have even taken them from the metro stations tunnelled so deep underground that they can serve as bomb shelters. In each huge, circular chandelier only one bulb burns, yet this underground seems torrid with light compared with the steep street up which we walk to get a view of that Dnipro whose tributaries I memorized so many years ago. It is something I have never experienced before, being in a blacked-out city at night, and the occasional gleams from streetlamps that haven't yet been plundered only make the darkness thicker. As we walk towards the parapet, I can make out the shape of a man huddled near us, the kind of man who was hanging around the currency counters in the souvenir shops. All the warnings friends, relations, self-pronounced authorities gave me before I left Canada come back in a rush: *Five years ago theft was virtually unknown there, and now it's the only way people can make ends meet; one young man, visiting from Edmonton, got so badly beaten up he had to spend eight weeks in hospital.* I try to remember the word for dangerous in Ukrainian, but it doesn't come, and it's too dark to open the pocket dictionary, which has already proved itself as good as useless. My tongue is a sieve – all the language I thought I had pours through it, silent and fickle as water. If the man were to attack us, I would not be able even to cry out.

Maryna doesn't seem concerned. She takes my arm and leads me to the edge of the parapet, from where we look out to a sleeve of darkness, roughed by the occasional light from a barge pushing down the river. No gold or fur or honey on those barges, and no Constantinople at this river's end. Maryna turns me so that I can see a gigantic, feebly lit arch a hundred yards across from us. It's part of the monument built, she explains, to celebrate the eternal friendship that has always linked Russia and its little brother, Ukraine. This time there is no mistaking her tone of voice. When I buy a pack of postcards the next day, I see that the green shape I took to be an overcoat two giants had hoisted high over their heads is really the five-pointed Soviet star, streaming glory behind it as Russia and Ukraine stride forward into the Dnipro.

My first day in Kiev I am too keyed-up to eat. Maryna takes me to a shop where the people queuing up far outnumber the cakes on display; to a café where I can buy a piece of bread with sausage, or a dish of plums and cream, but each time I shake my head, no. I offer to buy her something, but she refuses, and I am too stupid with jet lag and culture shock to understand the complicated etiquette of the situation. It is impolite to eat by yourself; it is necessary to break bread with a stranger, or even, as we finally do in the smoky bar of a hotel somewhere on the Khreshchatyk, for me to take a few walnuts from the little plastic bag Maryna has pulled from her purse; to eat the apple she has also brought, and to down some of the orange-crystal drink she chose for us at the bar. The apple is like the windfalls the deer find in the farmer's fields behind our house: small, red, pocked with small brown scabs. The flesh is streaked subtly with red, as though your lips are bleeding as you bite into it.

As we sit at a small table in the smoky bar, trying not to watch the American rock video on the screen over the counter, I discover there are gaps between us other than our lack of a common language. Maryna is nineteen; young enough to be my daughter. She is beautiful, and she wears her beauty as she does her mulberry-coloured winter coat: as a defence against more things than I will ever understand during my short stay here. Against the raw November air, yes, but more importantly against the knowledge that no matter how clever you are – and she is very bright – no matter how much Faulkner and Joyce, Kant and Hegel you have read in translation, you will never know a world in which things are not in chaos and crisis – in which, if you're a married woman, you have the time to read and even write books, because you don't have to spend hours every day lining up to buy milk and bread, a bit of meat and a few vegetables, all at different shops. Because there is still paper to print things on, strong, smooth white paper, enough to write first and second drafts, to crumple, half-used, and throw away. Because you inhabit, by right, a world in which you don't have to spend three hours every day getting back and forth between the centre of the city and the two-room apartment in which you live with your parents, at the edge of town: two rooms, not two bedrooms. Maryna studies journalism at the university; her boyfriend studies computers; if they are lucky, their combined salaries might amount one day to forty dollars a month. The ticket on which I flew from Frankfurt to Kiev cost seven hundred dollars.

Everything here boils down to terminal arithmetic: the minute amount you have, opposed to the enormity of what you need. Every moment that I spend in Kiev I will hear a double clock ticking: one hand striking off the minutes I have left before I leave; the other grabbing on to, squeezing one by one, the endless minutes all the others have to stay behind. In Ukrainian, the word for freedom – *volia* – rhymes with destiny or fate – *dolia*. People here are finally free citizens of a country free at last, after so many hundreds of years, so many different forms of tyranny, but the new freedom seems hardly to be distinguished from the old enslavement. All the people I will meet in the next few days will be free only to live out their destiny; being fated to remain here, whatever happens, whether the streets of Kiev run with blood next Sunday as the cult leader Maria Dev Khristos predicts, or only with the cold November rain, bringing with it a new devaluation of the currency, a dozen more beggars in the street, the world ending in its slow and slipshod way, and far too unpredictably for anyone to do a thing to change it.

I have two scandalously cheap nights at the Ballet and Opera Theatre (my front-row seats cost the equivalent of sixteen cents each). The building is glorious – after all those dim, hushed streets on which I seem never to have heard a car sound its horn, or greetings exchanged, it is like stepping into a flourish of trumpets. We are early, so we walk round and round the balconies that look down to the foyer, distinguishing the gilded names of composers scrolled in Cyrillic script: Mussorgsky, Rimsky-Korsakov, Tchaikovsky, Glinka. The colours here are all the more luxurious for being subtle: cream and just enough gold that you feel yourself gleaming under its light. As we take our seats in a box overlooking the orchestra rows, I make out families with rafts of little girls in party dresses and, in their hair, those wide, white puffs of ribbons which my sister and I, seeing them in photographs of old country aunts and uncles, used to call whirlybird bows. In the interval I will see these same small girls doing jetés in the corridors off the foyer, snowboots barely encumbering their feet as they twirl over polished marble.

Tonight it is *Lebedene Ozero – Swan Lake*. The program feels like a relic, its paper the regulation recycled onionskin. As I look at it more closely, I see that it *is* a relic, nearly three years old. Someone has simply taken a pencil and crossed out the names of those dancers no longer with the company, and pencilled in their replacements. It doesn't seem to matter; the dancing is extraordinary, the delicacy and finesse of movement galaxies away from all the shoving and pushing and crushing of bodies into metro cars. I have never seen *Swan Lake* before, I tell Maryna, and she is astonished; she rarely goes to the ballet these days, she says, because she has already seen everything in the repertoire a dozen times over. When a production from anywhere outside the country comes to the theatre, it is impossible, she says, to get a ticket. People would rather go without a day's food than miss a play or opera from the world outside – a world as enchanted to Kievans, I imagine, as the lake to which Siegfried has now returned in search of his swan queen. He performs an extraordinary set of leaps, rushing after the malign enchanter who has the swan queen in his power. He grabs and lifts him, holds him high for what seems forever, and then dashes him to the ground, tearing off one of his long dark wings as he does so. There is something fiercely transgressive here, the climactic moment of the whole ballet this *pas de deux* between prince and magician – and then the villain dies, and the white queen nestles in the prince's arms, and the theatre rocks to cries of *brava, brava!* I know *Swan Lake* is supposed to end tragically, and yet here are the lovers reunited, safe in the eye of a storm of applause. Strange, I think: sentimental. Like changing the end of *Lear* so that the old king and his daughter live together, happily ever after.

Podil is the part of Kiev I fall in love with. Once it was a cluster of wooden huts at the base of the hill on which the ancient city rose: palaces, churches, ringed within a wall crowned by the Golden Gates. Now it's a maze of three-storey, stuccoed buildings painted deep rose, leaf green, azure, or the quiet yellow of mustard seed. In Podil you find the city's most exclusive shops: perfume, cosmetics, flowers, silks and brocades. You also find here the only real cafés; we stop for lunch in one that is decorated like a Ukrainian cottage, with embroidered cloths draping the windows and a replica of a traditional clay stove, painted with folk motifs. There are no waitresses; you line up at the small counter and wait, and wait, till you can grab your chance to buy sausage or sardines on toast, pastries, drinks made from the syrup in which wild plums are preserved. Then you rush with your booty to one of the long, always-crowded benches; every so often one of the cooks rushes out of the kitchen and grabs the cigarette from someone's lips – you are not

Pecherska Lavra (or Kievan Cave Monastery)

supposed to smoke here, she says, and grinds the cigarette into the floor, whereupon she exits with a flourish of her dishcloth, and the smoker lights up again.

We walk all around Podil, stopping every few moments so that I can take a photograph, though my fingers are so cold I can hardly press the button. But this is a Kiev I hadn't known existed, an old town in which there seems to be no trace of the five-pointed star, or the sugar-cube building style favoured by Stalin. Before we leave Podil, Maryna takes me to a craft shop hidden in an alleyway, and here I find at last something I want to buy and take home with me. Clay figures, painted white or *café au lait*, and decorated with spiralling patterns: a cossack on horseback; a ram with curling horns; a fox lady in a long skirt, one hand up to her face in a gesture of mock astonishment; a small, beautifully shaped horse, the thousand-year-old symbol of Kiev.

I buy almost the entire stock, not caring that the pottery is delicate, that it will take a miracle to bring all these figures home unscathed. And yet I do – the only damage is an epaulette knocked off one of the cossack's shoulders. It's not till I get home that I discover each of the figures is a whistle – that if I lift the fox lady or the ram to my lips, I can blow a sharp, pure note. The sound I never heard on the streets of Kiev – the sound of a policeman's or a child's whistle.

You cannot leave Kiev without visiting Pecherska Lavra, the city of golden domes rising from a steep hill overlooking the Dnipro. On a cold, wet Sunday morning we ride the packed metro cars and jammed trolleybuses to what was once the Greek Orthodox equivalent of Vatican City. Once inside the scrolled and gilded gate, we are in perceptual heaven. Monastery buildings whitewashed, baroque, their reflections floating like swans across the rain-slicked cobblestones. Elaborately fashioned lampposts, filigree gazebos, rich purple asters blooming in the gardens – everything inside these walls is magic.

And all of it is built upon the caves below, the first of them hollowed in 1051 by a monk returning from a pilgrimage to the monastery of St. Aphon in Greece. He was quickly joined by others: the icon painter Alipiy, and a healer, Agapit, who tended whole flocks of the city's sick. We tramp – a host of us – down a sloping corridor of whitewashed wood, our only view to the exterior an occasional window cut into the wall, screened by wooden rails painted a rich blue, through which we glimpse a blur of golden leaves and brilliant black trunks. At last we crowd before a narrow door and push inside, five or six at a time, Maryna holding the sleeve of my coat so that I don't get left behind. I haven't yet learned to shove assertively enough; it is a survival skill, here. The alternative, it is becoming clear to me, is to be trampled, suffocated as we are now, bottlenecked into a stifling cell where a young, black-skirted monk, his dark hair curling against his lard-pale face, directs us to a tray of candles.

Beeswax, and thinner than my little finger. I light the long, fragrant candle and push myself closer to Maryna, who has crossed herself and is already entering the narrow corridor into the caves. The floor slants abruptly – the only light comes from our tapers, and yet I can see clearly, where the corridor branches off, a throng of people, some fifty candles strong, are having a service of some kind in a niche we are not allowed to enter. Instead, we pass farther down the corridor, farther inside the earth, pausing every few feet beside a ledge cut into the wall. On each ledge is a tight triangle of mummified flesh, no bigger than a tall child, and draped in rich brocade. Sometimes there's a pair of tiny leather shoes sticking out, with tiny leather feet inside. One of these mummies, Maryna tells me, is the monk Nestor. I think of the place I first heard his stories: a basement whose atmosphere was not unlike that of these catacombs through which I press now, forbidding myself to give way to hysteria, claustrophobia, nausea, despite the heat and sweet scent of the candles, despite the sheer mass of bodies heaving in front of and behind me. Finally, we reach the farthest point to which we are admitted: the cells in which the most devout of the monks had themselves walled alive. In each cell a small, semicircular window has been cut; here bread and water would be left each day; perhaps, too, a beeswax candle like the ones we are holding in our hands. The windows are glassed-in now, and curtained with floral prints that look as out of place here as would a tea trolley or whatnot stand. Of course no one lives here now, and yet I want to ask, just to make sure. Perhaps there are people in this city – that young, fanatical-looking monk, for example – to whom the idea of a life within these walls, a steady supply of bread and water, would seem a luxury.

For there are more beggars at the Lavra than I have seen anywhere else in Kiev. Women who are not old, standing just inside the doors of the churches, singing hymns, humming snatches of the liturgy, and holding out small pails into which alms can be thrown. A crippled man, the stumps of his legs wound round in dirty linen bandages. Maryna brushes past the beggars as if she doesn't even see them; I follow suit, guiltily, for I can't help seeing them, and would put something into their pails except for the fear of offending, or seeming to criticize my guide. I wonder about her gesture before entering the caves: making the sign of the cross. She has not done so on entering any of the other churches we have visited; why here, on the threshold to the caves? Because we are going underground, into the sleeping city of the dead, and it would be dangerous not to make some small, propitiatory gesture?

Later, at the cathedral of St. Sophia, standing before the sarcophagus of Yaroslav the Wise, about whom Nestor wrote with such splendour in his chronicles, I find myself wishing for tiered trays of candles in crimson glasses; for priests swaying censers full of the sweet, smoky incense that, long ago, used to be the scent of Sundays for me. Trappings, regalia, circumstantial décor; not the faith that caused my great-grandmother to bow before the icons and kiss the floor in front of the priest's hem every Sunday. That kind of faith I do not want; cannot imagine. Will it return to these churches, as the crises deepen and disaster looms – a Russian invasion, or another Chernobyl? If only there were candles to light and say a prayer by, in this ancient sanctuary which has been sacked and destroyed and rebuilt, turned into a brewery and now nothing more than a museum. And always under the gaze of the blue-draped Mother of God, her hands outspread in either horror or blessing, and a small, embroidered towel tucked into the sash at her waist.

It happens to be the fiftieth anniversary of Kiev's liberation from the Nazis, in 1943. Today, the boulevards are full of blue and yellow flags, and hung with banners saying, "Remember those who struggled for your freedom." I wonder if they've been recycled from the Soviet era; if not the banners themselves, then the words and very tone of discourse, everything stamped with the mark of exclamation, exhortation, as if people couldn't be trusted to think or remember for themselves.

From the Khreshchatyk – once the Champs-Elysées of Kiev, filled with luxurious shops, theatres, cafés, until the Soviets blew it up in their retreat from the invading German army – all traffic has been cleared, so that people can take part in some kind of distance race. There are more and more vendors with booths and tables, and a version of our Dickie Dee wagons: two women in simulated Ukrainian dress (plastic aprons with embroidery stamped on them, plastic ribbons hanging from the equally plastic wreaths in their hair) push baby carriages full of ice-cream bars. Voices drift in and out over the loudspeakers, but no one seems to be listening.

Through all the flags and banners, I am looking for traces of the city that has been invaded and sacked and ruined so many times: in 1240 by the Batu Khan's Mongolian hordes, in 1941 by the Nazis, and in 1986 by a subtler form of annihilation – the radioactive winds blowing from Chernobyl, 130 kilometres north of the city. When I meet Maryna's mother, I ask her about the events of April 1986, and she tells me it was two weeks before anyone in Kiev was told what had really happened. Children, she said, went out to pick mushrooms they would eat for dinner that night. Mushrooms are a sacred food here, mushrooms that you pick in the woods outside the city, carry in wicker baskets all through jam-packed metro rides, and cook delicately in cream or butter; one of the few luxuries available to anyone able to go out and harvest them. The children of Kiev were evacuated for a period of six months after the explosion at Chernobyl: Maryna would have been twelve in 1986. I try to imagine a city without children, a whole summer in which the playgrounds and schoolyard soccer fields, the duck-shaped paddle boats and fairground rides stand silent, motionless. How parents would have felt, learning that for two whole weeks they had been pouring glasses of contaminated milk for their children, urging them to drink up, to become healthy and strong. Not feeding them the potassium iodide tablets necessary to protect the thyroid gland from absorbing radioactive iodine. And I remember something I once heard, which hits me in the face each time I see a child on these streets: that the incidence of childhood cancer of the thyroid, almost unheard of elsewhere, has reached epidemic proportions in Ukraine and Belarus.

I am looking for traces, in these streets down which we hurtle in the swaying trolleybus, of the thousands of children who, along with their parents and grandparents, cousins and aunts and uncles, walked to their murder, fifty-two years ago. The trolleybus takes us along Zhitomyrska and Artema streets, and then down roads so dreary that not even every blossoming chestnut tree in Kiev could rescue them. When the Jews of Kiev were marched to Babi Yar it would have been early autumn. They'd have walked by many of the apartments we are passing now; by this shoe repair shop, and that post office, though the weather that day was unseasonably warm and clear, nothing at all like today's grey mist. It is the right weather in which to come here, though; the right season, too, with the trees planted round Babi Yar divested of their leaves, standing bare, black, utterly vulnerable. We leave the sidewalk, with its regulation kiosks, and enter the path that leads to the monument, a huddle of gigantic figures blackened by the rain to the colour of basalt. Men struggling, a woman at the very top, holding up a child that no one and nothing is about to save. The figures are mounted on what looks like a concrete bunker

A view of the Babi Yar monument

projecting towards the continuation of the ravine, on the other side of the road that rings the monument.

It's not the sculpture that moves me, but the place itself, the circular ditch or moat in which the figures are placed, and around which we walk in the fine, chill rain, through a carpet of willow and maple leaves. The only sounds come from giant crows, cawing and hopping between the trees encircling us. Stark, black crows against grass that is still lush, and long and green. The buildings we had passed on our way down were glum, the grey of rain-soaked concrete, but here the colours are bright, clear, uncanny. Like the silence, the completeness and closure of the circle whose circumference we walk. There is a kind of ramp up to the monument, marked with thin, zigzag ridges; at the end of the ramp are three plaques, one in Ukrainian, one in Russian, and the last in Hebrew. They replace the Soviet-era version, whose words did not so much inscribe as erase: "To the victims of fascism." At these new plaques, people have left fresh flowers and there are *kar-bovantsi* wedged between the letters in the three different alphabets. I can understand flowers, but the gesture of leaving money here, small paper pieces curling in the rain, puzzles me. I remember the custom of placing coins on the eyes of the dead, and think of the people I have seen going about their business on the streets of Kiev this morning; imagine them with paper money where their eyelids should be.

Once more I take photographs, half a roll, clicking and adjusting the shutter as Maryna waits patiently, trying not to shiver. We are going on to her parents' apartment for dinner; there will be hot food, and tea and wine to drink; books and conversation. Yet it takes me forever to finish; I take pictures of the crows, the drab apartment blocks, the distant woods where the ground slopes precipitously – a ground full of blood and bones and bullets. All the Jews of Kiev, and after them, the others: resistance fighters of all political stripes, writers, actors and singers from the Ballet and Opera Theatre, cocktail waitresses from restaurants frequented by the Nazi élite. And the half-starved members of Kiev's Dynamo soccer team, which, cheered on by a stadium full of equally starving people, had been foolish enough to win its match against a team of sleek and shining-muscled German soldiers.

On the long trolleybus ride to her home, I pluck up the courage to ask Maryna a question: *Are you an optimist?* She says yes, and then, *What else can you be here? How long could you survive if you were a realist?* Her response brings back to me a picture of the Ballet and Opera Theatre, with its gilded names of the great composers, its marble hallways down which small girls, with immense white bows in their hair and heavy snow boots on their feet, do pirouettes, their arms extended as enchantingly as those of the prima ballerina they've just applauded till their small hands ached. The pride, the delight that parents here take in their beautiful, vulnerable children: the necessity of leaving the two-room apartments into which as many as six people and three generations might be crammed, of going out in your finery to watch, to become, something magical, beautiful on stage. The packed theatre, the cries of *brava, brava!* falling like ticker tape from the balconies. And I understand now the reason why the swan doesn't die at the end of the ballet, but returns unharmed to her lover's arms. I begin to understand the power and the terrible hope of happy endings.

It snows the morning I leave; one of nature's falsifying gestures, utterly theatrical. A line from Mavis Gallant comes into my head: *Snow, the first clean thing in a dirty year.* Everything goes without a hitch. The official shows up to bid me goodbye and to kiss my hand, or rather my glove. Maryna accompanies me to the airport; we talk very little in the car, but once I'm at the check-in counter we hug, and tell each other we will meet again soon – if not in Kiev, then in Canada. I find my customs declaration, my baggage passes inspection, my passport is duly stamped, and I am walking back out onto the tarmac, under the B movie control tower, getting back into the Lufthansa jet which is already a different world, *outside*, incarnate in the small, foil-wrapped package of macadamia nuts the steward offers me. *The world's most exclusive nut*, the package proclaims, and I believe it. Our plane takes off, and another glides in, perhaps discharging my *semblable*: a returned Canadian-Ukrainian inheriting my shock at first stepping off the plane at Borispol, into that equation of dirt and the simplest means possible to remove it. A jet plane filled with crumpled serviettes and smudged plastic surfaces – a galvanized tin pail, a straw whisk, a kerchiefed woman prematurely stooped, her empty pail weighed down with the knowledge that she will never sit down in the seats she cleans, belt herself in and fly out, fly away.

The first few days of my return, I rise each morning at three-thirty, still on Kiev time. I have given away most of the things I brought back with me: books for my family, clay figures for my friends – except for one fox woman, which I've kept for myself. Outside, the sky is pitch black, and the windows throw my reflection back in my face: pale, sleep-starved, raggedy-looking in my nightgown and a huge woolen shawl I've pulled over my shoulders – the black shawl with roses Maryna's mother gave me as a parting gift.

I shut myself into the parlour, the one room where I'm sure no one will hear me. I take the fox whistle from the table, put it to my mouth, and blow, again and again, as if at last I am fluent in the language I never learned by heart; as if they could hear me all the way to Kiev, signalling a message I can't yet decipher, a connection I can't help but feel. The way you're supposed to feel twitchings in an amputated limb, long after it's been severed. So long ago that it could be some stranger's body, gesturing inside your own.

THOMAS KING

# The Open Car

My brother and I grew up in a small town in central California. My mother ran a beauty shop out of our house. She worked long hours, and what I remember most was that we were the only family in the neighbourhood who didn't have a television or a car.

That's what my mother wanted. A car. A convertible. When we got a car, she told Christopher and me, we could put the top down and get away. We could go on a trip. We could travel.

Three weeks ago, I had to go from Toronto to New York, and because I had some time before and after my meetings, I persuaded Helen that we should travel by train. I pointed out that a train trip would give us a chance to relax and see the countryside. She reminded me that I was simply terrified of flying and would do anything to stay off a plane.

Which is true.

Nonetheless, I prevailed on her generous spirit and bought two rail tickets for New York. It was a twelve-hour trip, and Helen was sceptical.

"What are we going to do for food?"

"They have food on the train," I told her. "It's got to be as good as anything you get on a plane."

Helen packed apples, grapes, ham and cheese sandwiches, water, juice, cookies, yogurt, crackers into two plastic bags, lugged them on the train, and arranged them like small pillows around our feet. Just as the train pulled away from Union Station, she remembered we had to cross a border.

"We have to eat all the apples before we get to Niagara."

"How many do we have?"

"Eight."

My mother believed that travelling was broadening, that by visiting other people and other places you became more tolerant and understanding. And she believed that travel was magic.

I ate two apples. Helen ate one. When we arrived at Niagara Falls, and the American border guards came on the train, we still had five apples.

The border is the part of the trip that Helen doesn't like. Leaving Canada and crossing to the States. She is a staunch nationalist, and the only pleasure she takes in going from one country (home) to the other (the evil empire) is in telling the guards (when they ask) that she is Canadian. She was hardly in a mood to give up five perfectly good apples, I can tell you that.

Outside the train, two station wagons pulled up with German shepherds in the back seat. These were not pets. At the time, I supposed that they were drug-sniffing dogs, but I wasn't sure, and I wasn't going to ask.

The guards worked their way through the train in twos, coming along the aisles slowly, checking passports, asking questions. There was a young black man sitting in front of us. He was, from the sound of his voice, from the Caribbean, and when they got to him, the guards stopped.

My mother travelled through her music. Every Sunday morning, she would stack records on the phonograph spindle, and, when they had all dropped onto the turntable, she would lift them off, turn them over, and begin again. They were musicals, for the most part, and operas – *Carmen, La Traviata, The Desert Song, South Pacific*.

There was a globe in the living room, and while the music played and my mother sang along with each piece, Christopher would find Spain and Italy and Arabia and Tahiti on the map.

One of the guards began asking the man a series of questions – where he was from, where he was going, how long he was going to stay.

And more questions.

Did he have any cigarettes. Any liquor. Any drugs. How much money was he carrying. Did he have a job. The guard asked the man about marijuana several times, each time hooking his lips around his fingers and sucking on an imaginary joint with practised ease to demonstrate exactly what they were looking for.

The man's responses were low and flat, so much so that neither Helen nor I could hear the answers even though we leaned forward in our seats on the pretext of looking out the window.

Evidently, the first guard couldn't hear the man either, for he became irritated and then angry. The man continued in his low, patient way, until finally the guard stopped him and motioned for him to stand up.

"Get your bags and your identification," the guard told the man, "and see immigration in the open car."

The man got his duffel bag from the overhead, smiled at the guard, and walked slowly towards the back of the train. The guard watched the man go. Then he took two steps forward and leaned in to Helen and me. Helen settled into her seat and locked her feet around the food.

"Citizenship?"

"Canadian."

"Canadian."

"Where are you going?"

"New York."

"New York."

The guard smiled at Helen as if she had just told him she thought he looked spiffy in his uniform and then he tipped his hat, just the way the sheriff always did in the Westerns I saw as a kid.

"Have a nice day," he said.

That was it. No liquor, no cigarettes, no drugs, no money, no job. No apples. No open car. As the guard stood by our seats, just before he moved on to the next person, I had two competing emotions.

First, I was appalled that they had not taken us to the open car, where Helen could have told them what they could do with our five apples. And, second, I was relieved.

We stayed at the border for about an hour. Just before the train rolled out of the station, the black man returned to his seat. He was still smiling as he slung his bag into the overhead. He sat down next to the window, put his head against the glass, and went to sleep.

I was about fifteen when my mother got her first car. It was a pink Plymouth Fury convertible with enormous fins and a cutaway at the headlights that made it look a little like a shark. My mother was proud of that car. On days when she finished work early, she would put the top down and drive it around town, slowly, as if she were in a parade. She always wore dark glasses and a long yellow scarf that floated above the back seat.

Just as soon as the car was broken in properly, my mother told us, we would pack up our stuff and go on a trip.

New York was fun. Not as clean as Toronto and a little scarier – and Helen pointed these differences out to me – but fun. Even Helen had a good time, though she was not unhappy when we got back on the train to come home.

We did not take much food with us on this part of the trip. Helen forgot about it until all the stores near our hotel had closed. We walked around the area, but nothing was open.

We were reduced to boarding the train early the next morning with nothing more than a pitiful bag of bran muffins, four little bottles of orange juice, and six bananas.

About six months after she got the car, my mother announced that we were going to take a trip. She got a road map from the gas station and laid it out on the table. Christopher and I watched as she worked her way down the coast and through the mountains, circling places as she went. Later, she took a ruler and measured out the distance, converted it into miles, and figured out how much the gas would cost to get there and back.

Then she folded the map up and put it away.

When we got to the border at Niagara for the second time, we were met by Canadian border guards.

"Watch this," Helen told me as the guards came on the train.

Actually, the Canadian guards looked pretty much the same as the American guards.

"Look around," Helen said. "Do you see any dogs?"

There were no dogs, at least none that I could see. But there were people standing on the platform taking pictures of the train.

"Maybe they can't afford dogs."

Why do we travel? Obviously, because we can afford to. Time. Money. Time and money. Perhaps it is a particular inclination – curiosity, romance, distraction. Perhaps it is nothing more than that.

I have friends who travel regularly, and when they say travel, they mean trips that involve great crossings – oceans, continents, hemispheres – and visits to great cities – Paris, Rome, Bombay, Tokyo, London. They leave home with vaccinations and visas and return with colour slides and colds.

As I recall, the Canadian guards had guns. Helen disputes this vigorously. In any case, they came through the train in twos, asking the same questions that the Americans had asked. And when they got to an East Indian couple, they stopped.

Every week, on Saturday (as long as the weather was good), we would get up early and wash the car. We washed it twice with detergent and then rinsed it gently with the garden hose, so we wouldn't get water on the upholstery or hurt the finish. Christopher and I crawled around under the seats, picking up twigs and leaves, little stones, lint, and pieces of a bubble-gum wrapper, while my mother took an sos pad to the whitewalls and scrubbed them until they glowed.

We told her we'd like to go to Donner Lake or to the ocean, and my mother said that that was a great idea.

The East Indian man told the border guard that he and his wife were Canadian citizens.

"Do you have any proof of citizenship?"

The man smiled and nodded his head and handed the guard two passports. The first guard looked at the passports for a moment and then handed them to his partner, who flipped through the pages, looking at each one in great detail.

"What's the purpose of your visit?"

"We live in Toronto."

"How much liquor are you bringing back into Canada?"

"None."

"Cigarettes?"

"No."

"Presents?"

"Nothing."

The first guard turned to his partner. Then he turned back to the couple.

"Get all your bags and your identification," the guard said, "and take them to immigration in the open car."

One day, my mother walked over to my aunt's house and left the car sitting in the carport. I grabbed the keys from the hook and Christopher got the map and we jumped in the car and put the top down, just the way we had seen Mom do it.

Then I started the car, left it in park, and revved the engine a couple of times. It was exciting sitting there behind the wheel, with the top down, Christopher calling out the towns we were passing and the towns we were coming to.

We had only been driving for about five minutes, when the car suddenly shuddered, coughed a couple of times, and died. I tried starting it, but it was no use. Christopher and I got out of the car and put the top back up. I hung the keys back up on the hook and Christopher put the map away.

The next day, my mother tried to start the car, but nothing happened. Later Mr. Santucci came by. He poured some gas into the tank and tinkered around under the hood, and in about an hour the car was running just fine.

When the guard got to us, I was ready for him.

"Citizenship?"

"Canadian."

"Do you have any cheese?"

I must admit, the question threw me, and had I had my wits about me, I am certain I could have come up with a clever response.

"No," I said.

"Have a nice day," said the guard.

My mother never travelled. She stayed home. I think she would have liked to travel, but she had my brother and me and the beauty shop. My father travelled. He started travelling just after Christopher was born and never came back. Perhaps he is still travelling.

Customs cleared the train, and the East Indian couple returned to their seats. As we pulled away from Niagara, I want back to the open car to see what we had missed, which, as it turned out, wasn't much. The open car was a cramped affair with a bar off to one side where you could get frozen hot dogs, pizza, hamburgers, nachos (microwaved while you waited), and a variety of drinks.

It had all the ambience of a small bus station. There were no tables or chairs, nothing convenient for an intimate conversation or an interrogation. Whatever you wanted to eat or do had to be managed standing, and I wondered what the immigration people could have done to the black man and the East Indian couple in a room like this.

When I got back to my seat, I told Helen about the open car.

"Did they have any yogurt?"

"They had pizza."

"Salads?"

"Hot dogs."

My mother no longer wants to travel. At least that's what she tells me. When Helen and I went to New York, my mother flew to Toronto to watch the kids. Have a good time, she told us. If you want to stay a few extra days, don't worry about anything.

So I told her about the car and what Christopher and I had done. When I finished the story, she looked at me and shook her head. The Plymouth was a hardtop, she said. The Pontiac was a convertible. And the Plymouth hadn't run out of gas, it had been a problem with the alternator. John Varris fixed that, she told me, not Mr. Santucci. If you're going to tell a story, she insisted, at least get the facts right.

We waited and ate when we got back to Toronto. A nice little restaurant on Queen. As we sat there waiting for the server, Helen began to laugh.

"What do you think the Americans would have done to us if they had found the oranges?"

"You mean apples."

"What apples?"

After we ordered, Helen slid a guidebook across the table. "We should go there next," she said, and she spread a map of Ireland out across the table and began running the coastline with her finger, stopping here and there to read a description from the book.

My mother was right. The Pontiac was the convertible.

MYRNA KOSTASH

Table Manners

Amsterdam, 1981

Drinking scotch, then hungover next day. Nightlife in Amsterdam: cigarettes and scotch, stretched out on pillows talking with Leo until birdsong comes in through the window. I squint and see chimney pots in black silhouette against the pink sky.

Norrie, Leo's friend, claimed last night he was the world's greatest living English-language poet. Not being up on my poets, I didn't argue. He claims, also, to be on the lam from the British police, which is why he sleeps in the office of a Dutch graphic designer and cadges meals with Leo. When he goes to the bar, he borrows guilders so he can buy everyone a drink. We spent the afternoon at his favourite, the Hoppe. He remembers my name by writing it on his wrist, but his own poems he forgets mid-recital. He tells stories instead, mainly of Glasgow and of long, featureless benders when strangers have saved him by plucking him out of his own vomit in the gutter. He would do the same for the similarly afflicted.

He grew up very poor. Eating eels scooped from the Glasgow sewers. So, when Leo prepared for us tonight a meal of smoked eel, Norrie and I flatly refused to eat it. Leo went out to the butcher's and came back with goat.

On the Museumplein a band of students stood silently, holding aloft the Irish flag. I watched from the bar. Every minute or so they did a slow pirouette, turning in place, so we all could see what they bore on their backs: a black-and-white photo of Francis Hughes, the IRA militant, second to die in the hunger strikes in Ireland.

The Dutch eat, but they do not get fat.

## *Návplion, 1983*

Travelling solo is my choice, but I did not turn down the young man with curly hair and black leather jacket who joined me last night in the very crowded taverna. (I had lost two chairs to the boisterous army recruits, but no one had made a direct approach.) He was an American and, in the style of Americans, especially the youthful and the attractive, he told his story virtually without prompting, in full confidence I would be interested. His father died of AIDS last spring, and it was the inheritance that was permitting him to travel around Europe, in a state of tenuously suspended panic that he might himself have caught the disease in the baths of New Orleans. He – Eugene, this big-shouldered, soft-lipped youth at my table – had always been gay, but it wasn't until he had moved to New York's Lower East Side in 1975 that he lived openly and exuberantly as a gay man. Now he's in love with Patrick, son of a Vietnamese woman and a scion of the Philadelphia bourgeoisie, whose photograph he extracts from his diary.

Patrick is a willowy, olive-skinned boy in a wind-flapped coat on the deck of a boat, reaching out to someone who has been scissored out of the picture. It is the young and the hairless who appeal to Eugene; Greeks are not his type. As for women, he doesn't hate us, but sometimes he deeply resents the way beautiful women can manipulate straight men. Eh bien! By the same token, he is, he admits, putty in the hands of beautiful boys.

We have supper together again today. Eugene's sister is a feminist in Boston who has submitted to therapy to ease the pain of being fathered and brothered by gay men. His cousin in North Carolina is a Maoist organizing textile workers. Now that Eugene is "out," no longer just a "petit bourgeois shit," the cousin has taken to writing him long letters in which he explains himself and his politics. This is not Eugene's cup of tea. He has only a high-school education, and his last job was as a bill collector, shaking down poor folks for library fines – an employment that deeply shames him now in the telling. He takes a kind of refuge in his pedigree – eighth-generation descendant of a man with a land grant from the Spanish in Louisiana. The line has been mixed through the years with English, Scottish, and French blood ("*not* Cajun"), and was eventually forced off its land during the Crash of '29. Eugene has been back to look at the plantation, a big house and sugar refinery now owned by the descendants of a former overseer. He's climbed up the lip of the levee and stared at it from across the Mississippi.

When he asks me to tell him a story, I stay within the general theme of progeny and dispossession: I tell him about Agamemnon, Clytemnestra, and the bloodied House of Atreus.

## *Noufara Bar*

I ride the wheel of Dimitri who, only a couple of weeks ago, I did not even care for. But then we went out from the wine shop for something to eat, and he laid his hand on my arm, reaching across the table to do so, and the *weight* of that simple act bore down on me with such swiftness that it has displaced my pleasure in being alone, my pleasure even in my narrow, white-sheeted bed. Dimitri, ten years younger, a little soft, like a fruit, with languorous movements, is rather more female than male in the way he radiates his appeal, never *moving* to take what he desires. He smiles coquettishly at me as he pours apricot liqueur from a wooden jug, and speaks of French films, jotting down in a little notebook he keeps in the cash drawer all the English words I use he's never heard before. Example: to nag. Apricot glazes his upper lip. I want to lick it off. Instead I stick my tongue down into the little glass and flick apricot into my own mouth.

## *Návplion, 1984*

I ate last night with Kostas and his buddy George, husband of Pat the Englishwoman. George, sucking noisily on a fishhead and talking in his excellent, almost cocky English of the twenty-year-old American he fucked the other night. Not to mention the three hundred French women he's had. Pat is a saint. George says so himself. He claims she doesn't know a thing about his philanderings. (It's true. I've been at coffee with her, and like so many of the other foreign women married here she believes she has married the exceptional Greek.) "She loves me. She loves to stay at home. She's not the least bit interested in women's liberation. Women are only oppressed if they want to be." So saith the Greek husband, sucking on a fishhead.

# Odessa, 1984

Sergei suggests an ice cream, but the parlour is full. We go back to our hotel and take a table against the back wall. Neither Sergei nor Lev seems the least bit concerned to be seen in our company. Sergei pats his jacket pocket. Lots of rubles. He's paying. Soviet champagne. Georgian brandy. We don't dance. I go up to my room. I come back. I slip books to Sergei under the table, shielded by the long overhang of the white tablecloth.

Eleven o'clock. The restaurant closes. We stroll over to a park and sit together, four in a row, on a bench, and pass the bottle of ouzo up and down the line. We are the only people in the park except for an old woman who is scrabbling about in the bushes for empties. I am staring at her when Sergei starts in on the Red Army and I tell him to shush. We get up. We leave the empty behind.

We arrive by taxi at Sergei's house in Suvorov Street. Before going in, the men piss against the wall; then Sergei takes me to an outdoor privy in the apartment's courtyard, cavalierly waiting for me outside while I hold my nose and crouch above the hole.

In his room, Sergei has the makings of a party. Cassette tapes, brandy, tea in big cups, desiccated cake, a slab of baloney. He asks me to dance, and we wiggle around the narrow space between his bed and the wall. At three o'clock we fall into the street. There is no such thing as a taxi. Lev flags down the first vehicle that comes along, a van full of young people. They deliver us to the hotel without having said a word.

Last day in Odessa. We try once more to effect entry into a restaurant defended by a bulky doorman at the curtained entry. He is

immovable. We bob and weave around him, hoping to see someone we know inside. What we see is a fistfight, punches to the
nose, between customers and management. We walk briskly over
to a café that offers drinks and ice cream. It is cavernous and
awash with spilled liquors. But it is peaceful. Lev asks me about
feminism. I answer as we dance.

## Dublin, 1986

So, where is the poetry? Here in the buffet of Heuston train station, a red-eyed woman with a gimp leg clears away the crockery
while lumpy men and women snore in heaps on the benches in
the waiting room. All the talk that swirled around me on the boat
last night from Liverpool was of drink. This morning even the tea
is not tea but some insipid concoction that spits out of a machine
at the press of a button. Whatever happened to the Irish teapot?

This is very far from Warsaw.

*It is Saturday morning in Warsaw. What is Konrad doing? Shopping at
the market with a string bag stuffed in his pocket as he picks over
strawberries and (radiated) young radishes for his ailing wife who sits
at home in a dark room, curtains drawn against the painful light. . . .
Later he will sit in his study, writing a report for the Minister, then join
his wife in the darkened sitting room to listen to a recording of Schubert. Perhaps there is a small dog at his feet. A piece of torte on a porce-
lain plate, the tines of a fork smeared with chocolate cream. A painting
hangs behind his head, the portrait of the artist as a nude young
woman.*

A week ago he was dancing with me, around and around in an elegant little waltz on the wooden dance floor. I was an angel sent

down to make him dance. When last he danced, he had a girl in his arms with whom he swooped around the floor of the smoky, post-war jazz club, their bodies hot with trombones and vodka while the last of Stalin's pickings folded up behind the prison doors.

## Aegina, 1987

Eleni's house is at white-washed right angles to the sea. I look through lace at the windows in the morning, watching Eleni and her lover on the patio. He is a fisherman and he has laid out a plate of grilled sardines for their breakfast, pulling down a branch of the lemon tree and snapping off the fruit that he will squeeze with a theatrical flourish over the tiny oily corpses. A crock of olive oil rests at Eleni's bare foot. I see a drop on her ankle, glistening in the sun.

The big rooms in Katerina's place are furnished in shambles: unkempt beds and bare floors, odd, disintegrating bits of Turkish furniture, dark, unlit walls hung with small oil paintings obscured by the dust of ages. In the garden the geraniums have gone wild. Andreas, the artist, has come to visit, plans for his island home rolled up under his arm, on his head a fisherman's cap. Wound around with a long green scarf, he sits gravely on a patio chair, his left hand holding the small white coffee cup as though it were a bird. He was once a great beauty, Katerina will tell me later. He has recently reconverted to the Orthodox faith, and his rapture is clear to me, luminous behind the white stubble of his aging cheeks.

## Amsterdam, 1981

A street market near the Rijksmuseum where I buy yellow melons. Moroccan women in robes. Blonde girls in white cowboy boots. Cups of filtered coffee with yellow cream. Plush Turkish carpeting on the café table under this book.

The Dutch are slim and fair. The women are small-breasted. I already feel the longing for larger, darker people, who eat.

ALBERTO MANGUEL

# After Carthage

In the mid second century B.C., in a senate hall now long fallen
to ruin, the Roman orator Marcus Porcius Cato, cranky with old
age and wary of the revived prosperity of a North African outpost
of Rome called Carthage, called on his fellow citizens to raze that
barbaric civilization to the ground in order to preserve Rome's
own immortality. A precursor of conservative nationalism, Cato
also ranted against the influx of Hellenic culture, which he saw
as a noxious foreign influence, and against the financial freedom
of women, which undermined, in his view, the stability of the
state. But to Cato it was Carthage that represented the greatest
threat to the *mos majorum*, the "ancestral ways" of Rome.
"*Carthago delenda est*," he repeated again and again. "Carthage
must be destroyed."

It was. In 149 B.C., the year of Cato's death, Rome declared war
on Carthage. Not a brick was left standing. Even the hill on
which the ancient African city rose was levelled and salt strewn
among the rubble. Years later the Romans themselves built a new
city on the site, and today the few remains that have been dug up,
in what is now one of the most fashionable residential districts in

With Rachel Manguel in the suburb of Tunis
known today (alas!) as Carthage

Tunis, bear the mark of Cato's people. Of Carthage, not even the
dust remains.

Instead, there is fine dry sand in the air, though the desert is
miles away. The sand air smells of oleander. The landscape here is
green, rich, soft. We are travelling south across Tunisia, along a
road marked by the absence of anything Carthaginian: all the way
from Tunis, the capital in the north, to the holy city of Kairouan
or al-Qayrawan, eighty miles away, the only landmarks are the
elegant traces of Roman imperialism – a solitary column, the
arches of an aqueduct. But even these are *memento mori*, remind-
ers that Rome, as all empires must, passed away in its turn. The
history of what is today called Tunisia begins with the Hegira,
the flight of Mohammed from Mecca to Medina, in the year the
infidels count as 622 A.D.

Ali Ben Meftah Ali, driving our battered Kairouan, is a Muslim, "but not a good Muslim," he explains. He was born to a

nomad Bedouin family and grew up in the desert, "where they're not so strict about these things." He taught himself to read and write, became a teacher, then a hotel administrator, a wholesale T-shirt merchant, and now a taxi-driver-cum-guide. He carries both a Tunisian and a French passport because he lived in Paris for several years. His wife is French. He has an eleven-year-old red-haired daughter, Souh-Kei-Nah, who, on a previous excursion, taught my daughter, Rachel, blonde and twelve, to write her name in Arabic. Today, however, Souh-Kei-Nah is in school and Rachel is sitting in the back, alone. The sky is as blue as a blue glazed tile.

A Berber folk song wails on Ali's cassette player. A sign in French and Arabic tells us that Kairouan is still twenty kilometres away. For the Muslims, seven trips to Kairouan are the equivalent of one trip to Mecca, and Ali has been there more times than he cares to remember. "Who knows," he says. "Maybe it will do me good."

Founded in the mid seventh century, shortly after the death of the Prophet, Kairouan became 150 years later the capital of the whole Arab West, a centre of military power, religious scholarship, and commerce. But in the eleventh century, as a result of Bedouin incursions (Ali tells the story with a touch of pride), Kairouan declined and the seat of government shifted north to Tunis.

Tunis is merely a modern city; Kairouan belongs, at least its central core, to the Middle Ages. We arrive in a white public square with squalid palm trees and slowly moving crowds. Ali parks the car outside the butter-yellow wall encircling Old Kairouan and we walk in. There is a scent of tamarind and nutmeg in the air, and of wet wool, the former rising from the spice stalls huddled against the wall, the latter from the many carpet shops displaying their wares on the sidewalks. A bearded man with a black turban growls something at us as we pass. "Crazy," says Ali by way of explanation. "A fundamentalist," he adds. "Crazy with God."

Ali suggests we stop at the carpet shop of a friend of his. Rachel, he believes, will enjoy it. When I decided to take Rachel on this North African trip, she and I talked about the different people that over the centuries invaded this part of the world. We've seen Roman Carthage and the extraordinary Roman city of Duggah, which for several centuries was one of the most famous cities in North Africa, but we haven't yet had a sense of the present, the world of Islam, here in Tunisia. Ali, whom we met in Tunis, told us that if we saw nothing else, we must see Kairouan, Kairouan the Holy.

Ali's red-haired daughter has never been to Kairouan. Her mother is afraid that she will fall under what she calls "Arab influence." "My wife wants Souh-Kei-Nah to have only European friends," Ali says wistfully. "My wife doesn't even want her to play with her cousins. My younger brother lives in the apartment below us, and his wife is very good, but not accustomed to a big city like Tunis, so she's very shy. My wife won't even speak to her and told Souh-Kei-Nah that my brother's children were all beggars."

The buildings of Kairouan are cut out against the sky like geometric shapes drawn by an unsteady hand – the rectangle of a house, the semicircle of a dome, the triangle of a peaked tower. The carpet shop is a large square fitted with latticed doors. Every inch of floor and wall is covered with carpets, of every conceivable size, colour, and design. All carpets produced in Kairouan are hand-made, and the government rates the carpets according to the craftsmanship. Even if prices are fixed, haggling, as in any Arab country, is *de rigueur*. A man who looks remarkably like Peter Ustinov comes out to greet us. We are led into a room in which the carpets, Ustinov says, "will be unfurled for our plea-sure." We are invited to sit on cushioned benches. A veiled woman brings Ali and me coffee on a copper tray. Rachel isn't offered anything.

For centuries, carpet-weaving has been a family business in Kairouan, a very lucrative business in the hands of only a few fam-ilies. No one can agree on when the industry began; according to one of the stories, the people of Kairouan learned their craft from spiders at the beginning of time, when (Allah be praised) men and animals could teach one another their skills. Here in the store, the variety is dazzling: there are wool carpets and silk car-pets, thick many-knotted carpets and carpets thin as raffia mats, large ones to cover an entire dining-room floor or decorate a wall, and prayer rugs big enough to accommodate only a single one of the kneeling faithful.

According to the Koran (88:16), the true believers who enter paradise are promised cushions, couches, goblets, springs of fresh water, and above all *zarabiyya*, rich silken carpets, on which to recline. More than any other piece of furniture, carpets provide a cleanly defined and yet immensely complex context for human activity, an indoor and perennial garden (carpet designs in turn influenced the layout of Oriental gardens), a private but not walled-in place, an object of contemplation whose pattern can be seen in an infinity of ways, depending on the choice made by the seer's eye. The carpets of Kairouan, though famous even before the Bedouin invasion, became influenced by the techniques and requirements of nomads rather than sedentary people, and incor-porated into their production other patterns and new shapes. The carpets displayed today in Kairouan are mainly of the kind seen in those mysterious executive penthouse offices of New York and Toronto where no one ever seems to do any real work, but there are other, stranger kinds: carpets that serve (we are told) as camel blankets, as tent bands, as door surrounds, and Ali tells me his family had such carpets hanging in their tents when he was a boy, looking after his father's goats. Most of the carpets Ali's friend unrolls for our inspection seem to be of the executive kind. I end up purchasing only a small carpet, blue, with a white-and-rust-coloured pattern. I have the uncomfortable sense of having fallen in Ali's esteem.

Nevertheless, as we leave, members of Mr. Ustinov's family come to shake hands with us. Suddenly we hear a commotion in the street. Outside, a group of boys run by, shouting. Mr. Ustinov shouts something after them. "Bad," he says, and Ali nods agreement. "They are influenced by things on television and the European music they hear," Ali tells me. "Before, young people behaved differently."

"The fundamentalists have a point, you know," he says pedagogically. "In Saudi Arabia the jewellers leave their shops open while they go to prayers. And no one touches a thing. You know why? Because thieves have their hands cut off!" Ali shows me how by drawing his right hand over his left wrist. Mr. Ustinov laughs.

"Now the mosque," says Ali.

Kairouan is a holy city on two accounts: first, because just outside the wall lives the religious fraternity of Sidi Sahab, and Sidi Sahab guards the tomb of one of Mohammed's companions, Abu Zam'a al-Balawi, known as the Prophet's Barber, on whose clothing – Ali tells me – a few sacred hairs from the Prophet's beard were found; second, because in the very core of the city rises the great Aghlabid Mosque, which is to North Africa what the cathedral of Chartres is to France. We can visit the mosque at certain times, when the faithful are not at prayers, and even then we are not allowed inside the sanctum. Ali leads us into the courtyard, a vast walled compound of stones smoothed by the passage of innumerable devout feet. In the centre is a sundial which started registering the hours of service one thousand years ago and below which lies a deep cistern with enough water for the entire city. From the courtyard we peek into the domed prayer hall glittering in the darkness with glazed tiles and copper ornaments.

A Catholic church, in spite of seeking communal reverence, seems to encourage the individual relationship to the godhead, with distinct seats in the pews, private places for confession, intimate chapels within the larger edifice, nicely suited for a divine *tête-à-tête*. In contrast a mosque is above all a place of congregation, of a crowd showing its devotion as a whole, of a people who find in their coming together the power of a faith that demands unconditional surrender to God's will. Islam doesn't distinguish between the religious life and the practical, everyday life: the law, *shari'a*, embraces all human activity, of which the devotions in the mosque are only part. In a cathedral, the space is determined by the architecture; in a mosque, the presence of the people defines the space. With one exception: a large fretwork partition cuts off a section of the great hall. Rachel asks Ali why it's there.

"That is the women's section," says Ali. "They can follow what happens through the little holes in the wood."

"Why can't the women be in the hall with the men?" Rachel wants to know.

"In our religion," Ali says, "women have other roles. They're not supposed to pray with the men."

Rachel puzzles over this. "Why do you think that is?"

"Because our religion says so," Ali answers.

"Yes, but what do *you* think?" Rachel insists.

"I'm a Muslim, I do what my religion tells me," says Ali.

"And don't the women mind being kept to one side?" Rachel is not giving up.

"They, too, do what their religion tells them."

"I don't think that's fair," Rachel observes.

Later, in a small restaurant lined with cracked tiles and reeking of frying-oil, under a poster of Bart Simpson holding a can of pop in his hand, Ali tells me that this is also what his wife says. "She thinks Arab society isn't just. She thinks we're all uncivilized. For her, if I don't behave like the men in France, I'm a brute. Well, in Paris I was never happy. My wife's parents treated me like dirt. And one day I woke up to find that someone had painted on our door a sign that said FILTHY ARAB, WE'LL HAVE YOUR SKIN. My wife laughed when she saw it. An Arab woman would never laugh if they insulted her husband."

We are having lunch: chicken and chick-peas in a spicy tomato sauce served in soup plates on a chequered vinyl tablecloth. This is Tunisia, where fundamentalism hasn't yet become as powerful as in other places, so we are drinking wine with the meal. Flies buzz around the basket of French bread.

"You couldn't have wine in Saudi Arabia," I say to Ali.

Ali dismisses my response as if he were waving away a fly. "Wine or no wine," he answers, "with the fundamentalists you know where you stand." Then he adds: "I wouldn't tell you this if you were American, because Americans don't want to hear what other people have to say. But this is the truth: the United States wants to see us destroyed. They want all Arabs destroyed. They see us as a threat to the West because we are so many, and because we obey our leaders. So they want to wipe us off the face of the earth. Not with guns, like they did in the Gulf War. They wouldn't do that again. They're too clever. They'll destroy us with television, and clothes, and songs on tapes, and sexy pictures. We can't let that happen.

"Already, we can't remember the ancestral ways, the way my father lived," Ali goes on. "When I lived in the desert, as a boy, nothing ever changed. That was good. I didn't know much but I knew everything I had to know. And then a brother of mine convinced me that I wanted more. Now I have a bad wife, a job that pays badly, and maybe I'll lose my daughter. I'm not a really religious man, but I think we Arabs can only survive in the hands of the fundamentalists."

For a moment I image this paradox: a man echoing, across the centuries, the same doctrine the enemy of his people fomented in another language and in another place: that one civilization can survive only if another is obliterated. Cato and Ali would not have found one another incomprehensible.

"We have no rules any more," Ali insists, and finishes off the wine. "Can you live without rules?"

In the street outside the restaurant the black-turbaned man "crazy with God" is shouting again.

"I don't understand why he's so angry," Rachel says.

A group of men, followed by several veiled women dragging a gaggle of children, pass us on their way to the mosque. "Pilgrims," Ali points out reverently. The turbaned one holds out a hand and one of the men throws him some coins, but they rattle to the ground. Black Turban falls to his knees to pick them up. The pilgrims trudge on. One of the children looks back at the kneeling man and laughs. Ali sees the child and shakes his head.

DAVID MCFADDEN

# Mr. Looney

He was known around town as Timmy, the town being Cahir, where he had spent his entire life. But he was a man who deserved great respect, and in his manner of speech and very demeanour he demanded great respect, and so I called him Mr. Looney. He was also known as old Looney, because he was seventy-six, recently widowed, and lived in a small, dark, damp, musty house with sagging bookshelves, sagging armchairs, and a sagging floor, on a side street off the old town square. From the age of sixteen, he had dedicated himself to studying the history of Ireland, a fervent amateur with no time for the academies. He spoke slowly, evenly, deliberately, and soberly, with a tough, rich accent. He never smiled.

"It is not generally known that this is the most historic part of Ireland," he said.

"You mean County Tipperary?"

"I do."

"Why would it be more historic than the other parts?"

"There are many reasons for that. Even the Celts, when they came in here to Ireland, it was here that they stayed. Just outside the town of Cahir was one of their main bases. That's going back,

173

for they arrived in Ireland in 504 BC. There were eighteen kings of Munster who resided just outside of town. And then later they moved to Cashel."

"Is it known where they are buried?"

"It is not . . ."

"No idea at all?"

"Well, I think I know. But it hasn't been excavated yet."

Mr. Looney's main theme was the poverty of knowledge on the subject of the history of Ireland. Very little was officially known, because very little had been excavated. For every Newgrange that had been discovered, excavated, studied, written about, renovated, popularized, and put on the tourist maps, there were thousands more that were known only to lonely amateurs like Mr. Looney, who had been exploring the countryside with a passionately obsessive and studied eye for six decades.

From his inspired guesses about the nature and meaning of many of the unexcavated mounds of various sizes and shapes that he was familiar with, he weaved intricate theories that were potentially disturbing, even revolutionary, and conjectures that were sometimes a bit confusing.

I had driven north from Mount Melleray, back over the Knockmealdown Mountains, along winding roads offering heavenly views of the Tipperary plain bathed in bright, cold sunshine, past dead sheep that had been hit by cars, and down to Cahir. Pity the season wasn't a month or so more advanced and that the beautiful rhododendrons, everywhere in bud, were not in full blossom.

Mr. Looney invited me in. He was dressed in what turned out to be his everyday attire: black pin-striped suit, black shoes, burgundy cardigan-style wool sweater with matching tie and socks, and a white shirt. He didn't waste time getting down to business.

"The main monument of Ireland is Newgrange. If you were in

Newgrange, and you went to the trouble of walking around the mound, you'd find it's exactly three hundred paces. And it's about thirty feet high. Now, I'm working on a mound here . . ."

He was referring to the burial place of the kings of Munster in a field somewhere just outside of Cahir.

"I have it located. I've had it divined. . . . I don't know if that's a new word for you . . ."

"No, it's not. You're talking about dowsing."

"I am. Excavation without going underground."

"Well put."

"The place I'm working now is exactly six hundred paces to walk around it."

"Double the circumference."

"It is."

"And how tall is the mound?"

"It'd be about fifty or sixty feet."

"Twice as high."

"It is."

"Have you spoken to anyone in charge of excavations about this?"

"I have not. The trouble, here, is this. Now, I've made a number of finds. I've walked the fields and I'm always on the lookout for something. Mounds and that. I reported an important find here in 1961, and they came along and they declared it a national monument – the mound and twenty acres surrounding it."

"And?"

"And they haven't come back."

"And what was that find?"

"It was a court cairn. A mound that's more or less pear-shaped. And there's a souterrain passage in that for burial."

"How far back would that go?"

"That would have been built in 4000 BC."

"And it still hasn't been excavated?"

"It has not, they never came back. Now that's the trouble in Ireland. You report something and that's it, that finishes it. I have found sites around here that they don't know anything about. They haven't money. That's the problem. They'll take the place over all right, but they haven't the money, they haven't the knowledge, and they haven't the people."

At first, when Mr. Looney said the word Tipperary, I thought he was saying "the prairie," because he pronounced it something like that. Tipperary is a relatively flat, prairie-like county, bordered by mountains. But the word Tipperary is said to come from the Irish Tiobrad Arann, meaning the well of Arann. Mr. Looney tended to pronounce *th* as if it were *t* (and sometimes as if it were *d*), and *t* as if it were *th*. He also tended to roll his *r*'s and his *l*'s and to insert an *r* or an *l* where it wasn't required. Water, for instance, was invariably "wortle." And he claimed to be able to tell by accent which county someone came from.

H. V. Morton – the author of *In Search of Ireland*, which I was using as a guide on my travels – wouldn't knowingly have had much to do with Mr. Looney, and Mr. Looney could not remember having heard anything about Morton or his books, but I have an uncanny feeling – close to certainty – that their paths did cross at one time. And in such a way that it did no less than seal Mr. Looney's fate. I had asked Mr. Looney how he became interested in studying the history of his region.

It was sixty years earlier, he said. Coincidentally, Morton would have been on his whirlwind tour of Ireland – including a brief stop in Cahir. Mr. Looney was sixteen years old and working as a clerk in an office in town.

"The windows were open, and the old characters of the town

would sit outside the window on long benches. And I would hear some very interesting stories being told."

One day a very distinguished English visitor stopped and asked one of the old gentlemen for the directions to Cahir Abbey.

"Never heard of it," the old man said.

"Sure, now, I thought there was an abbey in this town."

"Oh, no, there's nothing like that here."

By this time the young eavesdropper was becoming a little angry. He went out, but the visitor had gone on his way. He approached the old man and asked him where he lived.

"On Abbey Street."

"Abbey Street. I thought so. And when you open the door in the morning what's the first thing you see?"

"Oh, my God. The Abbey! I never thought of that . . ."

Mr. Looney went back in and went back to work, but he couldn't stop thinking about the incident.

"Later that day, on thinking this thing over, I decided that no man, no matter where he came from or who he was, would come into my district and ask me a question I couldn't answer. And that's how I started to got interested in my parish and the history of it and the history of the whole locality, not only of Cahir and South Tipperary, but of the whole South of Ireland – south of a line running from Dublin to Galway, which is roughly half of Ireland. I've travelled it all, and I know the history and background of all those parts. The unfortunate thing is that very few people ever ask me anything about it."

I didn't ask Mr. Looney anything more about the English visitor. Even if I'd had a picture of Morton to show him – which I did not – I probably wouldn't have. How reliable would his memory have been after a brief glimpse of someone sixty years ago? Besides, he apparently heard Morton's voice but didn't see his face. As far as I was concerned, the visitor could have been none other than H. V. Morton. I was in search of Morton, and I had discovered him, if only in the resounding impact he had unknowingly made on the life of one individual human being.

Morton's visit to Cahir was brief. But it had been a lovely day, the sort of day when old men like to sit out on benches and chat, and he liked the town immensely. He found it "bright, clean, hopeful, vaguely busy . . . peaceful and drenched in the sanity of the eighteenth century." He mentions the castle, the bridge, the river, "the square as wide as a parade ground, and the warm afternoon sunlight."

But he doesn't mention the abbey.

Perhaps because a certain old codger, sitting in the warm afternoon sunlight, had told him it didn't exist.

"The Polynesians were the first here," Mr. Looney was saying. "They came from Greece. We did a lot of trade with Greece and with the Middle East in pre-Christian times. There was a big trade with the Mediterranean."

"What about the Celts?"

"The Celtic people originated on the Tibetan-Indian border, and they moved from there to Ireland along the southern part of the Mediterranean and into Spain. Milesius, the King of Spain, sent his three sons in here to conquer Ireland. They arrived here in 504 BC."

On the wall in Mr. Looney's house was a painting showing a dolmen, a smaller version of one I had seen at Browne's Hill. Mr. Looney said he had discovered the dolmen hidden on a wooded slope just out of town, and the painter, a local crony, had painted it for him.

"It's a huge capstone," he said.

You couldn't really got a sense of size from the painting. But the capstone looked as if it were just sitting on the ground.

"Is it still supported?"

"It is, actually. But poorly. It was interfered with in some way. But it's a very good example of a capstone. Perfect, in fact."

"And you haven't reported it."

"I have not."

He started talking about beehive huts, which he pronounced "hoods" and described as "old drystone buildings of the early-Christian period . . . little huts for living in, monastic cells. There are a lot of them around here, but I haven't divulged the location of any. You can put in a very interesting day around here, I tell you."

Sitting on Mr. Looney's desk was a stack of old leatherbound books that looked as if they had been borrowed from the county registry as part of whatever current project he was working on. I picked one up and flipped it open. It showed a town that had a population of two thousand in 1821.

"The population of that town today is five hundred," said Mr. Looney.

He offered to take me out to Athassel Abbey on the River Suir, which he pronounced "sure" as in "certain." We hopped into his little red Nissan. In *Ryan's Daughter*, Sarah Miles uses the term "certain sure," meaning "very sure," as in "I am certain sure you'll like this story," but I never noticed the term being used in the real Ireland.

"See that church?"

We were buzzing along the Waterford road, heading east out of Cahir. The church was in ruins and covered with vegetation.

"That's the old parish church. There's a wall down the middle of it, like, and it's known as a screen wall. And that screen wall, it divided the Catholic and the Protestant services. The two were held together, then. You can see there were two belfries on it."

"Are there a lot of them like that around?"

"You'll have a job finding a second one of them, I tell you. I came across another one of them down outside Killarney. As for this one, the last service held there was Protestant – in 1795. A Catholic service would have been held just before then."

We passed a gloomy-looking crossroads, a T-junction actually, one of those landscapes that make you think inexplicably of death and sorrow, a *crux commissa* or Saint Anthony's Cross, and Mr. Looney said three men had been hanged there a hundred years ago or so.

"And just about four years ago, the bloody follow who didn't know any better took down the posts they were hanged on."

We had pulled over to drink in the gloom.

"He was bulldozing the field. And it's a tradition, even now with the posts removed, that the people will never walk past here. They always went out of their way to avoid walking past here."

"What were the men hanged for?"

"Land agitation."

"Oh, God!"

"Yes, there was a lot of that in those days."

"So the people around here must have sympathized with them tremendously."

"Well, everyone did. Because, see, like if you go back to, say, even up to 1912 or 1913, you'd have a big job going around this, the most prosperous part of Ireland, finding a man with a ten-pound note of his own. There was no money. Even people working, the wages was practically nil. It was a battle of survival. I have copies of the actual paysheets – the wages was one shilling and sixpence per day. Nine shillings a week. And if you were able to supply a cair and box with yourself, you got one pound a week."

"A cair and box?"

"By that is meant a horse and cart for drawing stones and that."

Mr. Looney said 160 men were hired in those days to work on the railroad in Cahir.

"And that was the wages they were getting. They had to walk in the nine miles from Clogheen and be in by eight o'clock in the morning. And they walked home at six in the evening. And then be in again the following morning. And they fought at one another to get the job. If a fellow fell out, there were dozens waiting to take his place."

"No wonder there was so much emigration."

"Yes."

We parked the car by a stone wall a mile from the village of Golden, and walked three hundred yards across a spacious green field, down to the River Suir, where the ruins of Athassel Abbey sat quietly in the warm sunlight like a lucid dream.

"This abbey was ruined during the Reformation," said Mr. Looney. "The tourists don't come here even in the summer."

"How far are we from the Rock of Cashel?"

"About seven miles."

"That may be why; there's no shortage of tourists there, even this early in the spring."

Mr. Looney had been a teetotaller and non-smoker all his life, and in spite of his years, he scampered up the crumbling stairs of Athassel, leaving me to eat his dust as I stood in the church choir, staring at the tomb of a thirteenth-century Norman knight. When I caught up with him, he was silently gazing out a small window over the mythic countryside without panting. He was about five-eight, and had a sort of Richard Nixon-Barry Fitzgerald look, but without the quivering jowls.

He didn't say anything, but I later realized that where he'd been gazing there had been an ancient town which had disappeared around 1350, and of which no trace remained. "Disappeared" is a euphemism. Brian O'Brien burnt the town to the ground in 1329.

"Powerful weather," said Mr. Looney.

"A brief respite from the cold rain."

"Summer will be a while yet."

Over his bald head, he had a few strands of feathery white hair which were brushed back and which would puff up in a breeze, so that they reminded me of the lonesome arches of a ruined cathedral, like St. Patrick's on the Rock of Cashel.

"The Normans would come up the Suir in flat-bottomed boats," he said. "They even had their own bakery. But there was a lot of trouble with drink and with women, here."

He said Athassel Abbey was also known as St. Edmond's Priory.

"The terrible thing was, their libraries were destroyed. From all their manuscripts, there are just a few scraps remaining at Cahir Abbey. I've had a terrible problem trying to find anything written about Athassel St. Edmond's."

He said that pigs had been brought into the ruined abbey on three different occasions by three different individuals over the years, and in each case they didn't thrive. It might have had something to do with the consecrated ground.

"Would this be pretty consistent throughout Ireland?"

"It would not. These places aren't usually interfered with in that way."

As we got back in the car, a young man on foot, and with a large backpack with a Stars and Stripes sewn on, was coming along the road. He scarcely glanced at us, and we didn't say anything. He climbed the stone wall and made his way down to the abbey alone.

I hadn't actually met any tinkers yet, but had heard a lot of different shades of opinion about them, and was about to hear more. Also, they had been the focus of a recent spate of unpleasant stories in the country weeklies and small-town dailies, in a mean and amateurish journalistic style that was shockingly one-sided.

"The tinkers were dispossessed during Cromwellian times and never got resettled," said Mr. Looney.

"This has the ring of truth."

"The tinkers are the travelling people. They maintain the old Irish customs. The thing is slowly breaking down, but when they marry, the bride and groom never meet until the wedding day. And the children are looked after first. Not one adult will eat a bit until all the children are fed."

"But they are not liked, the tinkers."

"The farmers like these people. They are strictly honest. They live by very strict pre-Norman codes."

I was very impressed with Mr. Looney's take on the tinkers. He thought of them as a somewhat distinct race with ancient values that the rest of us had forgotten. Most others saw them as layabouts, thieves, and wanderers.

I had no idea where we were by this time – some farmer's lane. A group of smiling rustics gathered around the car and said, "Hello, Timmy, how are you bein'?"

They waved us on. We drove slowly past the farm buildings and up a slight hill to an uncultivated area. A little below the top of the hill was an ancient roofless stone chapel, very small, about thirty by fifteen feet. Mr. Looney said it was built in the seventh century. A window over the high altar seemed to be lined up with the rising sun at the spring solstice, which was close at hand.

Below the chapel was a small group of stone crosses. Mr. Looney called them high crosses, but they didn't seem tall enough to be called high. On one had been carved six lines in ancient Gaelic.

"No one has succeeded in deciphering it yet," said Mr. Looney.

He said there were no figures of Christ on the crosses or even in the churches until the twelfth century.

"See this stone?" he said. It was under a metal bracket so it couldn't be removed. "Saint Bechaum came to this chapel and asked for butter. He was refused, so the butter turned to stone."

"And this is it?"

"It is."

Farther down, there was a small clochan, a stone beehive hut with an extremely narrow opening, again in the direction of the rising sun. The capstone that might have been on top – or, more likely, a wood-and-straw roof – had been long missing.

On the floor inside was a large flat rock with two round basins carved into it so smoothly it might have been natural. Mr. Looney said it was a balaun stone which would have been used for baptizing the pagans.

"And in pre-Christian times, they were used for grinding corn, is that right?"

"There's another one in Cahir Abbey," he said.

People in Ireland sometimes say there's as much anti-Papist feeling among the Catholics of the South as among the Protestants of the North. For instance, Saint Bechaum was Mr. Looney's favourite saint, but . . .

"Saint Bechaum travelled most of Ireland," he said. "He was an itinerant preacher. He was well known in Rome – involved in changing the dates for Easter. No one knows where he's buried, but I've found traces of him all over Ireland . . ."

I marvelled at the large number of Irish saints.

"Yes, and of all the saints we have – hundred and hundreds of them – only three are registered in Rome. Even Saint Patrick is not registered in Rome. I guess he didn't pay his fee."

As we slowly walked back to the car, it occurred to me that the area under cultivation had perhaps at one time been the site of an expansive village of stone huts. What we had seen had been merely an untouched remnant of a vast clearing of the huts over the centuries. Mr. Looney enthusiastically agreed. Emboldened, I asked about the Blarney Stone.

"Would it really cause me to become eloquent? If there's the slightest chance . . ."

"The Blarney Stone? Ah, that's only folk stuff. That's just a gimmick."

"Well, what about the Little People?"

"That's different," he said.

His face softened, and he began to tell me a story I was to hear many times on my travels, a story that was part of an extensive living mythology, one that the academics and professional historians were beginning to find, in the main, correct.

"Now before the Celtic people came here, there was a tribe of people occupying Ireland. They were called the Tuatha Dé Danann. They were small people. Like, in early-Christian times a tall Irishman would be five feet six inches. But these were small people."

"Smaller than five-six?"

"Much smaller. And the Celts were bigger people and they were all blond. The Tuatha Dé Danann built those forts you see. And when they were under pressure from the Celts they'd disappear. And that's how this thing came about with the little people and all disappearing into the earth. They used to go down into their souterrains, their underground chambers and passageways. They just disappeared into nowhere. That's how the thing about the little people came about."

"When did they become extinct?"

"The Celts finally defeated them and slaughtered them all. That's the way it was in those days – even up to Cromwell's time. Massacres. Ah, but the history of Ireland has never been written."

# Searching for Stevenson

"And what would you like from Edinburgh?" I asked my friend; I was leaving shortly for the Book Festival there.

"Well," he said without stopping to think, as though the answer had been waiting a long time for the question, "a little bust of Stevenson, if it's no trouble." Like me, my friend is a writer; unlike me, he is also a collector.

"No trouble," I said. "A wee bust of RLS it is, then."

The day after arriving in Edinburgh, I prepared to discharge my duties at the Book Festival while the clouds discharged rain. I was scheduled to give a lunchtime reading. The Festival brochure assured its patrons that lunchtime readings were a real bargain: "The best value in town – the price of your ticket includes a filled roll." The comestible was the clincher that would tilt the undecided and send them rushing pell-mell to the reading.

What might it be like, I wondered, to look from stage height upon rows of masticating mouths: would I be treated to privileged glimpses of mayonnaise, bits of lettuce, and shredded chicken? Would the rolls be crusty, thereby igniting a concatenation of crackles and crunches, and multiple mini-avalanches of crumbs?

Would the aroma tickle my nostrils and make my stomach rumble? Would the rumbles be picked up by the microphone? Would there be toothpicks? Would I, in short, feel like some watcher of the skies when a new planet swims into his ken, or like stout Cortez, silent, upon a peak in Darien?

The proceedings of the entire Book Festival were being conducted under canvas, in Charlotte Square Gardens. There was a jolly carnival atmosphere about the place. It managed to shrug off the rain shower that was now faintly thrumming a military tattoo on the seven or eight large tents. Just inside the entrance to the one where I was to read, a depleted platter sat upon a table of white ash. Looking somewhat abandoned, three forlorn filled rolls rubbed elbows within the platter's vast expanse.

I scanned the audience from the back of the tent and noted with relief that the edible section of the lunchtime reading was mostly consumed. My gastronomic fears bad been unfounded – only one person was still chewing. And when it was time to take the stage, the stubby end of that final filled roll, too, had performed its vanishing trick.

The rain continued to practise restrained drumrolls as I read from my novel. Every now and then a wind gust, whipping the drizzle, broke the monotony of the rhythm by injecting a few bars of syncopation. Most of the audience smiled tolerantly and looked skyward. Ah, yes, they seemed to say, the sun was shining this morning, but we're paying for it now. These, I guessed, must be the seasoned veterans of Festivals past. And the few who were irritated by the pitter-patter were obvious novices with unreasonably high expectations such as proper acoustics and a decent sound system.

The traffic around the Square did its bit, too, in dashing the hopes of the fastidious. Rising and falling in concordance with the traffic lights, it posed an interesting challenge. But I managed to float with the automobile tide, manoeuvring my voice around obstacles and taking evasive action by incorporating the gear-grinding lorries into the punctuation. This, however, made the full stops abnormally long, at times; the sporadic silences imparted a pseudo-Pinteresque quality to the text.

Halfway through the reading, I reached a sombre section: the protagonist's best friend had died in hospital, and arrangements were being made for the funeral. At that instant, the sounds of reggae music began creeping into the tent. Well, no, not quite creeping – they stomped in determinedly as though they owned the place, making my audience and me feel that we had no business being there.

And my audience – my kind and faithful audience that had gazed heavenward with such understanding – now squirmed in their seats and exchanged disapproving looks. Who had been so stupid as to leave the door open? their faces inquired in silent indignation. Everyone frowned and turned around to look. But the door, of course, was firmly shut.

Now this door, which sealed the entrance to the tent, was not a rudimentary tent flap nor a hasty hatch flung harum-scarum into a canvas hiatus. No, it was a proper door, and a fine specimen of its kind, too, polished and hewn of solid, well-grained wood, complete with hinges, door-jamb, lock, gleaming brass knob, and threshold. All the accessories that help to make a Scotsman's home his castle. In fact, it was a most accomplished door which would have done justice to any middle-class dwelling, regardless of ethnic background. It was a multicultural door, a good door, a strong and faithful door; a movable barricade of weight and substance, forming a bulwark against thieves, encyclopaedia pedlars, real-estate agents, and the winter cold; a benevolent barrier to keep in the warmth of the hearth, the dog, two children, cooking smells, and all the memories of a happy family.

But, alas, besieged by reggae, this handsome door was revealed in all its helplessness, mournfully out of place. For it was a door without walls. And a door without walls is a doomed door. It is a door without a future. Open or shut, its case is hopeless. It is a door yet to find worthy employment, a door severely in need of relocation.

And so, there it stood in all its empty finery, flanked by canvas to left and right, a pitifully over-qualified door. It waited like a spire in search of a church, or a minaret that had misplaced its mosque.

Someone in charge hurried out to try and mute the sounds of reggae. But reggae is nothing if it is not loud, and she returned with an I-did-my-best look upon her embarrassed face.

The irrepressible rogue music, we learned later, had escaped out of another tent – a very important one, for it even had a title: Beck's Famous Spiegeltent. The Festival brochure invited visitors to "enjoy the cafe/bar and cabaret throughout the day in the splendid Beck's Famous Spiegeltent, brought specially to the Festival from Holland."

For a moment I considered abandoning my reading in favour of leading a sing-along of "Loch Lomond" and "Roamin' in the Gloamin'" and, of course, the ever-popular "I Love a Lassie, My Bonnie, Bonnie Lassie." And it would not have been entirely irrelevant, for the protagonist of my novel loves to sing, and these songs are among his favourites.

Then I thought better of it; my audience, in its present mood, seemed capable of belting out the lyrics with a vengeance, and I had no wish to be unfair to the reggae crowd or cause an incident. Besides, I had been invited to read, and not to impersonate Sir Harry Lauder.

So we gamely endured the hour. During the book-signing

session, a number of people congratulated me for managing a fine reading despite the overwhelming odds. I thought about "The Charge of the Light Brigade," and was grateful to them for their kindness.

The official purpose of my trip was behind me. Now I was free to explore the city and search for a wee bust of Stevenson.

"It's closed for lunch," murmured the museum attendant apologetically, when I tried to enter the basement room marked Robert Louis Stevenson. It was just past two, and he said downstairs could be viewed after three. So I went upstairs, to the Robert Burns and Sir Walter Scott sections, which were open. Stevenson, Burns, and Scott had separate lunch hours.

I was in Lady Stair's House. Built in 1622 by a prominent merchant burgess of the city, read my map-guide, it contained portraits, manuscripts, and relics relating to the three writers. A sign warned visitors to exercise caution when ascending the stone stairway, for in Lady Stair's House the steps did not rise equally. It was a seventeenth-century architectural feature, explained the sign, and had been preserved during restoration of the house. The function of the dissimilar step was that of a built-in burglar alarm: to make an intruder stumble, thus warning the occupants.

I went up and down the stairs several times, but could not trip, for the two deviant steps had been painted white. It was like being told the punch line before the story.

Finding the basement room still shut when I had finished upstairs, I walked the Royal Mile and examined a few souvenir shops in the High Street with the bust in mind. Earlier in the day, the guide on the Award Winning Green & Cream Open-Top Double Decker Edinburgh Tour Bus had explained that the Royal Mile, which extended from Edinburgh Castle to Holyrood Palace, was really more than a mile: "It's a shining example of the generosity of royalty, you know," he had said.

Almost every shop displayed pewter busts of Burns and Scott, along with miniature editions of their works. Then there were lists of surnames with corresponding clans and tartans, scotch-taped to a prominent wall, enabling visitors from the New World to locate their roots in a jiffy. Bushy-bearded Highland dolls in kilts and sporrans overran the shelves, bearing generic labels like MacGregor and Buchanan and MacLeod. But I did not spot a single Stevenson among them.

There were pocket-sized versions of bagpipes, models of haggis, little glass Nessies, videocassettes of Highland Dancing Made Easy in Ten Simple Lessons, plaid scarves, plaid socks, plaid ties, and anything else imaginable in plaid. But of the one who was the object of my friend's veneration, there was never a trace. It seemed quite an unfair state of affairs – squads of Scotts, battalions of Burnses, but not one solitary Stevenson.

It's no use going to Switzerland and grumbling about the Alps, my friend always says, the one who requested the bust. But surely a little spot could have been found for RLS, a tiny bit of shelf space, so I could be done with my friend's shopping. Although, given the choice, he (RLS, that is) would probably have preferred this benign neglect to the alternatives on sale.

In my place a man of action – someone like my much-mentioned friend, perhaps – would have fired off deliciously pungent letters to the Edinburgh Tourist Board, the Chamber of Commerce, and the Lothian Guild of Souvenir Manufacturers (with carbon copies, in the last instance, to head offices in China and Taiwan). I, instead, kept searching in silence.

Next day, I returned to Lady Stair's House, and the Stevenson room was open. Among the usual collections of dark inkpots and warped pens, a straight razor caught my eye. It had belonged to

Stevenson's grandfather, who had been nicknamed Beardie, explained the label. Why Beardie? Because he had sworn not to shave ever again until Bonnie Prince Charlie was restored to the throne.

Then there were Stevenson's things that had been brought back from Samoa: riding boots, stirrups, a crop, a palm-frond fan, a hat, walking sticks, guns. None of these had an explanatory note as interesting as Beardie's razor. The attendant wandered into the room, and I asked if he knew where I might be able to buy a little souvenir bust of Stevenson.

He held his hands behind his back and swayed a little, like someone appreciating a landscape. "Hmm. I'm sorry, but I'm merely on loan here for two days from the City Art Centre, and not so well-acquainted with this museum." He stroked his ginger moustache. "Might be something in the shop upstairs, though. Let me ask the fellow there."

I should have told him I had checked upstairs the day before, but I wanted to see him climb the stone stairway, the one with the uneven burglar-tripping steps. He completed the ascent without mishap, and was back moments later. "They only have a Walter Scott. Have you tried the shops in the High Street?"

"Yes, I looked in them yesterday."

"You should ask," he advised. "If there is no demand for Stevenson, the shopkeepers might not have him on display. But there could always be something in the back."

"Yes, that's a very good idea," I said.

He began strolling with me from exhibit to exhibit. "I could let you have that one for five thousand pounds," he joked, when we came to a two-foot bronze of Stevenson standing. We laughed and strolled on. The stern law-enforcement quality of his black uniform seemed increasingly out of place in that quiet little room.

On the walls were charts with snippets of biography, and one in particular was of a caretaker reminiscing about the little Stevenson, who would always follow him about the grounds, full of questions, never without his tiny stub of a pencil, stopping dead every now and then to scribble "goodness kens what" in his little notebook.

I asked my new friend if he could read the bits in dialect with the proper accent. "I don't know what you mean," he answered, testing me, his tone a mix of defence and challenge.

"These lines look so rich," I said. "I can hear them in my head but cannot make them sound the way they should."

His reluctance melted when he became certain that my request was spurred by genuine interest and not intended to poke fun. There was an old map of the country, and he pointed out the place in the Highlands where he came from. At my prompting, he spoke a few lines in the brogue that was native to his region, and then, to show the difference, followed it with a few words in the border accent (the one with England, that is, he clarified). Before I left he treated me to a beautiful recitation of a Burns poem that began:

Ye flowery banks o' bonnie Doon,
How can ye blume sae fair?
How can ye chant, ye little birds,
And I sae fu' o' care?

His voice, the words, something about Lady Stair's House, all made me nostalgic for places I had never seen, which was a bit silly, though I did not think so then.

"Good luck with the Stevenson bust," he called, as I passed through the courtyard and into the street.

A piper played at the corner, his hat at his feet. The skirl of bag-pipes filled the air like a flock of lazily gliding birds. The sun was shining as I emerged from Lady Stair's House. We'll pay for it by evening, I thought. A quick learner, I had already assimilated the local method of weather forecasting.

Yesterday, the shops between here and St. Giles' Cathedral had been examined. Today, I decided to tackle the ones in the opposite direction, towards the Castle.

"Would you have a little bust of Robert Louis Stevenson?" I asked at the first place, "something like those, perhaps?" pointing to a glass case where half-a-dozen Walter Scotts pouted in pewter.

"A bust of Stevenson?" His tone made me feel like Oliver Twist asking for more. I quickly added that it was for a friend, nothing really to do with me.

"Ah, a gift." He brightened. "Would you like to give your friend a Burns instead?"

"Do you think he might notice the difference?" I hedged, reluctant to dismiss him outright.

He pondered the possibility for a bit. "Aye, that he might. That he might."

In the next shop, the woman's suggestion was more to the point, though a trifle impractical. "You must come back next year," she said. "The shops will be full of Stevenson souvenirs then – 1994 is his death centenary."

The third place had none of the cheap tourist stuff, and was more in the nature of an antique store. If I found a bust here it would be expensive. But I asked my question of the shopkeeper, who could easily have been the model for some of the bushy-bearded Highland dolls I had seen.

"Stevenson. Robert Louis Stevenson," he said, spacing the names carefully, as though to make sure we had the right man.

I nodded, that's the one.

"A fine writer," he continued. "A very fine writer. *Treasure Island. Kidnapped. The Strange Case of Dr. Jekyll and Mr. Hyde.*" More confirmation of the man's identity. I nodded again. "And didn't he go abroad and live in a faraway foreign land?"

My hopes were rising. "In Samoa," I said. "He died there."

"Ah, yes, Samoa." His eyes grew distant now, even romantic, before he continued, "I'm sorry, I don't have what you're looking for. But may I ask you something personal? May I ask why you want Stevenson's bust?"

"It's a gift for a friend who adores his writing."

"Oh, I see." He seemed disappointed. "Shall I tell you what I thought? I thought, from your skin colour, that you yourself might be Samoan, which might account for your interest in the man." He was amused by his own admission. "And where do you come from?"

"Canada. And before that, India," I volunteered, without waiting for the routine follow-up question that was forming on his lips.

"But you can always pretend to be from Samoa," he laughed. "Claim that your family were Stevenson's neighbours on the island. You could write a history of it, become a Stevenson authority." We laughed some more and then I left, too lazy to explain that Samoans and Indians are about as interchangeable as the Scots and the English.

A souvenir store across the road, larger than most, was enticing shoppers inside by offering a taste of shortbread: a man stood in the doorway with a plate. I asked him my question, and got the expected answer. But this time I persevered: "Don't you have any souvenirs of Stevenson? A postcard, perhaps, of the Stevenson museum? Or his childhood home in Edinburgh, or his house in Samoa? Anything?"

A shop attendant who looked like the shortbread man's

brother or twin brother (though not identical) overheard me. "This shop is full of Stevenson souvenirs. Overflowing with them," he greeted me, flinging his arms around him to indicate the merchandise. "You're in luck, my friend."

I was willing to listen.

"This thimble, for example," he said, extricating it from a tartan sewing kit. "It is the exact copy of the thimble that Stevenson wore while darning his socks after a day of hard writing. It was his way of relaxing."

I couldn't help laughing, but he continued solemnly, picking up a plaid-covered tea cosy. "And this is a perfect likeness of the one with which Stevenson kept his teapot warm."

Now the shortbread fellow, too, got into the spirit of things. "And this mug is the exact model – down to the last detail, mind you – of the one in which Stevenson poured his tea after it had steeped." In a confiding voice he added, "He liked his tea quite strong."

"And have you seen this? A superb copy of the sunglasses Stevenson used to wear – the sun was bright in Samoa, far too bright for someone accustomed to the cloud and fog of Scotland."

The two passed the gag between them with ease, like a seasoned vaudeville act. They covered all the items within their reach. Shoppers formed a circle to listen. Scarves, ties, wine glasses, teaspoons, dolls, bracelets, pens, ashtrays, cigarette cases, keychains, photo-frames, all were integrated into an instant hagiography and given the Stevenson seal of approval.

Finally, the one who had begun the entertainment picked up a plaid-handled toy revolver, cocked it, and raised it above his head. "And this gun, produced in our finest workshop, is the exact replica of the one with which Stevenson, alas, shot himself in the head."

"Ah, yes," I interrupted, thinking I had him now. "But Stevenson died of a cerebral haemorrhage. I read it only this morning at the museum."

"Of course, that's what it would say in the museum, wouldn't it?" he said patiently. "For is it not the perfect euphemism for blowing out one's brains? Mind you, it's always in the souvenir shops that you get the real story, not in the museums."

My search for Stevenson had ended, I decided, and my friend would have agreed with me. Besides, after this bravura performance, everything else was bound to be anticlimactic – good thing I had taken in the Highland Regiments and the Edinburgh Military Tattoo the night before at the Castle.

People began drifting out of the shop. The shortbread man held the plate before me: "Won't you try a little piece? It is the exact same recipe that Stevenson used."

"Aye, that I will, thank you," I laughed, and went to look for a cup of tea that would complement the shortbread while I pondered the questions of mortality, memory, monuments, and the manufacture and management of fame. I was grateful to my friend for having endowed me with the quest. Without it, my time in Edinburgh would have been the poorer; instead, I felt as exhilarated as though I had returned from a lengthy ocean voyage to Samoa, the sea-spray still moist on my cheeks, the tang of salt upon my lips, and clutching with great care against my chest the sweet, freshly baked transubstantiation of RLS.

DANIEL DAVID MOSES

# Rain in Hawaii

The graduate student greets me at the airport with apologies for the rain.

We haven't seen blue sky in six weeks, sighs his girlfriend.

But I can't complain. I'm just in from Canada, where we talk, mocking our situation, even in the temperate south, about six months of winter. It's March, the first week of spring in nineteen ninety-one, and though the snow's gone and frost is coming out, at least in Toronto, colour has yet to come back.

The island of Oahu under rain was a warm body, green and flowered, even through cloud from the plane. And now the city Honolulu, drizzled on in the distance, seems organic, rocks in a tropical garden.

And I'm the guest here, the exotic one, a red Indian.

On the short walk to the lot and the graduate student's sturdy little car, for the first time in seasons, my skin feels damp, my forehead drips, and suddenly I'm sure I'm shining with sweat.

The car swings onto the expressway, and overhead through the see-through, snapped-down sun-roof, the clouds part and show just for a moment the blue of the sky.

What a tease, the girlfriend mutters from her front seat.

But later it's begun again, the downpour a rushing noise on the roof of the restaurant where my new friends and I are eating Japanese.

We're talking about my work and theirs, about the reading I'm here to do tomorrow night at the university, about what I should see of Hawaii in my bit of time here. We're talking about the life in my home city, and New York, and how isolated they feel here.

It really is the frontier, she says.

All I need do at this end of the long day, after the hours of flight and the hours added by time zones, and in this twilight of paper lanterns, is close my eyes – I'm that ready to dream. But the sake clarifies my hunger, and the flesh colours of sushi bloom on my plate, my palate.

So the Japanese are the cowboys? The student grins.

And the rain plays the car for a drum when we drive, seeing the sights of the night city. It also beats against the ocean face and the leaves, against the flat and the mountainsides, against houses and their eaves.

So how is it that, in the dark off Diamond Head, lights glow in the rain? Is it phosphorescence?

No, the girlfriend tells me, the true surfer goes out boarding the waves at every opportunity.

So why are so few tourists here, a mere scattering dodging drops on the slick streets along the strip? Isn't there usually more spend-ing of the green stuff at the feet of the famed tall hotels of Waikiki? The lights here are lit but so few of the crowd are.

The fear of the war in the Gulf, the girlfriend tells me, keeps the people away.

But that war's on the other side of the world – I begin.

We're Americans, the grad student sighs, as if explaining every-thing.

We swerve away from the strip and up a street to the heights as the rain comes down, the centre line reflectors like electric fish under the rushing water.

And up there we shelter beneath the gutters of the girlfriend's house, and watch a blackness, a cloud of whispers and winds, moving in from the night and the ocean. It blows between the mountains and covers up first a hill of stars; a suburb where smaller streets and houses are. Then it's closing in on the bright towers downtown, putting their stories of light out too.

The clouds finally part for me four days later on Hawaii, the Big Island.

My guide to the Kilauea crater welcomes me like a brother, says one of his foremothers was Algonquin, from Canada too.

In the orientation centre, a display pictures the volcano as a goddess, Pele, and as a tornado of heat rising through the earth's crust, a storm of magma.

Prayer sticks have been placed at the edge of the crater, just beyond the wooden barriers. Under my fingers the grain of that wood is risen, weathered by acid air, by a frost of sulphur.

So somehow both of us do end up red-faced, burned, from the sun glaring there off the bare fields of lava or from the vog, the volcanic fog, or maybe from both.

On my last afternoon on the island, I seek shelter from that high sun under palms.

I'm at a beach on the south coast, hoping with my hosts for the success of the handsome young man I met and ate dinner with the evening before, a Native Hawaiian who had tried, he said, to be an American. He did school and business like he was supposed to, but ended up in his twenties divorced, a recovering alcoholic. Now he was trying just to be Native again.

I scramble from rock to rock a short way out into the bay, and look back and up at the green fields and mountain. How hard it must be to learn now how to carve, how to drum and sing, to remember a way of life, with all this land overturned into plantations.

Down on the beach, my hosts are easy to spot, two light faces among all the dark ones, all crowded along that narrow strip of lava-black sand by No Trespassing signs.

And here in the loud, bright surf at my feet, great sea turtles are riding in on the tide, eyes wide and steady as many grandfathers'.

Much later, my wonder is how we all manage to keep on living so absorbed in ourselves, with the storms of creation right under our feet.

# What Do You Want to Know For?

I saw the crypt first, though it was in a cemetery to the left of the
road, on my husband's side of the car.

"What was that?" I said. "Something strange."

I had seen a big mound, an unnatural lump, blanketed with
smooth grass.

We turned back, though we hadn't much time. We were going
to visit friends who live on Georgian Bay.

There it was, set in the middle of the little country cemetery.
Like a woolly animal – huge and somnolent, prehistoric. We
climbed a bank and unhooked a gate and went around and looked
at the front end of this thing. A stone wall between an upper and
a lower stone arch, and a wall of bricks within the lower arch. No
names, no dates, just a cross roughly carved into the keystone of
the upper arch. At the other end earth and grass covered the wall.
Some stones protruded – they were probably set there to hold the
earth in place. No markings on them, either, no clues as to what
might be inside.

We returned to the car.

A couple of days after this, I had a phone call from the nurse in
my doctor's office. The doctor wanted to see me, an appointment

had been made. I knew without asking what this must be about. Three weeks or so before, I had gone to the city breast clinic, to have a mammogram. There was no special reason for doing this, no problem. I have a mammogram every year; I have reached the age when that is recommended. But I had missed last year's, because of travelling.

There was a lump deep in my left breast, which neither my doctor nor I had been able to feel. We still couldn't feel it. The doctor said that it was shown on the mammogram to be about the size of a pea. He had made an appointment for me with a city doctor who would do a biopsy. As I was leaving he touched my shoulder. He is a friend, and I knew that his first wife's death had begun in just this way.

I had ten days to put in before I saw the city doctor. I filled the time by answering letters and cleaning up my house and going through my files and having people to dinner. We went for many walks and drives. I got it into my head that I would like to see the crypt again and find out something about it. So we set out, sure – or reasonably sure – that we knew which road it was on, But we did not find it. We took a parallel road and did not find it on that road either. But surely it was in Bruce or Grey county, we said, and it was on the north side of an east-west road, and there were a lot of cedar trees close by. We spent three or four afternoons looking for it and were puzzled and disappointed. But it was a pleasure, as always, to be together in this part of the world looking at the countryside that we think we know so well and that is always springing some surprise on us.

This landscape is a record of ancient events. It was formed by the advancing, stationary, and retreating ice that has staged its conquests and retreats here several times, withdrawing for the last time about fifteen thousand years ago. And a glacial landscape is vulnerable. Much of what gives it contour and variety is made of gravel, and gravel is easy to get at, easy to scoop out, always in demand. These back roads we ride on come from chewed-up hills and terraces. Ridges of hills are replaced by extensive holes in the earth, and the holes, once they are exhausted and deserted, grow grass and bushes. So instead of a long line of interesting humps, a miniature mountain range (that's what an esker looks like), you get, eventually, a succession of picturesque irregular hollows. It's as if a part of the landscape was trying in a haphazard way to turn itself inside out. The hollows are pleasant and sometimes spooky, as their steep sides grow velvety with new grass. But the tracks of the glacier are gone for good.

So we have to keep checking, taking in the changes, seeing things while they last.

We have special maps that we travel with. They are maps sold to accompany a book called *The Physiography of Southern Ontario*, by Lyman Chapman and Donald Putnam, whom we refer to, familiarly but somewhat reverentially, as Put and Chap. These maps show the usual roads and towns and rivers, but they show other things as well, that were a complete surprise to me when I first saw them. Long snakes or tails or ribbons of a beautiful purple colour, and brown spots like freckles, except that they are not round but lozenge-shaped. These are sprinkled thickly or sparsely, usually on a light tan background but sometimes on splotches of clear blue or on smaller splotches of murky grey. These dark grey areas are swamps, and the clear blue splotches show where a lake once was, an ancient lake that left a deposit of clay. Sometimes there is a patch of dazzling yellow adjacent to the clay, and that is a build-up of sand. The purple ribbons are moraines and the brown lozenges are drumlins. The tan background of many drumlins is called, appropriately, drumlinized till; there is also an area of undrumlinized till, appearing as a spread of dreary middling grey, and a lot of bevilled till, a soft pleasant green, stretching along the shore of Lake Huron. Eskers are fluttering strokes of a sharper green. Orange-gold networks, richly complicated, are the spillways, old watercourses. Red strokes and red interrupted lines are the bluffs and old beaches. And my favourite of all these kinds of country I have left till last. Dark brown it shows on the map, a chocolate-burgundy colour. A series, usually, of big and little blobs. It is called kame moraine, sometimes just kame.

Eskers are the easiest things to recognize, when you look around. They look like miniature mountain ranges, as I've said, or like a dragon's back. They show the route of the rivers that tunnelled under the ice, at right angles to its front, depositing gravel as they went. A little mild river, a creek, will be running along beside them now, a direct descendant of that old battering torrent.

Moraines show where the ice halted on its long retreat, putting down a ridge of rubble at its edge. And kame moraines show where a heap of dead ice sat, cut off from the moving glacier, earth-stuff pouring in through all its holes and crevices. Or perhaps it will show where two lobes pulled apart. So both moraines and kame moraines are hilly, but moraines are hilly in what seems a reasonable way, while kame moraines are wild and bumpy, with an unpredictable rhythm, a look of chance and secrets.

Drumlins, those lozenges on the map, are probably the easiest things to spot, after eskers. Not by their size. Some could qualify as big hills but others barely rise out of the surrounding fields and swamps. You spot them by their smoothness and by their shape which is that of a half-buried egg. And the glacier did lay them down like eggs, neatly and economically getting rid of the burden of material it had scraped up in its bulldozing progress. The drumlinized-till plain that surrounds them is not really smooth, but it is smoother, on account of this dumping, than the

David Kilgour

undrumlinized till that lies where the ice didn't consolidate its load, dropping it more or less constantly as it proceeded. The bevilled till, which was worked over by the strong waves of the shallow melted ice water, in the far reaches of the old lake, is smoothest of all. Clay is flat but not smooth – lumpy-looking, something sour and cold about it. Heavy soil, coarse grass, poor drainage. The sand country adjacent to it can stretch out flat or rise in rounded hills. This is the delta formed by the moving stream, dropping material into a still lake. It grows tobacco, dry-floored pine forests.

I didn't learn any of this at school. I think there was still some nervousness then about being at loggerheads with the Bible. So my knowledge is untainted, fresh. I get a naive and particular pleasure from matching what I can see on the map with what I can see when I look out the car window. Also, from trying to figure out what something is, before I look at the map, and being right at least half the time. Sighting the boundaries is a hard job, at least when it's a question of those different kinds of till, or of the point where kame takes over from moraine. But there is something more than just this keen pleasure of identification. It's the fact of these separate domains, each with its own history and expression and favourite trees and crops and weeds, its special pull on the imagination – these little countries lying snug and unsuspected, like and unalike as siblings can be, in a landscape that's usually disregarded, or dismissed as drab agricultural counterpane. It's the fact you cherish.

I thought my appointment was for a biopsy, but it turned out not to be. It was an appointment to let the doctor decide whether he would do a biopsy, and he decided that he would. He had looked only at my most recent mammogram. Those from 1990 and 1991 had not yet arrived from the country hospital where they had been done. The biopsy was set for a date two weeks ahead. I got my instructions about how to prepare for it – not eating, as if for real surgery, which I had to realize it was.

I said that it seemed quite a while to wait.

At this stage of the game, the doctor said, two weeks was immaterial.

That was not what I had thought. But I did not complain – not after a look at the people in his waiting-room. I am over sixty. My death would not be a calamity. Not in comparison with the death of a young mother, a family wage-earner, a child.

We were becoming absurdly stubborn about finding the crypt. I went to the town library to look at the nineteenth-century atlases, to see if perhaps the cemeteries were marked on the township maps. They seemed to be marked on the maps of Huron County townships, but not on those of Grey and Bruce counties. (This wasn't true, I found out later – some were marked and I just didn't find them.) But in the library I met a friend, who had dropped in to see us shortly after the discovery. We had told him about the crypt and given him some rough directions as to how to find it, because he is interested in old cemeteries. He said he had written down the directions when he got home. I had forgotten ever giving them. He went straight home then and found the piece of paper – found it miraculously, he said – and there he had written down some words. *Peabody, Scone, McCullough Lake.*

Farther north than we had thought – just beyond the boundary of the territory we had been so doggedly covering.

So we found the cemetery again, and the grass-grown crypt looked as surprising, as primitive as I had remembered. Now we had lots of time to look around. We saw that all the old stones in one section had been collected and set in concrete, in the form of a cross. Most of these were the tombstones of children. In any of these old country cemeteries the earliest burials were likely to be those of children, and young women dead in childbirth, and a few young men who had drowned or been killed in the sort of accidents that happen when trees are being cut down, barns put up. There were hardly any old people around to die, in the early days.

The names were nearly all German ones, and many inscriptions were in German. *Hier ruhet in Gott.* And *Geboren*, followed by the name of a German town or district; then *Gestorben*, with a date in the seventies or eighties of the last century. *Gestorben* – here, in Sullivan Township in Grey County in a colony of England in the middle of the bush.

*Das arme Herz hieniedan*
*Von manches Sturm bewegt*
*Erlangt den renen Frieden*
*Nur wenn es nicht mehr schlagt*

It's odd how you think you can read German, even when you can't. I thought that this said something about the heart, the soul, the person buried here being out of harm's way now and altogether better off. *Herz* and *Sturm* and *nicht mehr* could hardly give me problems. But when I went home and checked the words in a German-English dictionary – finding them all except for *renen*, which could easily have been a misspelling of *reinen* – I found that it was nothing so comforting. More like – the poor heart buried here could get no real peace until it stopped beating.

*Better off dead.*

Maybe they got that out of a book, and there wasn't much choice.

Not a word on the crypt itself, though we searched more carefully than before. Nothing but the rather clumsy-looking cross. We did find a surprise, though, in the northeast corner of the cemetery. A second crypt there, much smaller than the first, this one with a smooth concrete top covering it, no earth or grass. But a good-sized tree, a cedar, growing out of a crack in the concrete.

Something like mound-burial, we said. Some custom out of central Europe, pre-Christian.

In the same city where I was to have my biopsy there is a university, and since it's the university where we were students, we are allowed to take books out of its library. On our next visit there I went into the Regional Reference Room to read some books about Grey County and whatever I could find about Sullivan Township. I read about a plague of passenger pigeons that had destroyed the crops, one year in the late nineteenth century. Also of a terrible winter in the 1840s, which lasted so long with such annihilating cold that people were living on cow cabbages dug out of the ground. (Were these ordinary cabbages, kept in a pit, or something coarser and leafier, like skunk cabbage? I don't know.) A man named Barnes starved himself to death, so that his family could eat his share, and survive. A few years after that, a young woman wrote to her friend in Toronto that there was a marvellous crop of berries, and when she was out picking them the day before, she had seen a bear, so close that she could see the drops of berry juice sparkling on its whiskers. She said that she was not afraid and that she would walk through the bush to post this letter, bears or not.

I asked if there were any church histories. I thought there might be something about Lutheran or German Catholic churches that would help me. It is difficult to ask for books in reference libraries because you will always be asked what it is, exactly, that you want to know, and what do you want to know it for? Sometimes you even have to write that down. The best thing probably is to say that you are doing a family history. Librarians are used to people doing that – particularly people who have grey hair – and it is generally thought to be a reasonable way of spending one's time. But if you mumble that you are just interested, you run the risk of being seen as an idler, a person at loose ends, with no proper direction in life, *nothing better to do*. I thought of writing down, *Research for paper concerning survival of mound burial in pioneer Canada*. But I didn't have the nerve. I thought they might make me prove it.

I did locate a church that I thought might be connected with the cemetery. St. Peter's Evangelical Lutheran, it was called, and it was only a couple of country blocks west, a block north, of our cemetery.

We arrived on a Sunday morning just as the bell was ringing for services, and the hands of the clock on the church tower pointed to eleven. We learned later that in fact they didn't move, they always pointed to church time.

In Sullivan Township you remember what the crop-fields everywhere used to look like, before the advent of the big farm machines. These fields have kept the size that can be served by the horse-drawn plough, the binder, the mower. Rail fences are still in place – here and there is a roughly built stone wall – and along them grow maple trees, hawthorn trees, choke-cherries, goldenrod, wild aster, old man's beard.

The fields are unchanged because they are not worth extending. Two big moraines curve across the southern part of the township – the snakes here are swollen as if each of them had swallowed a frog – and there's a spillway between them. In the north the land is clay. The crops were probably never up to much, and where the country is put to any use at all now, it's pasture. The wooded areas – which everybody here has always called "the bush" – are making a strong comeback. In places like this the trend is no longer towards a taming of the countryside and a thickening of the population, rather the opposite. But the bush will never take over again, completely. It has only made a good grab. The deer, the wolves, which at one time had almost disappeared, must be on the increase. Even the bears, perhaps, with berry juice on their fur.

Non-farmers are moving in, and more will follow. The notion of farming fades, and unexpected enterprises replace it. SPORTS CARDS GALORE, one sign says. Two-door doghouses, offered for sale. Chairs are repaired and tires are sold. Antiques and beauty treatments are advertised, and surely don't pull in many customers from the empty roads. Brown eggs. Maple syrup. Unisex haircuts.

St. Peter's is large and handsome, built of limestone blocks. There is a high steeple and a modern glass porch to block the wind and snow, also a long driveshed of stone and wood, a reminder of the time when people drove to church in buggies and cutters. A pretty stone house, too, the rectory, surrounded by flowers.

We drove on to Williamsford to have lunch, and to give the minister a decent interval to recover from the morning service. A mile or so along the road we made a discouraging discovery. St. Peter's had its own cemetery, with its own early dates and German names, and that made our cemetery, so close by, seem even more of a puzzle, an orphan.

We came back anyway, around two o'clock. We knocked on the door of the rectory and after a while a little girl appeared, try-ing to unbolt the door. She made signs for us to go around to the backs and came running out to meet us on our way. The minister wasn't home, she said. She and her sister were here, looking after the minister's dog and cats. But if we wanted to know anything about history or cemeteries or churches we could go and ask her mother, who lived up the hill in the new log house.

We asked her name, and she said it was Rachel.

Rachel's mother didn't seem at all surprised at our curiosity or put out by our visit. She invited us into her house, where there was a noisy and interested dog, and a self-possessed husband just finishing his lunch. The house was a pleasant one – all one big room on the main floor, with a wide view of fields and trees.

She brought out a book that I hadn't seen in the library. An older history of the township – she thought it had a chapter on cemeteries. And in fact it did. In a short time we were reading together a section on the Mannerow Cemetery, "famous for its two vaults." There was a grainy old photograph of the larger crypt, which was said to have been built in 1895 for the burial of a three-year-old boy, a son of the Mannerow family. Other members of the family were buried there in the years that followed. One pair of Mannerows were buried in the smaller crypt in the corner. What was originally a family burying-ground had later become public and the name was changed to "Cedardale." The vaults were roofed with concrete on the inside.

Rachel's mother said that a descendant of the Mannerow family now lived in Scone.

"Next door to where my brother lives," she said. "You know

there's the three houses in Scone: there's the yellow brick one, that's my brother, and the one in the middle: that's Mannerows'. So maybe he might know something if you went and asked him."

While I was talking to Rachel's mother and looking at the history book, my husband sat at the table and talked to her husband. The husband asked where we came from, and then said that he knew Huron County very well. He had come there from Holland not long after the War (he was a man considerably older than his wife) and he had lived for a while near Blyth. He had worked on a turkey farm.

I overheard this conversation and I asked him later if it was Wallaces' Turkey Farm that he worked on.

Yes, he said, that was the one, and his sister was married to Alvin Wallace.

"Corrie Wallace," I said.

"That's right!" he said. "That's her."

I asked him if he knew any Laidlaws around Blyth, and he said no.

"You didn't know Bob Laidlaw?" I said. "He was in turkeys too, and he worked with Wallaces'."

"Bob Laidlaw? Sure I knew him. But he was from Wingham. He had a place up to the west of Wingham."

I said that he came from Blyth, or rather from the eighth line of Morris Township, and that's how he knew the Wallace brothers. They had all gone to school together at S.S. No. 1 Morris.

He took a closer look at me.

"You're not telling me he was your dad, are you? You're not Sheila?"

"Sheila's my sister. I'm the older one."

"I didn't know there was an older one," he said. But he was only slightly disappointed. "I never knew that. But Bill and Sheila, they used to be down working on the turkeys with us, in the fall. You never came then?"

"I was away from home by that time. By the time my Dad got into raising turkeys."

"Bob Laidlaw!" he said. "Bob Laidlaw was your dad. You see when you said Laidlaws I thought right away, Bob Laidlaw. But then I thought, he was from Wingham. So I said no. Because you'd said Blyth."

"There were lots of Laidlaws around Blyth originally," I said. "That's where they settled."

"Did they? Did they really? But up west of Wingham. I remember his place, sure."

Then we both said that it was a small world. We said this, as people usually do, with a sense of relief and refreshment. (Those who are not going to be pleased with this discovery usually avoid making it.) We explored the connection as far as we could, and found that there was nothing much more to be got out of it. But we were both happy. He was happy to be reminded of himself as a young man, fresh in this country and not knowing what might be ahead of him (though by the look of his lively wife and pretty daughter, you couldn't say that things hadn't turned out fairly well) and I was happy to find somebody who could see me still as part of my family, who could remember my father and the place where my parents lived and worked all their lives, first in hope and then in honourable persistence. A place astonishingly changed now, though the house is still there. The front yard and the side yard and the vegetable garden and the flower-borders, the hay-field, the mock-orange bush, the lilacs, the chestnut stump, even the lane to the river, have been buried by a tide of car parts and bodies, of gaudy junk. Smashed headlights, upended car seats with rotten upholstery and bloated stuffing, grills and fenders, over-turned truck-cabs, heaps of painted, rusted, blackened, glittering, whole or twisted, defiant and surviving, metal.

Rachel's mother asked us if we would like to see the inside of the church, and we said that we would. We walked down the hill and she took us proudly and hospitably into its red-carpeted interior. It smelled a little damp or musty as stone buildings often do, even when they're kept very clean.

She told us how things had been going there. The whole building had been raised up some years ago, to put the Sunday school and the church kitchen underneath. The church bell still rang out the death of every church member. One ring for every year of life. Everybody within hearing distance counted the rings and mostly they could figure out who it was for. The front porch of the church was modern, as we had noticed, and there had been a big argument when it was put on, between those in the congregation who wanted it and those who didn't. There was a split, finally. A part of the congregation went off to Williamsford and set up their own church there, though with the same minister. The minister was a woman. The last time they had to hire a minister, five out of seven candidates were women. She was married to a veterinarian, and she used to be a veterinarian herself. Everybody liked her fine. Though a man from Faith Lutheran in Desboro had got up and walked out of a funeral when he found that she was preaching at it. He could not stay and hear a woman preaching. Faith Lutheran was part of the Missouri Synod.

There had been a great fire in the church, some time ago, which gutted much of the inside but left the shell intact. When the inside walls were scrubbed down afterwards, layers of paint came off with the smoke and there was a surprise underneath. A text in German that didn't wash off, hidden on each of the side walls under the paint:

*Ich hebe meine Augen auf ben Bergen, von welchen mir Hulfe*
    *kommt.*
*Dein Wort ist meines Fusses Leuchte und ein Lieht auf meinam*
    *Wege.*

This time I could have got the translation right, even if it had not been written underneath, English for the present-day congregations.

*I will lift up my eyes unto the hills, from whence cometh my help.*
*Thy word is a lamp unto my feet and a light unto my path.*

Nobody had known that these German words were there, until the fire revealed them.

They had been painted over – perhaps at the time of the 1914-18 War – and afterwards nobody had mentioned them, and the memory of them had altogether died out.

In the stained glass of the church windows, we saw these symbols: the Dove (over the altar); Alpha and Omega (in the rear wall); the Holy Grail; the Wheat Sheaf; the Cross in the Crown; the Ship at Anchor; the Lamb of God bearing the Cross; and a golden bird, the mythical pelican which was thought to feed its young on the blood of its torn breast, as Christ the Church. The mythical pelican resembled the real pelican only in being a bird.

We did stop at the Mannerow house in Scone, but nobody answered the door. The house and yard were very tidily kept. In the yard there were flowering bushes and bright beds of annuals and a little black boy, sitting holding a Canadian flag. This is not intended or understood as any sort of racial insult in this part of the country. I am not sure how it is intended. Possibly people think that a little black boy adds a touch of sportiness and charm.

On the day before I was to have my biopsy, I got a call from the city hospital to say that it had been cancelled. I was to keep my appointment anyway, to have a talk with the radiologist, but I did not need to fast in preparation for surgery.

The radiologist said that when she looked at the mammograms sent from the country hospital, she saw that the lump had been there in 1990 and in 1991. It had not changed. It had not changed in the mammogram taken this year. Still the same lump in the same place, the same size. You could never be absolutely one hundred per cent certain that such a lump was safe, without a biopsy. But you could be sure enough. A biopsy was an intrusive procedure, and if she were in my place she would not have it. She would have a mammogram in another six months instead. If it were her breast she would keep an eye on it, but for now she would let well enough alone.

I asked why nobody had told me about the lump when it first appeared.

Oh, she said, they must not have seen it.

We made one more effort. We drove to Scone. We noticed how familiar Sullivan Township and the church and the cemetery and the villages of Scone and Desboro and the town of Chesley were getting to seem, how the distances appeared to have shortened. And we knew, even if we didn't quite admit, that we had found out all we were going to find out. There might be a bit more explanation – the idea of the vault might have come from somebody's reluctance to put a three-year-old child in the ground – but it wouldn't matter so much to us. What had been so bluntly compelling was drawn, now, into the pattern of things we knew about.

Nobody answered the door this time, either. I stepped into the little porch and tried the bell on the inner door, There was an armchair in the porch, and an afghan on the armchair. Potted plants on small wicker tables. Still nobody came. But I could hear some loud singing inside the house. A choir was singing "Onward Christian Soldiers." And now I could see the colours of a television screen in an inner room. The bobbing faces of a blue-robed choir against a sunset sky. I listened to the words of the hymn and knew that they were just ending the first verse. That made three or four verses more to go.

I let the bell alone, till they were finished.

I tried again. Mrs. Mannerow came – a short competent-looking woman with tight, greyish brown curls, wearing a blue flowered top to match her blue summer slacks.

She said that her husband was very hard of hearing, so it wouldn't do me much good to talk to him. Besides that, he had recently been in the hospital; he wasn't feeling very strong. And she didn't have much time to talk, herself, because her daughter was coming from Chesley to take her to a family picnic. It was her daughter's in-laws who were having the picnic; it was for their fiftieth anniversary.

She didn't mind telling me as much as she knew.

When she first married into the family she used to wonder. She asked them questions. Why did they bury their people like that, where did they get the idea? But the Mannerows all took it for granted, they didn't know why. They took it for granted because it had always been that way as far as they were concerned, and none of them ever thought to ask why or where their family got that idea of burying.

The vault was all concrete on the inside.

She did remember the last funeral they had in there. It was the last time they had it opened up. To bury Mrs. Lempke, who had been born a Mannerow. Then there was no room for any more.

The vault was all opened up at one end to put her in, and you could see what was inside. You could see the coffins with the names on them.

And a table sitting there in the middle. A table with a Bible on it.

And beside the Bible, a lamp.

It was just one of those old-fashioned lamps, that burned coal oil.

To think of it, sitting there just the same today, all sealed up and nobody going to see it ever again.

"Nobody knows why they did it. They just did."

"Do you think they put any oil in that lamp?" I said to my husband as we were driving home.

He said that he had been wondering that same thing.

The corn in tassel, the height of summer passing, time opening out with room for ordinary anxieties, weariness, tiffs, triviality. No more hard edges, or blamelessness, or fate buzzing around in your veins like a swarm of bees. Back where nothing seems to be happening, beyond the change of seasons.

MICHAEL ONDAATJE

Six Photographs

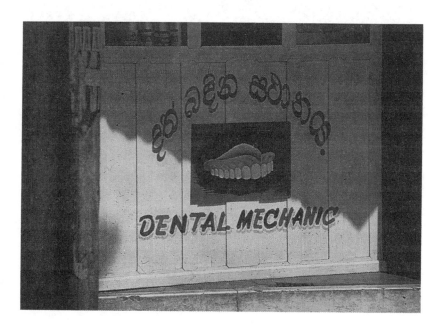

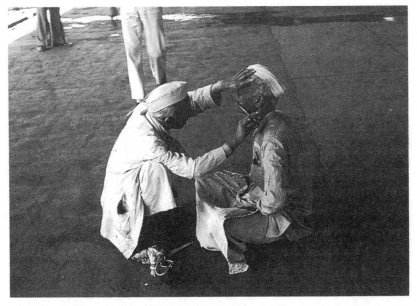

Tomorrow: a roundtable discussion on whether English will
continue to dominate the world

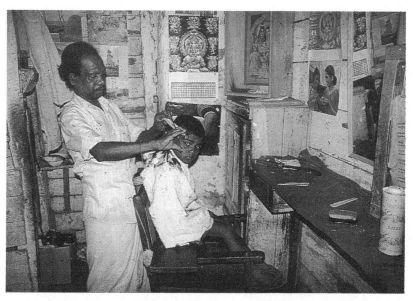

The Golden Age of Sculpture in Sri Lanka

Bouquet de Corsage

Any person who has auctioned asparagus.
*(Elimination Dance Surveillance Files, Italy, 1987)*

Baby Cinema

# Settling In

Black, black, black is the colour of a Mexican night. And my first impressions of blackness and carnations and small, brightly-dressed Indians – mother, father, and all the little papooses trailing the wide tree-lined boulevards of a European city – will remain, I am sure, stronger and sharper than those that will come later.

(I write this in 1991 from notes made in the sixties and wonder about the language. Is it usable today? Probably not. Although I ask myself why not. Papoose is a lovely word. A Narraganset word, so the dictionary tells me. I wonder, too, if it's right to say Indians? They themselves call themselves *los indios* – or did when we were there. But perhaps they no longer do. Or no longer want a gringa to do so.)

A. and I had a good flight, non-stop from Toronto. Marred only by the pretentious absurdity of the CPA meal. It was five courses dragged out over hours. Designed to please Canadian tourists, I trust, rather than a preview of what Mexicans expect. At the airport were the assembled embassy representatives, the Chef de Protocol from Mexican External and – surprise! – Walther and Johanna Hess of the German Embassy, whom we had known in

Australia. And what a hilarious encounter. Walther and A., who had shaken hands formally when they said goodbye to each other, now having both had Latin postings greeted each other with *abraços*, to the astonished delight of Johanna and me.

The hotel where we are staying is very modern, very Hollywood, and, to my taste, utterly depressing. It is dark and stagey with water falling and large plants growing in its darkness. Night plants? Are there such things? Our room looks out over the rooftops of this low city – flat roofs, bulbous here and there in a rather anatomical way, with concrete water-storage tanks. Coming in by air, the city looked grey. And grey it is, compared with the red tiles of Brazil, which are still bright in my eye, and the heavy smog which greys the sun.

Our first black Mexican night was splintered by the melancholy two-note whistle of police communicating with each other, and towards dawn, little chunks were gobbled out of it. "What's that?" I asked. "It's a turkey," A. said, waking from sleep. "A turkey! Here? In downtown Mexico City? In . . .?" "It's a turkey *anywhere*," A. said, and went to sleep again. And it was. It lived on an adjacent roof among the laundry.

The Canadian Residence where we shall live is a fifteen-minute drive from the centre of town along a fine boulevard, Paseo de la Reforma. Down its centre, on Sundays, the Don Quixotes ride in large felt sombreros, tilted according to personality – dour, cheerful, fierce. They wear wide little armless jackets – which give their torsos great breadth – and the most beautiful trousers imaginable, with embroidered or tooled strips running from waist to ankle, which make their legs look long and slender.

On each side of the grassy boulevard, an avenue flanked by rows of trees stretches as far as you can see. So coming or going you drive down a tunnel of green – young and delicate now, because it is spring.

Spring, here, is the hot season. Hottest at midday and cooling rapidly towards evening. Mornings are hazy; the thick smog hides the surrounding mountains. By afternoon, you can see the horizon with its sinister-looking volcanoes, their tops like sawed-off shotguns. On brilliant days, Popocatepetl appears, standing guard over the reclining figure of Ixtacihuatl, his sleeping bride. Popo, they call him, which in the context of an inflected language, sounds like the masculine form of El Papa, the Pope.

Down the Reforma, too, on a Sunday, with all the populace out, are the balloon men, looking as if they've descended by parachutes of multicoloured helium-filled balloons – painted or nippled or tufted – unlike any I have ever seen. And the Indians, scores of them, the men in straw sombreros, the women with pigtails, idling along the lovely boulevard.

The house is a headache. Ugly, to begin with. A great stone pile with a womb-like rotunda as in a hotel, with a curving staircase (terrazo, not marble) leading to a mezzanine. It has not had a woman in it for some time, and it shows it. Also, we are in the throes of a minor redecoration to make it ready for the Prime Minister, who is paying an official visit in six weeks. The government is loathe to spend money, so the minimum is being done. A mistake in my opinion. The decorator is a nice-enough boy but with the very worst qualities of Canadians – he has a deep reverence for the ordinary and thinks of furnishing a room as filling it with furniture.

On the outskirts of the city, on what was once a vast lava field, is a new suburban development – Pedregal. Many of its houses and the walls that surround them are made from chunks of lava put together with coloured cement of a dirty pink, blue, or green – a queer effect, the rough, brown-black lava contrasted with soft, powdery pastels. Sometimes the lava chunks are painted to blend with the landscape – a sere, dried-out, and wonderful world of grasses and plants with pods or tangled briers – all greybrown-black. And in their midst, a small bush, stubby-fingered, its finger-tips bursting into clumps of brilliant yellow; or the weird *colorin* trees, their trunks like stylized human forms posturing strangely below a burst of thin, whip-like branches. On them, perched bird-like, are bright artery-red flowers. And on little ponds, hollowed out of the lava, ducks float. The houses are low, almost subterra-nean, walled – a submerged ruin of a city. But chic. Ultra modern. Hermetic.

The old city, the Spanish city, is equally walled. *More* walled. You can't see the houses at all. Top Secret.

I shall have to develop a taste for this countryside. En route to Teotihuacán, the City of the Gods, the vegetation is totally grey. There are gums with gunmetal leaves; peppertrees which veil themselves in fragile grey-green; organ cactuses, which look as one would expect; and nopals, which grow one flat, spiny vegeta-ble disc out of the previous one and, from a distance, appear to be crocheted from coarse grey wool. Even the earth itself is grey, and the houses – made from the same earth patted into unbaked bricks – seem to be either unfinished or falling down. A world of rubble. But Pedregal, come to think of it, is not so very different. Rich man's rubble.

This beauty, if beauty it is, is in another scale entirely from the scale I know. Microtonal. Something to be learned.

The Palacio de Bellas Artes – imitation classical, domed, doomed, wombed – is offset, outside, by some trim little phallic cactuses. Inside – not content with the classical – art nouveau has been introduced: fans and flutings with zig-zag areas of glass and great,

sharply square pillars of toffee-coloured marble, their edges not
softened by sucking. Upstairs – and up stairs it was, as well as
down, for the elevators weren't functioning – we saw the Diego
Rivera room, containing mainly his very early work. Nothing that
I thought good. Some immense Siqueiros murals dated 1944
which are violent and horrible. Some softer, large, plum-coloured
Tamayos. A room of rather ordinary sculpture and one of early
Mexican chromos, which I've not yet developed an eye for. That
was all this great domed womb of a room revealed.

I grow suspicious about Mexican art. It may not be as good as I
had hoped. Or is it merely a matter of acclimatization? And yet I
remember an exhibition of Mexican art in Montreal in the forties
which I found rich and provocative. But perhaps it was its political message that so appealed to me then, matching, as it did, the
most political phase of my own life. I remember a cartoon in the
exhibition of a peon with a newspaper blown over his face, and an
old lady – or so thought I, a youthful know-all – saying, "Incomprehensible. Utterly incomprehensible." But *I* knew what it
meant. And I remember the colours of the paintings I saw then
being more vivid. Perhaps they were. Perhaps they have faded.
Perhaps they are dirty, and need a wash, housed as they are in this
polluted city.

The church of Our Lady of Guadaloupe dates from 1709. It was
here that the Virgin appeared to Juan Diego. He told the priests,
but they wouldn't believe him. When she appeared to him a second time, the same thing happened. The third time, he asked the
Virgin to give him some proof and she told him to pick some roses.
When he patiently explained that no roses grew on that rough
hillside, she urged him to do as she said. Before he had gone far, as
in a fairy story, he found roses in full bloom, and he cut them and

carried them in his apron to the priests. When he arrived with his story and dropped the flowers at the priests' feet, his apron was found to be marked with the image of Our Lady.

I first read this story in Graham Greene's *The Lawless Roads*, which I devoured in the late forties at fever pitch caused by my fascination with Mexico, my admiration for Greene's writing, and an anti-Catholic fury. My fascination with Mexico had been accidentally fuelled by some rather poor black-and-white photographs of the baroque interiors of Mexican churches taken by Marius Barbeau. Greene's telling of the Guadaloupe miracle was full, if I remember rightly, of Catholic political overtones that were beyond me then – as perhaps they are beyond me now.

Guadaloupe is, of course, the church of miracles, and on our first sight of it, we were astonished by the number of worshippers, inside and out. Many were enacting their bargain with God by approaching it across the plaza on their knees, carrying a lighted candle and a baby! One girl, in near hysterics, long past being able to navigate alone, was supported by family members who placed cloths in front of her to protect her bleeding knees.

Meanwhile concheros, near-naked men in feathers with anklets of bells, shook rattles and stamped their bare feet!

We explore less now that we have moved into the house. But we explore. What a curiously grey and dusty city. Many of the trees are gums with their dangling grey leaves. Colonial architecture is heavy. Modern public buildings seem merely large. But there is imagination and daring, too. The scale of University City is remarkable – immense swimming pools, football arenas, *haiali* courts. The library, an enormous cube, elongated vertically, is completely covered by mosaics of Mexican stone, the colours ranging from warm earth colours to white, grey, and grey-blue.

La Merced, a newly constructed market building in the city,

feels a mile long and is filled at street level with mounds of fruits of all names and kinds and colours and sizes: the usual watermelons, cantaloupes, oranges, grapefruits, apples, and then the tropical ones – papayas, mangoes, *mames*, and a myriad others I cannot yet name. Vegetables, too – red radishes as long as your forearm and very strange-looking root vegetables.

On the outskirts of the city you approach the small topless pyramid of Tenayuca – thirteenth-century Chichimeca – through a poverty-stricken village, some of the houses of which were undoubtedly built with stones filched from the pyramid's upper layers. Around its base a ring of serpents – mouths open, teeth showing – which vary only in size and colour.

The cathedral, built in 1523 on the Plaza de la Constitucion, once the site of the Aztec temples, is said to be America's oldest and largest church. Today, the whole building lists dizzyingly in two directions.

Taking up almost the entire opposite side of the plaza stretches the National Palace, constructed as a home for Cortés. Inside, interminable as the Devil's entrails, are murals by Diego Rivera – many of them still only in the cartoon stage but some fifteen or so are completed. I don't much like feature paintings, to use the expression a Russian once used to me. When I asked what he meant, he replied, "What do *you* mean by a feature movie?" As one would expect, the murals tell the painful story of the Spanish Conquest, depicting the site as it was at the time of the conquerors' arrival – a great salt lake stretching in all directions and the Aztec temple like something out of faerie.

Calixtlahuaca, farther afield but an easy drive, is famous for its rare, circular ruin, said to have been a training centre for Aztec priests in its latter days. Its Aztec days were indeed its latter days. Four different civilizations are displayed here like rings in the bole of a tree. The outer ring is Aztec; the next – built from a glowing rosy stone – is Toltec. About the previous two, nothing is known. Our guide, a villainous-looking fellow in a fine straw hat, had a great deal to say about the ruins and was very chatty – as were dozens of small girls in long skirts and rebozos, and dozens of small boys, all of whom materialized imperceptibly and silently like smoke. Our guide told us that Calixtlahuacans speak Spanish and their own language – "narwhal," I thought he said, but I was clearly wrong. It is *narhuatl*. His sample sentence sounded like the clicking of knitting needles and made me think of Van der Post's description of the language of the Bushmen. He also claimed to know Latin, and there and then he bent and picked up a stone and wrote in the dry earth two illegible sentences. He is self-educated and boasts a library of fifty books. He has eight living children, four dead, and none of them knows anything. All stupid, he says angrily.

The ruin overlooks a valley which is irrigated and very beautiful. *Maguey* grows here, and corn. The corn is green and young. We watched a man with his *pulque* equipment – not unlike bagpipes – suck the *agua miel* from the *maguey* and fill his pigskin. In the middle distance young men are playing football. In the background, too softened by dust to appear sinister, are the inevitable volcanoes. The afternoon light is golden. But the small cruciform building, decorated with rows of stone skulls, robs the gold of its lustre.

Why have we a Sun day and a Mo(o)n day? Only just realized it on the basis of learning Spanish. Monday is *lunes*. But of course, *lundi*. How was I so slow?

Our house is a headache. We're in the process of having it painted. I feel I have a tribe of Indians living here, all with paint pots and brushes. The chief, who is surely brother to Diego Rivera, delights me. All greetings are ceremonial. Why did the meeting between him and A., so full of dignity and feeling – A. learning from him, replicating his solemn, formal actions – nearly break my heart? I do not know. I do not know.

Plumbers are tearing out the walls of all bathrooms as it is impossible to get hot water out of the showers. So nice for the P.M. to sponge bath! And we fight dust, three kinds: the accumulated dust, dust made by the workmen, and dusty-season dust.

However, on Friday, market day, I managed to escape to Toluca, the capital of the State of Mexico. A good highway leads through the Park of the Lions (lions?) across the top of the world – grey, dry, mountainous, and patterned with *maguey*. This spike-leafed plant which grows a couple of feet high provides *pulque*, a kind of milky beer, as well as paper, needles, thread, and soap, according to our driver. The leaves look as if they are made of metal – stiff, long, and radiating from the base. It is cultivated extensively in this area. Farther on we passed a fish hatchery and great, scented pine forests. Then the miles of adobe walls bordering the road tell us we are in a village.

On Fridays the town of Toluca gives itself up entirely to market. Merchandise covers the sidewalks: Woolworth jewellery, nylon underwear, silk dresses, combs. But in the market proper in stalls with canvas tops are *serapes*, *rebozos*, baskets and pottery, and pieces of embroidery of stylized birds in various shades of red and pink. Indian women in braids sit beside their wares eating *tortillas*, while their black-eyed babies crawl about among the yolk-yellow, newly hatched chicks, the pottery and wooden spoons. Most of the Indians speak English, for it is a tourist market, and most think you are a *gringa*, which, here, means an American, so the absurdly low prices are, of course, doubled.

A dozen things I have meant to record have passed me by. For instance, the weekend we were at Cuernavaca, we were wakened by the Catholic Church calling the faithful by cannon fire at five-thirty; and just in case any fell back to sleep, they repeated this merry reveille on every half-hour thereafter. The cannon fire was accompanied by what sounded like a fine collection of dishpans beaten with wooden spoons. One member of our embassy who had been brought up in the arms of the Jansenists was almost insensible with shock after his first mass in Mexico. It was a saint's day and so, very special – giant rockets being fired from the still roofless altar and Indians in all their feathers dancing and whooping in the church itself.

On Sunday, A. and I took our sandwiches to Texcoco, a market town on the opposite edge of the old lakebed. There we had the pleasure of seeing a woman snake-oil operator pushing cotton wool up the nostrils and into the ears of patient Indians and producing miracle cures on the spot. I was sacrilegious enough to take her photo and was roundly abused for so doing. We moved off fast, anxious not to be taken as heretics by the believing crowd.

A market here is wonderful: pottery (good and bad), *tortillas* being cooked, little fluffy chickens, blankets, fruits, vegetables, Woolworth jewellery, sweets called *allegrias* (happinesses), yard goods, etc., etc., and all laid out on the ground and arranged so prettily in little piles, if piles are possible. We bought a cantaloupe and some tiny copper pots and pans for the children.

Then on to the Molina de Flores – the Flower Mill. It is an old mill, now a national park, and filled with the thousands of picnicking Mexicans who sling their multicoloured hammocks between the trees, the women with their black braids tied together at the back, the men in their big hats and with the inevitable jar of *pulque* and, for background, nopal cactuses and crumbling pastel plaster walls. Surprisingly, from ground baked as hard as their pottery and littered with Coca-Cola caps, grows a small delicate star-like flower, rather like a nude prairie crocus, and equally touching.

I have a very good bird book and am delighted with it. Have identified a canyon wren – large for wrens in my experience – who lives in the canyons of our house; a chipping sparrow – the same fellow we have at home; and a robin, also identical. I wonder what determines whether you become a permanent Mexican resident robin or a migrating one – for apparently there are both. And identical – but identical.

The gardener brought me a great thick hollowed-out bamboo filled with gardenias from Orizaba, his *tierra*. I am swamped, bathed, flooded with the smell of gardenias. Their white breath is all about me.

Yesterday Pablo, our second *moço*, a small-boned, neat little Indian with a triangular head rather like a snake's, had the misfortune to run into me when I was in nothing but pants and bra. Since then he has gone about in a myopic trance, looking for all the world as if he could see nothing closer than the horizon. Today his eyes are quite bloodshot. I only hope I haven't induced a traumatic blindness.

Today A. and I set off for a group of small villages a bit off the beaten track where, the book said, there was embroidery and weaving to be found. We were once again in maize country. In the villages the small adobe houses cluster close together around the immensely domed fortress-like churches. At Almoyo del Rio we had to leave the car and climb a steep and roughly cobblestoned hill in search of the embroiderers. An old man led us to the house of Conception Mireflores (Behold the Flowers). She and her sister fed their children from the breast in between showing us their handwork – strands of coloured wool drawn through white cotton cloth to make repeating designs, rather like the dancing girls you can cut from a folded strip of paper. Their house was poor, but it had light and electric irons and a sewing machine. Otherwise it consisted of a few chairs and a double bed, and its walls were covered with pictures cut from magazines. In the courtyard outside, a small naked boy was having his hair washed while the two more recent arrivals had hair like the finest black silk.

We bought some work from the Mireflores and trudged on up the cobblestoned hill to the main plaza, where we had the good luck to meet one of the strangest brass bands marching along the rough street. Such brasses! Dinted, dented, and quite grey green with neglect those trumpets and trombones and bugles. Each player played his own tune – touches of "Hail, Hail, the Gang's All Here," mixed with a well-known military march the name of which escapes me. Their pandemonium accompanied and escorted a small group of young men and women headed for the city hall for a civil marriage, we can only think. It was surprising to us that although I was carrying embroidery done in the village, no one came running with wares or trying to peddle. We only saw the embroideries when we specifically asked, and then we were shown them with the greatest consideration and courtesy – chairs being drawn up for us first. And so we bought some quite lovely things from those orange-coloured Indian women with their dark hair in plaits. And none of it looks nice in this godforsaken house we inhabit!

July 1 is over. A lot of work and nothing like as good a party as in Brazil. But then, we haven't the facilities. I am glad it is behind us.

We still limp along without a cook and me trying to teach the upstairs maid the rudiments. Meanwhile we have a new cook's helper whom I suspect of all kinds and manners of laziness. She walks like a water plant and *that* seems ominous.

Last week, driving back from Puebla, we quite suddenly saw Popocatepetl and, recumbent at his side, his sleeping bride, Ixtacihuatl. It was rather like magic – now you see them, now you don't. Even when we got home, there they were, snow-topped and very clear outside our windows, almost within reach. Other days one can see range after range of mountains stretching off into the distance interminably, but not far enough to include them. Then they appear. And they are *right there*. And beautiful. One would learn to be very proprietary about them – perhaps even affectionate.

One of the things about Mexico that never fails to surprise me is the sight of women vendors sitting on the sidewalk, their five tomatoes or mangoes or their peanuts in front of them. I remember the first I saw and thought, poor soul, no legs. I wonder if she was born that way? And then, before the thought was ended, there was another woman with the same ghastly handicap, until at last it became clear that they couldn't *all* be legless and propped there but that there is something odd about the way they sit that makes them appear to be trunks. I never got used to it.

Went the other day through a narrow door and into the inevitable courtyard which opens out behind it, and in through another narrow door and into a grotto of artificial flowers sold by Jesus Tamayo. How to convey the wonder of it? The flowers are totally without guile. No attempt is made to make them look real. They are meant to look artificial and they are fresh and charming – every imaginable kind of flower. It is as if a child god had got cracking and begun again. They quite literally cover the walls and ceilings of three small rooms – no containers visible – just flowers, flowers, flowers, a grotto of flowers and the air so sweetly sprayed with perfume.

In its own way, just as wonderful as a candle shop.

All candles here are hand-made of tallow. There are shops that make nothing else. They make candles of every size and shade and description. They will match any colour sample and make them in any diameter or height, from pencil slim to great thick candles for use in church. But most wonderful are the decorated ones. A length of candle at the top is left bare. About a quarter of the way down is a row of small tallow flowers, immediately below is a row of bigger ones, and so on, until an inch or so from the base there is a row of large flowers – the whole looking like a pyramid of flowers. Sometimes the candle and the flowers are different colours, sometimes the same; sometimes the candles are small, sometimes large. But they are all unfailingly lovely, never garish, never clumsily made. An astonishing art form.

Independence Day. It is wet and cold. Last year it was hot and sticky. And last year, at this time, I was frantically pushing the last toothbrush into my suitcase in order to fly to Canada with Sevigny, Associate Minister of Defence, who had been here for the independence celebrations.

How different the two years! Last year, because it was the 150th year of independence, it was a special celebration with four special trains carrying the invited guests to Hidalgo, where the liberty bell was first rung. Rather a gloomy and flat performance. Dressed in full evening dress, we sat on bleachers in the black night. The face of the church was floodlit, and at eleven o'clock, as is traditional, the president pulled the bell rope and shouted, "*Viva Mexico!*" and the crowd shouted back, "*Viva!*" But it was depressing somehow and lacked feeling.

This year the celebration took place, as is customary, in the Presidential Palace in the Zocalo. The men wear business suits (to honour the revolution) and the women full evening dress (to honour themselves!). Inside the palace a human corridor of special guests forms, down which march the president and his wife – although she was not marching this year, having just had a heart attack – and the members of his cabinet and their wives, those of them who get there in time, that is. Then the human corridor forms a line and marches past the president and cabinet ministers.

From then on, those who can cram onto the small balconies off the upstairs windows do so; the others melt into one another in the long and overcrowded reception room. We jammed onto a balcony. It was a bleak night with intermittent downpours, but all the buildings facing the Zocalo were decorated with the red, white, and green of the Mexican flag and illuminated by strings of white lights that traced their outlines. It was beautiful. In the immense concrete square below us, the people massed, dressed as Mexicans dress, in highly coloured clothing, all shapes and sizes of sombreros, with many wearing masks.

As the intensity of the rain increased, umbrellas appeared, and coloured plastic sheets which groups of people held over themselves. And as the rain continued, the crowd thinned to a few brightly coloured lonely figures in the immense black square. But as eleven o'clock approached, the square filled again, despite the rain – a dense, multicoloured crowd, moving like wheat in a wind. And in their midst, here and there, the queer geometry of the great frames which hold fireworks and look like machine-age trees.

At eleven the bell was rung – just as Father Hidalgo had rung it a hundred and fifty years ago, as if summoning his people to Mass. And the president's voice rang out, "*Viva Mexico!*" and the voice of the crowd replied, "*Viva!*" Then the president's voice again,

"*Viva la Libertad!*" and the voice of the crowd, "*Viva!*" Whether or not he still cries, "*Mueran los Españoles!*" I don't know because by now the noise level had made it impossible to hear what was being said. The rocket "trees" were firing off their coloured fireworks into the black sky, fire balloons were being sent up from the cathedral, and it was no longer possible to make out exactly what was happening. But it was impressive. This immense crowd of Mexicans standing drenched to the skin and reliving their liberation from the Spaniards. One Mexican woman behind me, dressed in sumptuous satin, looked down onto the crowded square and said, "*Que bonito is mi pueblo.*"

This morning we went to a wreath-laying ceremony at the Independence Monument. The president and his cabinet sat on a dais, we – a step down – on chairs arranged on a street-side stand, and a further step down, their hair in plaits, selling their little piles of peaches, sat the tattered vendors of flags and national colours. Then to the great parade outside the National Palace, where we sat on uncovered bleachers. Last year we had had to protect ourselves from the sun as best we could; this year we were armed against a rain which, luckily, only threatened. The parade began with armoured cars, tanks and trucks, and motorcycles. These were followed by the cadets, the reserve and the permanent army, the firemen, the charros, and the rural defence. Overhead, the air force: ordinary planes floating in a kind of noiseless formation, like a sequence from a silent movie, contrasted with the death scream of the jets which were painted with neon paint, and the curious giant hover of the dragonfly helicopters.

The cadets wore uniforms of various colour combinations, some with long jackets, some with short, some with tight pants, some with loose; band members with a multitude of coloured chenille tassels hanging from their arms; permanent army troops in slaked earth colours (the parachutists in a kind of yellow clay colour with white scarves and white gloves so that they appeared already wounded and bandaged); others in varying shades of grey and khaki – the colours of war; and still others in even darker colours – the colours of decomposition. Some moved in a semi goosestep, some in an ordinary walk with an occasional high kick, or a stamp. Their individual walks were immensely varied: the over-erect who leaned backwards; the over-anxious to get there who leaned forward; the wet pants walk; the tight boots walk. On and on they filed around the Zocalo, which was now covered with squares of red, green, and white paper, which occasional small whirlwinds lifted in a twist and let fall. Each time the Mexican flag passed, we rose. The flags took various forms: ordinary; silk "shields" on sticks; and what I can only describe as stuffed flags, made from felt or some heavy material and wired onto the flag-staff. Running about among the onlookers were groups of girls in white carrying white enamel slop pails filled with water for the thirsty.

Firemen in scab-red open jeeps changed the mood of the parade. Some mounted troops blew weird solemn music on their bugles as they passed. This was almost medieval in feeling. And then, more wonderful still and still more weird, mounted buglers blowing the same strange music, riding little low unkempt horses and dressed in curious, apparently divided dresses of buckskin, their immensely long trousers covering their feet, heads tied up in red bandannas, sombreros slung behind, machetes upraised, and the provisions for a long siege tied to their saddles – serapes, lassoes, baskets and bags. They felt as foreign as Tibetans, like some wild mountain horde, unwashed, unbrushed, and untwentieth century. Shades of Genghis Khan. They originated in Michoacán during the revolution and have been maintained since as rural defence troops. There were numbers of them. Enough to sustain the mood for some time and to make one feel that Mexico is a foreign country indeed. Finally came the *charros* in their tight, embroidered or silver-medallioned trousers, their little boleros and great felt sombreros, their richly tooled and decorated saddles, their brightly woven and coloured bridles. They were followed by girls in full skirts riding sidesaddle, and by children – the tiniest of all a little Indian girl, her hair in plaits, who looked no more than three.

For me the whole parade was worthwhile for the sake of seeing those rural defence troops. The music they played, "La Marcha do los Dragones," made your blood run black and very slow.

Yesterday Leonora, Norah, and I set off with Guillermo to a harvest festival in the village of Leonora's cook, Antonia. A wonderful day. High sky and great puffy clouds. Followed the Toluca road, then cut off to the right under the Nevada de Toluca. The little village was nestled in against the hillside – the usual small village with a domed church and mud streets.

Antonia's father is a landowner. He has nine hectares. His house is made of adobe, and its one room is finished with two double beds and a table. We were greeted by her father, a big open man in a dirty shirt, and her mother, a snub-featured woman with pigtails, quick and quiet moving. Antonia brought us *tequila*, salt, and lemon, and we sat around the table with her father and his *compadre* and drank. Outside the house were lobelias, chrysanthemums, geraniums, begonias, growing in whitewashed tin cans, and opposite was a loosely slatted structure with smoke coming out the slats. This was the kitchen. An immense, tall corn crib set up in the yard was about half-full of ears of what we call Indian corn. As we sat drinking, the burros and horses were coming in from the field laden with sacks of corn, and the young men heaved the heavy sacks onto their shoulders and climbed a rickety ladder and dumped the ears into the crib.

None too sober from the series of quick little glasses of *tequila*, we left the men and went over to the kitchen to watch the preparations for lunch – as best we could, that is, for the smoke from the wood fire burning on the earthen floor was nearly blinding. A pretty girl was sitting on her haunches making *tortillas* in a double-handled wooden press and putting them to heat on a large flat plate over the flames. Her press was the only piece of modern equipment of any kind I saw, and it was not very modern at that – only a primitive step up from patting the dough by hand. Beans were boiling in one pot, and *mole* – a special spicy sauce – was cooking in another. This feast had been a week in preparation, and it was all going to be carried up into the cornfield for the peons who were on the last lap of the cutting.

Shortly before we set off for the fields, I asked Leonora where we would find a lavatory, and we were led by one of the girl-cousins across the yard and behind a couple of cactuses. I saw a little hut with smoke coming out of it and thought it was the backhouse and that they were burning incense, and I was pleased by the pleasant, inebriated idea. However, as I found myself almost ankle-deep in human excrement, I realized that I was in the lavatory, that this was it, and that the hut was the neighbours' kitchen. The fact that everyone could see us seemed secondary compared with the basic problem of hygiene. Leonora had previously told me that I need never worry about anything I ate or drank at Antonia's, as her people were very clean people. I didn't remind her of her words as we squatted behind the *magueys* among the flies, nor later when we returned and waited among the flies for the food to be put in baskets.

Finally everything was ready, and a great stream of us set off – all ages and both sexes – through the village, down two barrancas, across one river, and up, up, up into the hills. At last we arrived. Sacks were laid over the furrows where the corn had been cut, and all the peons arrived and sat in a great circle. *Tequila* was passed around to men and women alike. Then rice with *tortillas*, followed by beef and chicken with *mole*. And *pulque*. The *tortillas* were delicious. I usually dislike them, as the corn of which they are made is treated with lime, and its chalky taste is repellent to me. But these tasted just like corn on the cob. I must say I was a bit uneasy about everything I ate after having seen the fly brigade, but there was little I could do about it. The *mole* and the meat were ghastly – meat very tough. The *mole*, which is made from chocolate, peanuts, and spices, is a bit too Mexican for me. I haven't yet developed a taste for it. The party was becoming very relaxed. *Pulque* was passed back and forth between us, but by this time everyone was using everyone else's mug, and I was none too happy about it.

Food finished, the cutters began again. For cutting the ears from the stalk, the women had small knives in the palms of their hands which were held in place by a loop over their middle finger, and they carried great loose sacks over their shoulders which hung down in front. When filled with corn, they were emptied into larger sacks tended by the men. These, when full, were mounted on the burros and driven back to the crib. The women worked fast, as, indeed, did the boys, who came behind with scythes and cut the stalks for fodder.

Wonderful good humour prevailed, and every now and again a great cry would go up when someone found a "cross." A "cross" was a stalk with three ears. Such a rarity was cut entire, and the person who found it raised it high and all the rest of us applauded. This was considered good luck for the finder, but to share his good luck with the rest, he had to provide *tequila* for the party. All the outsiders found "crosses" – Leonora, Norah, Guillermo, and me. I was done out of mine by a small boy who claimed it was his. He was not yet old enough to have learned the wisdom of keeping quiet and letting the guests pay!

Finally, with all the corn cut, we packed up again and started downhill. En route we picked handfuls of a special leaf, rough, like a cat's tongue, with which we washed the plates when we came to the river. The women told us that "we poor people" had many little economies. Unable to afford soap, they found other ways of cutting the grease.

I was immensely touched by the social sense of these people. They never left us on our own. They obviously wanted us to be happy. Their sense of being responsible for their guests didn't set us apart from their labours. When we offered to carry a basket, they let us. When we offered to wash the dishes, this seemed to them a fair division of labour. No nonsense about guests not working. Conversation was mainly about the children and the crops – simple, gentle conversation of a simple, agricultural people. Yet Antonia's mother told Leonora she didn't want her girls to marry, that married life was too hard and there were no good men. A girl was better off single. In this very *pueblo* a man had shot his daughter who stopped to chase a bird when she was meant to be bringing him his lunch in the field. Yet they laughed a lot – at nothing very much – the easy laughter of good humour.

Dusk was falling as we arrived back in the village. The corn crib was outlined black against the still-pale sky. The men climbed its ladder and dumped their heavy sacks. The women sat in the yard on painted chairs – dignified, erect, talking politely and quietly among themselves.

# Things Fall Apart

Cristine and I had decided to make the crossing from Nigeria to Cameroon by sea. From Calabar the nearest road into Cameroon was nearly a day's journey north, and was often closed because of the rains, or because of hostilities; while by boat, for a fare of eight naira, we could make it direct to Victoria inside of eight hours, free of border checks and bad roads and cramped buses. The boats departed at nightfall from a tiny wharf on one of the islands that Calabar spilled out to, stealing their way through the tangle of mangrove swamp that lined the coast to avoid the coast guard.

We'd arrived at the island several hours before departure and been befriended almost at once by a man who went by the name of Doctor, though as far as we were able to learn his only claim to the title was the tiny shop he owned on the island, where he sold a variety of over-the-counter pills and then the usual assortment of canned goods and plastic housewares.

"You don't want to go on those little boats," the doctor told us. "You'll die on those boats."

But as evening approached and the doctor's intentions toward Cris began to grow obvious, Cris became more and more anxious that we make an escape from his hospitality. At the wharf, with

the doctor still counselling delay, we eyed the lone boat making the journey that evening, a makeshift skiff of tarred wood with a flimsy outboard at one end, a half-dozen or so passengers already hunkered down for the trip within its bare-boned hull. The boat was moored twenty feet or so from the pier, and we had to balance our way across several other boats to get out to it. Half-way over we stopped a moment in panicked indecision, the doctor still urging us back from the shore and the boatman urging us onwards.

"You'll die out there!" the doctor said.

We stood staring at the boat for an instant as if searching it for a sign. Inside, a mother and her two children had already formed a sort of encampment amidst the luggage and contraband piled in the boat's centre, a tattered umbrella raised above them against mosquitoes and rain, and mats laid out for beds on the few planks of floor there.

"I think we should go," Cris said, and finally we heaved our packs aboard and took our place among the others.

By the time we were out of the harbour, the first commotion at the arrival of whites had passed and we seemed forgotten, made anonymous like the others by the growing darkness. There was muted conversation for a while in mixed Ibo and pidgin, interspersed with the terse instructions of the boatman, who sat perched at the rudder on the boat's only seat, to his scrawny Gilligan-like assistant; but then gradually the boat settled into silence, edging its way by moonlight into the first thickets of mangrove. The mangrove took us in like some fairy-tale forest, gnarled and ghostly human, great legs of root rising up to the beards of seaweed left behind by high tides in the upper branches. At every turn the mangrove repeated itself, a labyrinth of twisting estuaries and windless coves, though still we moved forward with only murky moonlight to guide us, all around us dim shapes looming and fading and then looming again.

Cris and I had made a space for ourselves toward the back of the boat; but there were only a few awkward floorboards there to keep us raised up from the water collecting in the bilge, our bodies gradually settling between the gaps and into wetness as we tried to arrange ourselves for sleep. We'd unfurled a sleeping bag to cover ourselves; as the night wore on and we penetrated deeper into the swamp, we had to bury our heads beneath it to ward off the mosquitoes. For a time I fell into fitful sleep, then grew vaguely aware of some problem with the boat's engine, an intermittent sputter and fail whose sudden silences made briefly loud the drone of mosquitoes and the lap of water against the hull. Well before daylight I was fully awake: the boatman and his assistant were tinkering away at the engine under the dim glow of a flashlight. Some terminal had broken or come loose, requiring wires to be taped in place to keep the engine running; but the boatman had only cellophane tape for the job, and we'd move along ten minutes or so after a repair before the heat of the wires burned the tape and the connection came loose again.

In these fits and starts we made our way through a last stretch

barefooted and bald, surveyed us scornfully from the prow. He seemed to feel no sense of rescue, only of interruption: we were offered passage back to Calabar if we wished, at full fare. There were some protests but the captain held firm, Calabar or nothing. Of our group the boatman and his assistant chose to remain behind, and, surprisingly, the woman with the two children – we left her sitting dignified and calm with her two charges inside her little encampment as if she simply could not be bothered at this late stage in the journey with having to heave herself up from her place to begin again.

We headed back toward Calabar. The scout leader – Joseph, we'd learned his name was – had followed the captain back to the rudder, still pleading for some sort of compromise; and finally he managed to broker one, the captain agreeing to let us off, for a fare of five naira apiece, at a small settlement where we could charter another boat to continue down the coast. Of our group, two chose to continue back to Calabar, leaving only five of us: Cris and myself; Joseph; a young man, Isaac, who was a student in Victoria; and another, Rotimi, who made a living smuggling portable ste-reos into Cameroon, one of which he carried in tow.

The settlement, tucked inside a marshy inlet, turned out to be little more than the elaboration of a single family, with a large, tin-roofed house and a few grassy outbuildings. Its overlord, brash and handsome and fierce, eyed Cris and me with a mercenary gleam as we got down from the boat. "Africa Man," he called him-self; he had the air of some renegade who'd fled justice or injustice to set up here a private fiefdom.

"Thirty-thirty naira," he said, thirty naira apiece, to get not to Victoria but only to where we could catch another boat farther down the coast. Within the usual scale of things, it was an outra-geous sum, but he held us hostage, marooned there on the shores of nowhere with his the only boat.

Joseph negotiated. The price came down eventually to twenty-five but then held firm. Cris and I offered to pay a greater share of the cost, since it was obvious our whiteness was a factor in the negotiations, but Joseph wouldn't hear of it.

"He wants to kill us, this man," he said.

For an hour or so we remained at this impasse, our group milling about listlessly on the verandah of our host's house while various children stole near to catch glimpses of Cris and me, and a few older women, our host's wives perhaps, went about their private tasks in the background. Then finally an agreement was reached: fifteen naira apiece, plus the cost of petrol. We boarded Africa Man's boat, sleek and new, with the luxury of a padded bench to sit on, and an hour or so later were left off at a ramshackle village down the coast. We had a hasty meal at a roadside stall, then asked after boats: fifteen naira again, we were told, and this still not to Victoria but only to the next town down the coast. The problem was petrol again – plentiful and cheap in Nigeria, though apparently more precious here – and a lengthy peninsula that had to be rounded to make the trip; but there was a path across the peninsula, we learned, that could get us to the next village on foot in about the same time as it took to reach it by sea.

We opted to go on foot, setting out an hour or so before dark. The brambled narrowness of the trail forced us into single file, Joseph and Rotimi in front, suitcase and stereo perched on their heads, and Isaac bringing up the rear. By the time we'd made the other shore it was nearly sunset, though we could make out a few miles down the seafront where the bush that lined the shore opened out to the village. We began to make our way toward it, though minute by minute the sliver of beach that formed our pathway seemed to shrink beneath us: the tide was coming in. We removed shoes, rolled up our pant legs, but still the tide kept rising, to our ankles, to our knees. Here and there great roots and fallen branches jutted out into the sea and we had to thread our way up through the bush and then back to the shore again, each time wading deeper into rolling water and falling dark.

By the time we came to the village, straggling in from a tide that had reached to our waists, it was truly night. The village seemed already to have closed down for the evening – there were a few flickers of cooking fires here and there and then darkness. Joseph managed somehow to locate the village headman, and we were allowed to stretch out for the night on the concrete floor of the schoolhouse. Muted voices reached us through the grillwork of the windows, the small stir our arrival had caused; but in the darkness it seemed impossible to say what nature of place we'd arrived at, what strangeness we had become. Cris and I settled into our sleeping bag with only the barest of conversation: we seemed to have retreated into our own separate versions of what was happening to us as if trying to guard what was most precious in the experience, this being so far from what was familiar.

In the morning we learned there was still no direct route from where we were to Victoria: we would have to make our way overland to where the road began. A guide from the village led us along a twisting jungle path to a settlement in the heart of the bush; from there, three canoes took us down a reed-choked waterway flanked by palms and great clusters of bamboo. We might have been some royal procession wending its way toward a sacrifice or feast, Joseph and Rotimi in front again, discussing arcane remedies and spirits and rites, and Isaac once more bringing up the rear.

We reached the outpost where the Victoria road began around noon. Joseph checked the harbour there and discovered our abandoned boat – it had apparently put in the previous afternoon, though under what conveyance we never learned. A bus was to leave inside the hour for Victoria, but at least two hours had

passed before we were under way, in an old wooden-benched vehicle that rattled like a tambourine over the dusty road. The road wound through a vast palm-oil plantation owned by some German concern; mile after mile the palm trees stretching out in their orderly rows, surreal after the amorphous gloom of the jungle. Then at some point a tire went flat, and we piled out of the bus while the driver crawled underneath it to retrieve the spare. The spare, it turned out, was flat as well – we would have to wait, it wasn't clear for what, though finally I managed to learn that the driver hoped to borrow a spare from another bus that should be passing by shortly. Shortly turned into an hour, then two. Cris and I had stretched out at the side of the road a little away from the bus; we seemed to have lost Joseph and the others now, who had quickly receded into the greater familiarity of the other passengers.

An army truck passed by and Isaac hitched a ride with it; Cris and I considered joining it as well, but before we'd decided it had moved on. A great passivity had overtaken us: arrival seemed anticlimactic now, the getting there having long surpassed in

significance the there that we were getting to; and already I regretted the part of me that had been focussed all along on destination, the blinkering that came from that, the missed details and lost possibilities. But as the afternoon stretched on, the thought of another night in the open, dirty and hungry and cold, seemed to rouse us. We began to walk toward Victoria, and then within a matter of minutes a jeep passed by and offered a lift. The driver, a doctor in Victoria, white-haired and spectacled, appeared diffident at finding two whites hitching at the side of the road.

"We came in by boat from Calabar," I said, when he asked about our trip.

"Ah." But though I would have welcomed an audience for the story of our trip I'd already begun to shape in my mind, the doctor seemed uneasy about prying any more deeply into our circumstances.

He left us at the Hotel Victoria, just beneath the slopes of Mount Cameroon, wrapped at that hour in late-afternoon mist. For a modest price we were able to get a small bungalow overlooking the sea; we showered and ate, then fell almost at once into dead sleep. In the morning, there was a great pyramid of mountain jutting out of the sea beyond our bungalow that had not been there the evening before. It must have been shrouded then by fog, which would have made it appear to merge with the sea and the sky. But in the first shock of its sudden presence it seemed simply to have risen up newly formed from the sea during the night like some wry tribute to our journey's end.

# Travel

Someone once said that the quickest way out of Glasgow was a bottle of Bols gin. Well I know people who have proved this all their lives with Captain Morgan rum. They never had to leave the room where they drank to travel on every ship that left the Miramichi. Fight in every battle.

As Owen Felltham said in the seventeenth century: fancy gives you wings to fly. So, at times, does cheap booze.

It can be argued also that we never go anywhere without bringing along what we most want to leave behind – namely ourselves. I have found this true enough on more than one occasion. Therefore we can say with some measure of certainty that we never do go anywhere. That where we are is as close to the centre of the universe as we are bound to get.

There is an Arabic saying that travel is a foretaste of hell. And when that line was first uttered they still had the luxury of travelling by camel.

What might they say if they had to travel across the international date-line, ending up in a small hotel room with a three-year-old child singing the theme song from Barney, at one o'clock in the morning?

"I love you – you love me –
We're a happy family –"

But I have travelled enough to know one thing. I can't stop now. And though the information I have stored up over the years has told me time and again – something like being continually hit over the head with a snow shovel – that it just isn't worth it, I'm sure I'll be on the road again in a month or two.

These are a few travel experiences I've had so far. I hit a hurricane off the coast of Africa when I was twenty, on a banana boat. I was a third-class passenger, and there was one life-raft for thirty-five of us – not that any of us would have been stupid enough to get into it. There were four lifeboats for the four first-class passengers – one lifeboat per person – and two lifeboats for the eight second-class passengers. We had one. We were all shoved into the stern of the ship, like mice – thirty-two African students, my brother, myself, and a cockney boy from London. Almost everyone was seasick. All except myself and the cockney boy – and to tell the truth I don't know why we weren't too.

At the height of the storm, when our Spanish captain was required to show nerves of steel, he was busy screaming his head off and telling the First Mate he would pitch him overboard. Running about with tiny tears in his eyes and laughing at the silliest things.

I've been stuck in the Kootenays in mid-winter, and there are fine people there, but to tell the truth I wanted to be home.

"My God, we've got you here now," my host said, with some surprise and wonderment, the very moment I arrived. "But with this storm coming in over the mountains – can't you smell it? – God knows when we'll get you out. No one hardly ever comes here in the winter, and we never thought you would. Better just make the best of it. How was your plane ride?"

"A little bumpy."

"Last plane came in – everyone puked."

I've been stuck on the tarmac in Baltimore for five hours, and in Dorval Airport for seven, and in Heathrow in London for almost three days, snitching leftover crackers from restaurant tables.

In Baltimore I had to keep convincing this little old lady who would wake up periodically that not only hadn't we landed, we hadn't as yet left the ground.

Once, on a particularly rough flight from somewhere to somewhere else in the middle of the night, the only thing I could hear – and it was, I believed, the last thing I would hear – was this little girl about seven. All I could see was her pigtails sticking straight up in the air tied in bows with two pink ribbons, and she was shouting at the top of her lungs:

"MOMMIE MOMMIE – MOMMIE MOMMIE MOMMIE – MOMMIE MOMMIE."

"Someone do the decent thing and slap her," I almost shouted, but then decided I better not.

On Qantas flights over the Pacific they have a screen set up which keeps feeding you information while showing the image of a tiny vulnerable plane inching across the ocean.

"YOU ARE NOW 4 THOUSAND KLMS FROM YOUR POINT OF DEPARTURE, at 38,000 feet."

"YOU ARE NOW 4 THOUSAND AND 20 KLMS FROM YOUR POINT OF DEPARTURE, at 36,000 feet."

"YOU ARE NOW 4 THOUSAND AND 91 KLMS FROM YOUR POINT OF DEPARTURE, at 35,643 feet."

It's a maddening experience, and after a while the man behind me started muttering (I'm sure he didn't think I heard):

"All right, all right – just keep it in the air."

There is one good thing about all of this – you can continually make up new blurbs for book covers for yourself which, although they are not lies, have almost nothing to do with the truth. Things like:

"Tossed by hurricanes off the coast of Africa; Storm stuck in the Kootenays; and Braved SHARK INFESTED water off the coast of Australia" or something like that.

If you aren't able to leave yourself behind when you travel you are at least able to take more of yourself with you, the farther you get from home.

For instance I come from the rocks in Newcastle, N.B., CAN-ADA. I come from the rocks. (They aren't really big – and really I don't know where they are, because I've never seen them.)

But once I leave Newcastle to go anywhere else on the Mirami-chi I am known as a Newcastler.

Once off the Miramichi I become a Miramicher.

In the Maritimes I am a NewBrunswicker.

In Canada I am a Maritimer.

In Australia or any place else I am a Canadian (once I tell them I'm not an American, which I usually do, unless I have just fin-ished making an idiot of myself).

The upshot of it all is this: If I really travel enough I might some day finally become a recognizable citizen of the world. Which won't make travelling any less fun than it already is.

# Subversion in the North

A traveller travels alone. To move around in a group is to carry your world with you. Alone, I find it possible to become an insignificant, even invisible, part of whatever I meet or see. Apart from the business of getting through the days – the physical and mental effort – it is a passive occupation. Groups, on the other hand, are active. Like explorers and armies, they come to impose themselves.

It was a strange idea, therefore, to gather together fifteen writers from fifteen countries along with five Canadian writers in order to fly them two thousand kilometres straight north to Baffin Island. They represented at tiny slice cut of the hundreds who had come to Toronto and Montreal for the International PEN Congress in 1989. What could those five hundred writers think after ten days in two southern cities except that Canada was a suburban society resembling the rest of the industrialized West?

The Northern trip was a consciously subversive idea. Baffin – the fifth largest island on earth, four times the size of England, 1,600 kilometres long – is simple proof that Canada is not what its urban élites pretend. They can live along the border and resolutely face themselves south, but any fool can see that this

In Igloolik, left to right: Edouard Glissant, daughter of Laurentino
Arnatsiaq, Nelinda Pinon, Betty Friedan, and myself

involves turning their backs on their own reality. Canada is as
much a part of the underdeveloped world as of the developed, of
the Third World as of the First. It is more of the North than of the
centre. What's more, the geography and the climate of the North
are such that it can never be developed. At least not in the way
we normally understand that term. The fifteen writers we hoped
to turn into witnesses of some small part of this reality included
the Nigerian novelist Chinua Achebe, Betty Friedan, the American feminist, the Burmese novelist Wendy Law-Yone, Duo Duo,
the Chinese poet whose exile had just begun, the leading French-
language Caribbean poet Edouard Glissant, and Blanche
d'Alpuget, the Australian novelist.

As for myself, the first time I had gone to the Arctic islands had
been a dozen years before and not to Baffin but to Melville, a good
thousand kilometres to the west and far to the north of both the
magnetic pole and the Northwest Passage, which Amundsen had
finally pierced in 1905. After seven years in Paris, I was coming

home to become Assistant to Maurice Strong, who had just been asked to set up a national oil company. It was January 1, 1976, and Petro-Canada consisted of himself and his room on the twenty-second floor of the International Hotel in Calgary. I arrived from France late on the evening of the second, made my way through the crowd of prostitutes in the lobby, where they had taken refuge from the cold, and registered, thereby doubling the size of the national oil company.

Two months later we were sent off by the government on a rather strange secret mission to Hanoi in the aftermath of the fall of Saigon. It seemed an exotic adventure.

A month later we were off again, this time to inspect the exploratory wells in the High Arctic. Hanoi quickly shrank into a commuter's jaunt.

We flew straight north, as far as a trans-Atlantic flight, from Calgary to Inuvik, near the mouth of the Mackenzie River on the Arctic Ocean. There, houses are raised on wooden stilts to prevent the heat they exude from causing them to disappear into melting tundra. And the population is a mix of Dene, Inuit and Southerners. Then on another thousand kilometres, up to Rea Point on the shore of Melville Island. The old Northwest Passage would have come up that way if the ships had been strong enough to force their bows through the solid ice flowing down from the polar ice cap.

Twice over the last twenty-five years, the United States has challenged Canadian ownership of the Arctic straits by sending first a giant oil tanker, then an icebreaker, through these waters, past Melville, effectively daring Ottawa to stop them. What the public heard was a diplomatic quarrel. The obscured reality is an oil industry idea that the Northwest Passage should become a route for reinforced tankers. Quite apart from the effect on the most delicate ecosystem in the world of turning the Passage into a commercial shipping lane, there is the obvious risk of an accident. No one knows what would happen if millions of barrels of oil were to escape and line the underside of the ice. What sensible people agree on is that it would be the worst accident imaginable, for the simple reason that the oil could neither be cleaned up nor disperse on its own.

When we arrived at Rea Point, the temperature was minus sixty. Exposed skin freezes dead in a minute. In that part of the Western Arctic the land is low and flat. Between the ice and the land there is no visible break – just a continuity of even whiteness, because the High Arctic is a desert where not a great deal of snow falls. If it resembles anything it is the central part of the Sahara.

The moment we landed I felt a need to move away from the handful of low huts. Not that they represented any sort of presence in such a landscape. They weren't even insignificant. More like houseflies when you are trying to think on a hot day. There was no need to go far. Perhaps fifty metres. Perhaps it was only twenty. Abruptly, it was impossible to measure the cold. Minus sixty or plus forty? Underfoot might have been sand or snow. The marginality of life could be felt like a great broom sweeping away any sense of self. The clarity as I walked out into the whiteness was astonishing. Terrifying. Revealing. The sense of time and direction slip away. Distances mean nothing. The outsider can neither judge nor imagine them.

The Western mind assumes that it can readily imagine anything. Its collective knowledge and experience have been fed by a millennium of exploration, global empires and scientific breakthroughs. Everything has been or can be reduced intellectually to a relative state. What is the North but a reflection of the South? A progress from hot to cold, from jungle to snow and ice, with, as always, the West's vision of itself at the centre.

Even Canadians take for granted that they know what the

northern half of their country is. Yet few of them have actually gone above the tree line, where even the ground is an illusion of earth dissolved in ice – this tundra so delicate that a vehicle crossing it once during the wrong season will leave marks for eternity as if an army of tanks had passed by. And even that north is a southern place compared to the Arctic archipelago. These islands are nowhere in the Western imagination. Nor are they open to comparison. They constitute an unparalleled extreme.

We moved on again the next day in a Twin Otter – the taxi of the North, loved because it can take off or land in what seems to be a few yards, if necessary on ice floes. I noticed as I threw myself cavalierly into a canvas bucket-seat that the others – the three northern oilmen flying with us – had carefully buckled themselves in and were sitting rather stiffly. Most of them, it turned out, had already crashed two or three times. One had recently crashlanded on a hillside of ice. They'd managed to fix the plane and take off again on the slope. The winds, the storms, the ferocity – all of this is incalculable. For those who don't pay constant attention, the elements are abrupt and definitive.

We hopped around in our air taxi from floating island to floating island – exploration camps built on ice which had been artificially thickened to ten metres by constant flooding. The men who lived and worked in these strange communities were emotional descendants of those who, a century ago, had gone into the woods and onto the prairies not so much ahead of civilization as to get away from it. When they strolled out onto the ice airstrip to greet us, in the cold which scientifically freezes skin dead in one minute, their jackets were often open, their gloves off.

Some of them we found living in tiny nomadic camps – three trailers dragged around hundreds of kilometres out on the arctic ice. These seismic crews were searching for oil by exploding dynamite on the ocean floor beneath them and measuring the vibrations. It would be difficult for a Southerner to come any closer to a pure, almost abstract freedom. The normal chains of civilization, whether Western or Inuit, were absent. These small groups advanced through a frozen, colourless limbo – itself meaningless apart from those odd explosions beneath the ice and the measuring of an unseen but vibrating sea bottom.

One trailer carried the dynamite; another was fitted with bunks. In the third they gathered to talk and eat. There was no alcohol. Food was here transformed into an obsessive religion. Great quantities of it were permanently on display and offer. There was a line-up of pies and cakes. Enormous roasts and turkeys waited side by side.

Once every few weeks, a plane materialized out of the void, dropped off a new crew, and carried the men away down to Edmonton or Calgary for a week. There, a few no doubt rediscovered families. But most gave themselves over to an urgent life of prostitutes and drink. These were frontier lives. Only a hypocrite would judge them in other terms.

As for their pursuit of oil and gas, it produced large reserves, most of which are now capped and invisible. Exploration has been wound down. The economic crisis combined with the rising environmental movement brought it to an end. So did the growing influence of the Inuit, who, in spite of contacts going back to the sixteenth century, had been more or less left alone until the early 1960s.

Of course, the missionaries had been unable to resist the possibility of new converts. And for much of the nineteenth century, the whalers had used the bays of Baffin while they exhausted the whale stocks. From these Scots and Americans, the Inuit got metal tools, cloth, rifles for hunting, the squeeze box for dancing music and various Western diseases which wiped out large parts of the population.

And then there was the frantic search for the Northwest Passage. A nineteenth-century folly, which had neither an economic nor a political justification. What could you do with a sea route which was closed almost eleven months of the year? Even during its so-called open season, ship after ship was ground up between cliffs of moving ice.

Ever since Martin Frobisher had fallen upon Baffin Island in 1576 and tried to find his way around in order to reach China, the expeditions had straggled across the Atlantic from time to time. They would dodge their way through the ice floes to reach Baffin, then opt to sail around this massive obstacle to the north or south.

In 1845, Sir John Franklin, with two ships and 128 men – the biggest expedition ever mounted – set off north around Baffin into a seventy thousand square mile maze of unknown islands. They were never seen again.

Suddenly the frenzy began. The pointless challenge of the Northwest Passage now had a humanitarian motive. Over a dozen years, fifty expeditions were thrown into the maze to save Franklin and, when that no longer seemed reasonable, to discover his fate.

In truth, most of the leaders of these rescue missions were as eager to win the glory that would come with finding the Passage as they were to find the lost men. Most of them were certifiable. Jules Verne captured their lunacy in his wonderful book *The Adventures of Captain Hatteras*, which in many ways was the first purely psychological novel. How could the North be other than a psycho-drama in *huis clos* for these explorers? Their attitude – that of the classic Christian conqueror – divorced them from any reality; particularly that tenuous, almost invisible reality which permitted the Inuit to survive in the southern half of the High Arctic.

Finally, there was Ottawa's decision in the early 1960s to

establish non-nomadic, permanent villages with health and education services. Undoubtedly, it was an invasion of Southern values. And yet the South was invading anyway. The cold war had brought a missile warning system. There were the miners and the oil men. Not to provide services would probably have been worse than providing them. There was also a desire to demonstrate that Canada was the effective owner of these islands.

This concept of ownership was at first incomprehensible to the Inuit, for whom life was a matter of movement and survival. They lived on the land. Used it. Philosophical and ethical questions aside, ownership was a luxury inappropriate in such a place. Yet when the Canadian government established a Southern administrative system in the North, the Inuit reacted with remarkable speed. Survival in such a place has put them constantly on the watch for changes, problems, opportunities. While whites hang stubbornly onto their way of doing things and fall back easily on theoretical national characteristics to justify doing the wrong thing, the Inuit adapt quickly.

In 1971, they organized themselves into The Inuit Tapirisat and began pressing for control of their own affairs. In Southern terms, that could only mean administrative control of the Eastern Arctic, with Baffin as the centrepiece. In the Eastern Arctic, 80 per cent of the population is Inuit.

This was the complex, impossible place into which we wanted to drop fifteen foreign writers. Petro-Canada had lent us a plane. During the seven-hour flight to Iqaluit – the capital of the Eastern Arctic – we tried to explain the delicate, unresolved nature of the North. The other Canadians – Alootook Ipellie and Minnie Freeman, both Inuit, and Dermid Collis and David Young – spoke from long experience. Their underlying message was that passersby should devote themselves to listening carefully.

The first night in Iqaluit, we were entertained by the local writers, artists and teachers. Iqaluit is a Southern-style town cut unnaturally into the rock surface of Frobisher Bay. It looks better in the winter. Inside the hotel, in a banquet room resembling thousands of others around the world, eating Northern food cooked in a European manner, it was as if we had flown but a short distance. Then a senior Inuit writer rose to welcome us with what quickly turned into an attack on the sentimentalism of Western "intellectual" fashions. We had encouraged the Inuit to break their self-sufficient nomadic cycle in the nineteenth century in order to trap furs for the European market. And now that they are irredeemably sedentary and dependent, in part, on trapping, we have decided that wearing fur is immoral. The result is poverty for the Inuit.

The surprise of the well-intentioned Southerners was obvious. The trapping problem is, of course, only a small part of the Inuit crisis. Having become sedentary, and serviced now by hospitals, their families have exploded in numbers, from around two children to eight. In the 1920s there were less than seven thousand Inuit. By the century's end, there will be forty thousand. The North is enormous, but it is not designed to support such a big population. What are they to do? What can they do? It isn't a place which can be converted over to a Southern economy.

There was a historic land settlement in 1990. The Inuit are well on the way, after a referendum, to a decentralized territorial government which they will control. Nunavut takes in the whole Eastern Arctic, but a good 80 per cent of its budget will have to be financed by Ottawa. Almost half the jobs in the territory involve working for the government. Indeed, what does the Southern idea of a job mean at this latitude?

The next day we broke into two groups, and mine, including Glissant, Achebe, Law-Yone, and Friedan, took off in a Twin Otter flown by childlike pilots – a Greek and a Russian – who had somehow ended up in the Arctic. We headed north and west across Baffin, itself undulating with great, dark rock surfaces below us and raw-looking in early September on the edge of winter. From there we began across Foxe Basin, where the water was still open, but littered with ice floating down from farther north. I kept going up to the open cockpit to ask the pilots to fly lower so that we could see the astonishing world below, but they seemed to be in an obsessive mood, fixed on their destination. I kept complaining. On a later flight over open water, the engines suddenly went dead, and the plane plunged down in a clammy silence. Someone vomited. Then the engines roared, and the Russian put his head round to look at us with a satisfied little smile. He pointed to the water: "You can see the whales." After six hours on that first day, we came to a small, flat island. On the edge of a bay there was a community – Igloolik.

It was here during the winter of 1822-23 that Captain Parry was iced-in while searching for the elusive Passage. The Inuit helped his crew survive, and two hunters – Iligliuk and Ewerat – drew maps to help them get on farther. This role of the locals is invariably ignored in our descriptions of exploration. Later in the century, whalers dropped in during the summer, and this tempted the Inuit to cut short their normal summer hunting. They stayed put on the coast in the hope of getting guns and tools. The Catholic mission came in the 1930s; the Hudson's Bay Company a few years later to buy fur and sell goods. But there was no real Southern presence until the school, the nursing station and the Mounties arrived in the sixties.

A quick glance at the houses, there, leaves a sense of familiarity. The government built them in a Southern suburban style. But then the eye slips beyond, to the rising, severe plane of rock, the dog teams pegged to the ground (Igloolik is one of the few communities where snowmobiles have not entirely replaced them), the beach lined with hunting canoes, the remains of seals and beluga whales frozen on the rocks and the bay filled with small icebergs. The way in which the sky seems to wrap around all of this creates the sense that you should not walk far beyond the houses.

We each slept in a different house. The classic entrance is unheated, to keep the seal, whale and caribou pieces frozen. There is often a big piece of raw meat out in the kitchen, because the preferred meal is raw and, if possible, frozen flesh. The explorers never seemed to understand that if they died of scurvy while the Inuit didn't, it must have had to do with what they were eating. The latter got their vitamins from raw meat and blubber. The Europeans' conviction of their own superiority led them to go right on boiling all the goodness away, decade after decade.

One of the things our group had come to do was to take part in a Northern writing program which involved computers and pooled printing resources. The organizers were hoping to bolster the Inuit culture with its own written literature which could be used against the Southern invasion. After all, on this island, far above the magnetic pole, few people can afford to fly out. But they can watch the full range of Southern television every day. This may be television at its most destructive; certainly, "Dallas" watched in Igloolik is television at its most surreal. There are problems of indolence in an artificially sedentary community – high levels of suicide, some drugs, other Southern problems.

On the other hand, a group in the village had made a video about their own lives, and everyone seemed to be writing a book for the publishing program. Some of the older women were writing short survival manuals, because the young who watched television were becoming confused about the reality in which they lived.

When we went to the school, a crowd was waiting to ask

questions about the role of books and the role of fiction. In many ways they understood better than us, because telling stories has always been part of their oral culture. One thing which is clear in this complex situation is that the Inuktitut language is remarkably flexible, perhaps more so than any Southern tongue. It proceeds by description, and therefore can absorb any new element. When the explorers arrived with clocks, they were immediately named *siqingujaq*, meaning "sun follower." The computer became *qaritaujag*, "like a brain." In an intentionally or unintentionally ironic comment on the explorers' obsession with sticking flagpoles in the snow to claim territory, they defined a flag as *saimati*, or "an item to make people happy."

We were invited to a banquet that night in the school auditorium. The whole community was there. The food was on three large squares of plywood in the centre of the floor. Three heaping piles of raw caribou, blubber, and char. We were invited to borrow a knife, take a large piece, sit on the floor, and carve away. When word got out that it was Edouard Glissant's birthday, the entire village sang happy birthday. Later during the trip, he returned the gesture with a poem, now published in a collection which celebrates the different places that have moved him. * Each has the title of a town or a village and consists of four lines.

> *Igloolik*
> Si loin dans le silence a rencontré sa main
> A secoué sa main dans la glaçure des abats, des peaux
> A regardé les chiens grossir entre les cordes, d'abois gelés
> A rentré au sec ce qui restait de viande et de petit jour

The next day we went out in a large, hide-skinned hunting canoe through the ice floes. It is one of those small but essential

---

*Edouard Glissant, *Fastes*, Editions du Gref, Toronto, 1991, page 26.

details of Northern life that the best drinking water is to be found in icebergs. The heat of the sun is magnified through the outer ice and creates inner cavities where the water is held.

When we reached open water, it became increasingly choppy and the spray began to cover our arctic gear. Eventually, the rough water forced us back to shore. I noticed that Betty Friedan had been very silent. After they had helped her out, she stood on the shore and said quietly, "I wondered at first why they hadn't given us life preservers." She was staring at the ice and the dark water. "Then I understood."

The North changes but remains unchangeable. It is a place where people move slowly and consider their actions with great care, knowing that most mistakes are definitive. Only a highly conscious society can survive. As for the rational idea of human control over the physical world, it makes no sense there at all.

CAROL SHIELDS

# Travelwarp

The bus between Buenos Aires and Rio took forty-eight hours, but it seemed there was no other way. Rail connections between Argentina and Brazil were non-existent, I was told, and travelling by air meant missing out on the great width of country in between. So, as the bus driver handed out blankets and pillows, I settled back in my seat and made myself as comfortable as possible.

That cramped seat became my home for two days and nights, and during that time I discovered a new truth: travel does not broaden the mind but instead narrows it. Narrows it to a tight haze of perception. To a numb opacity. To the soft-edged microchip of the present moment and the accompanying wish to escape or at least enlarge that moment.

My fellow bus travellers chattered away in Spanish and Portuguese, while I was sadly limited to English. Luckily, though, I'd a thick paperback for company, Jane Smiley's novel *The Greenlanders*, a book I'd had kicking around the house for months but hadn't found time to get into. This epic, with its huge cast of characters, is set in fourteenth-century Greenland and deals minutely, dramatically, with the life of the early Greenland settlers, their farms and villages and seasonal rituals. Greenland in the Middle Ages was a society not only positioned at the edge of the world, but poised on the cusp of decline, and Smiley writes of its final years with a beguiling mixture of erudition and empathy.

Frequently, during the forty-eight hour journey through South America, I looked up to see banana trees flashing by, or villages with sunlit squares, and then I would return to my absorbing saga and its struggling men and women. The world of the novel was solidly created, furnished, and inhabited, a world I entered willingly, shutting the doors behind me, or at least some of the doors. The pages felt curiously crisp and alive in my hands; there was an adulterous love affair, a murder of vengeance, a cruel banishment. Meanwhile, glancing up now and then, I took in the vast stretches of Argentina from the bus window, then a string of pollution-choked cities, and finally an astonishing glimpse of turquoise ocean. The printed images on my lap faded for a time, then rushed back in.

I read the final pages as the bus entered the suburbs of Rio, feeling by that time that I had one foot planted in twentieth-century Latin America and the other in fourteenth-century Greenland. It was impossible to say which was more securely rooted. The journey that I had expected to be linear, stern, and instructive had divided itself down the middle; its margins were blurred; real time had collapsed, and also expanded.

I remembered how, some years earlier, well-meaning friends presented me with a biography of Bonnie Prince Charlie to read during a coach tour of Scotland. I brought it home unread, having discovered that the last thing I wanted to do when I slipped into the hotel bed (freezing) under the reading lamp (dim) was to bone up for the next day's sightseeing. Far from desiring total immersion in Scottish culture, I looked for ways to blot it out for a few hours – first thumbing through copies of *The Spectator* that some other vacationer had left behind, and then diving into an abandoned edition of *The Grapes of Wrath*, a real find, coverless, underlined, the final chapter missing, but what did that matter so long as my icy Scottish hotel room was thronged with disenfranchised wanderers in search of California riches and sunshine. Another plane of reality was instantly available to me, an arm's reach away on the bedside table, offering a leavening of perception, balance, order, at the very least a backdrop against which I could define the dark, contradictory Scottish landscape, its tidy towns and wild purple hills and waterways.

For a good many of us, travelling is hard work. You would never guess from reading glossy holiday magazines that much of a traveller's time is spent being idle, bored, uncomfortable, hungry, sleepless, confused, lonely, and gravely concerned and frustrated by the rates of exchange. Cultural confrontation is often more exhausting than enlightening. The disturbing foreign currency, tissuey, vividly coloured, is constantly being handed back and forth in vague and disorienting commercial transactions, leaving the visitor – in the city of Fez, for instance – yearning to curl up with *Middlemarch* rather than venture out to taste Morocco's nightlife. After all, you've got yet another city souk to explore tomorrow, more traveller's cheques to cash, hearty postcards to write to the family back home – all this while you're still trembling with jet lag and reeling from a headache which you know perfectly well you can banish by applying a dozen pages of George Eliot, a journey back in time, a visit to gentle, suddenly familiar England with its landscape of hedge and yew and moss-coated church steeples, leagues away from Fez's sturdy palm trees and markets and mosques and the buzz of *here*. Switch on the reading light, if there is one, open to page one, and an hour later you are no longer *here* but *there*, and – with luck, and readerly faith – soon lulled into a deep, dreamless slumber, that most cherished heaven for travellers.

But a good book, even a mediocre book, that reads *against* the journey offers far greater dividends than mere escape; the right book can enhance the experience, multiply the impact, increase your psychic travel points, enlarging book as well as voyage – an act of alchemy that turns both to gold.

You have, after all, left home, and are primed for the exotic, for anything, in fact. (Isn't this what your travel agent promised?) Your antennae are up, your senses open. Otherness is what you're after. Difference. You've assigned yourself a suspense of time and structure simply by buying an airline ticket, by boarding a train, by filling up your car with maps and apples and bottled water. But don't forget your bag of books. Leaving home without a book is inviting a diminution of pleasure.

A book on Inca art, for instance, works nicely against a week in Boston. Or the endlessly enriching Jane Austen during a stop-over in Hong Kong. Or Kafka at midnight after a day of scuba diving off the Mexican coast. One set of perceptions is brought edge to edge with another. These juxtapositions of life and print startle us awake and keep away the travel demons: fatigue, despair, aching bones, primal angst, simple homesickness. The beaches of Hawaii can be brought into focus with a smart dose of Atwood; the Alps can be humanized by a chapter of Dickens or a story by Mavis Gallant.

I once experienced the vivid distortion of reading Paul Scott's *Raj Quartet* when travelling through Ghana in the early eighties. And V. S. Naipaul's *A Bend in the River* while on a tour of Japan. Such curious and random conjunctions of time and space can put a kind of torque on our comprehended vision of the world, doubling its power, tripling its dimensions, and confounding the traveller's careful itinerary.

A mere trip becomes a journey, a journey an odyssey. The sand beaches of Brazil, for me, will always lie in the path of a creeping glacier, and the medieval austerities of Greenland enlivened by the blinding glare of South American heat and the faraway music of drums and castanets.

LINDA SPALDING

Others

Doors to what?

Three years ago, my daughter and I spent her Easter break in Chiapas, that southern piece of Mexico just across the border from Guatemala which has been so much in the news recently. It's the home of those Mayans who live in the uplands, in the *selva* – or forests – and in small villages that are entirely cut off from the comforts of the twentieth century.

We'd reserved a room at NaBalom, a place established in San Cristóbal half a century or more ago as an ethnographic centre, and staffed by student volunteers from everywhere. But there'd been a mistake about our reservation, so, after half a week there, we'd lost our room and found a place for one night only at a cheap hotel. We had three days left, and San Cristóbal was packed with tourists. It was Holy Week. *La Semana Santa.*

After our long search for a room, we slept late despite the most chaotic racket – bells, buzzers, children and parents all reverberating off the tiles. By nine the maid was hammering at the door and shouting, Hoover! But we slept. Mother and child. I was slightly sick, so when we finally went to the café, I had a careful breakfast – *una torta con queso y aquacate.* Then we set off.

What were we looking for? The Maya. But having been instructed by a guide about the Mayans of this area – that they are genuinely, truly averse to "us" – we'd decided to look for ruins instead. Relics of the culture were, perhaps, more available than human encounters. The guide had taken us to San Andreas and Tenejapa, a village that was bombed by the Mexican government during the recent rebellion. It's famous for its weavers. What I remember of this place is a few tired buildings and a small co-operative in which women sold their beautiful work, all done with vegetable dyes. We'd gone in a small van, and the road was so dusty we'd put whatever cloth we could find over our faces in order to stay alive. But once there, we were kept under watch. The guide had taken us to Chamula, too; a village that serves as ceremonial centre to hundreds of Mayans from the forested hills. This had entailed purchasing a pass, leaving cameras behind, and following strict rules imposed by the community. Rules for outsiders. We'd discovered, in fact, that we were assumed to be dangerous, like people carrying disease. And that's how we'd felt,

A woman of San Andreas, weaving

surrounded by men in dark wool *ponchos* and women in blue *hui-pils*. (The Mayans dress communally – each village has its colour.)

However, never mind. If we couldn't meet the people or talk to them without causing offence, we would get as close as we could to their world, which was still connected to the stones of its past. There were very few parts of Chamula we'd been allowed to see, but certain things had been explained to us. The system of elders. The *curanderos*. The sacred drink called *pox*, pronounced "posh," which is used for ceremonial occasions. These Mayans chased the priests out of their hills long ago and converted their churches to indigenous places. More like a cave than a building, the church in Chamula has a floor covered in pine boughs. Tall, thin tapers are stuck to it, and it is there, between the boughs and under the ancient saints wrapped in silk and mirrors, that the *curanderos* work with eggs, a chicken, a bottle of Pepsi or a Pepsi bottle full of *pox*. The whole society is wrapped in silk and mirrors, but we were locked out of it.

It was Thursday of Holy Week, and although the saints and bells in the churches of San Cristóbal were covered, there were papier-mâché Judases hanging from doorways and balconies, and parts of the Passion being enacted on the streets. This city is colonial Mexico. Until the sixties (about the time of the PanAmerican highway) the Mayans weren't allowed on its sidewalks. Their communal lands have been broken up and stolen. Their forests cut down to make room for cattle-grazing.

After breakfast, we walked into the suburbs. We'd been told about an ancient site and we were going to spend an hour or two acquiring it for our memories, in the absence of other experience. I was carrying a heavy leather bag, which was full of tickets, passports, the camera, and other things we were afraid to leave in our room. It was going to be a long walk and we didn't have detailed directions, but we noticed everything we passed. Some workmen hammering on a roof. A Judas figure hanging just underneath them. The Judas was grinning, and his huge penis stood out stiffly. We knew he would be carried off to jail on Saturday and on Sunday he'd be burned in a huge bonfire. Still, he was disconcerting swinging there, and somehow I stumbled, losing Tampax from my pocket on the road in front of the hammering men. I was tempted to walk on, not to bend over and retrieve these female things, because the grins of the workmen were so like the grin on Judas' face.

We were heading for the *Ojo de Aqua*, passing grazing goats and the landmarks that had been part of our vague directions. We'd been told to look for children to guide us, but there were no children on the dusty road and no children by the spring, although it gathered at our feet exactly as we'd been told it would – small and earth-coloured, slow moving. Trees hung over it and there was even a short bridge. There were no children anywhere around, but there was a man walking with a small bag in his hand. "*Mix-oaquil?*" I said, trying to pronounce the name of the site.

He pointed to a great hill that rose up at the end of the path, and as we walked towards it, he began to follow us.

"Señor, we do not want to trouble you," I said in careful Spanish.

"I don't mind," he told us. But the mountain was steep, and soon we had to lift our knees and take high, climbing steps. The air was thin and I couldn't seem to get enough of it. I tried to take deep breaths. I was wearing a skirt, and my hem kept catching under my feet. The morning was clear and dry and hot. The trees around us were so dry that they cracked at a touch. The ground was baked into stone. The path up that mountain was as crisply chiselled as the steps of a pyramid.

Kristin, my ardent daughter, was ahead of me, wearing good walking shoes, and behind me the man who had pointed the way was still following silently. I climbed a little faster. I was longing to be alone with my child on this mountain and I wasn't pleased to have this outsider, this man, following so closely. It was impossible to speak, even if I had known what to say, but after a while I said, "Señor, you must go on; we are slowing you down."

"I don't mind," he said, again. He was short, but he took great strides while the mountain sloped up steeply and while I tried to stay ahead.

Once I paused to catch my breath and look back at the city. "It's beautiful here," I said, because I didn't know what else to say.

He nodded. "Where I live it is more beautiful."

He was close on my heels. Kristin took the heavy bag off my shoulder, but I still had no air, and sweat ran down my face and neck. The trees were smaller now and so was the view of the city below us, but whenever I paused the man would press forward, as if we were delaying him.

At last he slowed at a little concavity lined with stones. "Here," he said, pointing at a tumble of rocks.

"This?"

"Yes."

Perhaps once there had been something here, a village important enough to have buildings made of stone, but nothing remained of it, at least nothing our eyes could see. Everything had been buried centuries ago. It took an effort of will to imagine a village as it once might have been, and I gave up and sat down on the grass. Kristin reached into our bag and got out the can of apple juice we'd brought. "What is your name?" she asked the man.

"Salvador."

She handed him the can of juice and he put it away in his own bag, smiling his thanks.

"Wait," I said, "we are all thirsty. It's hot and we have climbed a long way."

He looked surprised, but he gave me the can and I tore at it and took a long drink, then passed it back to him.

He smiled. This business of drinking from the same can pleased him. "When you come to my house," he said, "I will give you a refreshment."

"Where is your house?"

He pointed into the distance, across the valley on the far side of the mountain we had climbed and up the side of another. "It is beautiful there," he assured us.

"Why did you go all the way to town?"

"To sell my fruit. I go every day."

I looked at his bag and considered it. There was one small bump under the cloth, one piece of fruit unsold and carried all the way back up the mountain with him. "It's a very long walk."

"No. Not long. Tomorrow I will walk to Chamula, which is a walk of ten hours."

Chamula! If Salvador was Mayan, then, where was his dark wool *poncho*? And the rest of it – his fear of us? We stood up and finished the can of juice between us. It would have been impossible to turn down his invitation now, so we set off slowly, across the valley which separated this mountain from the one ahead, passing a group of five or six men who looked at us strangely; Kristin with her unshaved legs and short pants, carrying my bag, both of us with our hair tied back, sweating ferociously, striding along in the path of a man who lived on the next mountain.

It was already growing late. And we were alone, except for the forest, with all these male strangers. And there was only a narrow path through the trees. I was still panting. I began to fear that I wouldn't make it, that the house was too far away. But we kept walking. Then we passed a group of women. There were four of them on the narrow path and they turned their faces away. "Will your wife be there?" I asked, but Salvador didn't seem to understand my Spanish. Neither of us was speaking a mother tongue.

We passed a herd of goats. Only a few. "Are they for milk?"

"No."

"What animals do you have, then? Cows?"

"No!"

"A horse?"

"Yes."

"But why not ride it to town?" As I spoke, I looked down the mountainside, all rock and shale. It was a stupid question.

"It is too hot for the horse," he answered.

We walked a long time. It seemed clear that we would never get back to San Cristóbal. I wouldn't be able to find the way; it was too far below us, even in its altitude, which had seemed so serious that morning. Kristin kept striding along in her businesslike way.

Far ahead there were some houses built of mud and thatch, but what else could be used here, where there were no streets, no traffic, no vehicles at all, not even a cart? Where a horse must be given to the mountain? "I have flowers," Salvador said. "I will show them to you."

I had no thought of anything at all, now, except this place, this time, these small, dry trees, this dry, hard, yellow mountainside. The sky was pale and clear. "Do you have flowers where you live?" Salvador asked, and suddenly there was a building made of blocks and painted white in front of us. There were a few other dwellings in the clearing, but they were wattle and thatch. This house actually looked out of place on this mountain, so far from anything in the world and so high above it. "Here?" We ducked our heads and entered a clean room with a bed, a plastic water container, a treadle sewing machine, and the cross that was here before the Spanish came, the cross that is not a crucifix but an opening into time. Around it, on the floor, pine branches and a piece of wood for burning candles, and the bromeliad, which is sacred to the Mayans and which grows in their mountain forests.

Two young children came to the edge of the door. I could see part of each face. Salvador spoke to them in words we didn't understand and they ran off. Then he brought in two small chairs for us and we sat down on them and he sat on the bed that was made of slats. We were thirsty again, but the water container was small and must have been carried a long way. And without the help of the horse. "Now," said Salvador, "we will have refreshment." As he finished this statement, the children reappeared with three Pepsis which he distributed. It seemed unbelievable. "Please see through the window," he said, as we drank.

I stood up and walked across the room to look out, down at the garden he had made on the mountain, a garden for beauty alone. Then I turned and we faced each other. The path into this clearing had emptied as we approached, I was sure of it. I'd felt the absence of people although he'd brought us through the forest as if we were not unwelcome guests. Now he got out a bottle and poured a tiny glassful of the clear liquid called *pox*. He passed the glass to us as I wrote our names on a piece of paper, and he showed us his identity card, which had his Mayan name spelled out in Spanish, although he told us it was inaccurate.

"Is your wife here?" Kristin asked.

Salvador indicated the doorway to a second, smaller room. The kitchen. "But she does not speak Spanish."

"Will your family go to Chamula with you?"

"Of course. You should look for us."

"Is it possible for us to come?"

"Of course."

We told him we would try. Then we said *adios* and thanked him. "Next year I will put in a floor," he said, as if we might be there to witness the event.

We began the long walk back to San Cristóbal, taking another excruciating route to the bottom of the mountain, where a taxi appeared and we got into it.

That night we moved to Sra. Gloria Rixy's house, a place where respectable women are allowed to stay. We have a room with three beds, no lock on the door. We had heard about Sra. Rixy the day before in a little café, and she had arrived in splendour during our lunch, looked us up and down to see whether our characters were sterling enough, and promised us a room. "*Si. Como no?*"

The next morning I flooded her bathroom because the top of a jamjar was blocking her shower drain. I didn't notice it. The water was cold and I was putting parts of my body under it gingerly. It was one of those showers that gets everything wet – the toilet, the sink, the whole room. The shower head was in the middle of the

Mayan crosses on a hillside

ceiling and there was no curtain, so the water ran out under the door and down the hall. I had flooded Sra. Rixy's dignified house. I apologized and asked humbly if we might stay another night.

We left one bag in our unlocked, communal room and brought the heavy purse, camera, tickets, passports. There was one restaurant open, just off the *zocalo*. Hot cakes, *huevos rancheros*. Then we rushed to the street. It was almost nine-thirty. We asked a taxi driver for a price to Chamula, and he told us it would be 15,000 pesos.

We passed Leonard, a friend from NaBalom, and invited him along, then we rode out of San Cristóbal at the tail end of a religious procession. It wasn't far by car – perhaps twenty minutes – nothing compared to the walk Salvador and his family were going to make. But when we were released on the outskirts of the village centre, our naive promise to look for them seemed suddenly ridiculous. We were surrounded by thousands of Mayans – thousands! – the men in their *ponchos* and the women in their woven *huipils*.

A sea of blue and black. And only *la gente*, according to the silver-toothed guard, would be allowed in the church. He had a long baton which he used to prove his point. We tried to see a little through the small doors. There were not many of us tourists, maybe thirty in all, and this included Mexicans, who were also not allowed to enter the church. (This is a place where tourists have been stoned to death for using cameras.) We could hear the sounds of noise-makers inside and see candles. There was a pool of water full of petals which was drunk from by those who passed by. It was hot. The elders were lined up outside the church. In a while they gave their ribboned hats to their wives, who stood lined up behind them, and went inside, taking positions around the altar, which was covered in a curtain of green leaves. We stood in the huge crowd, and then magically Paula and Mary Evlyn arrived, two more friends from NaBalom. We all stood in the sun, a head taller than *la gente*, until suddenly the whole front of the church was thrown open. What had seemed to be walls were actually enormous doors with smaller doors set inside. Now, over the heads of the celebrants, we could witness the sight inside.

What happened next was that Christ was taken off the cross with much noise-making – an ominous metallic whirring and the occasional sob of a shell horn. A purple cloth was held in front of the cross to hide the slow descent, a movement of inches. It took forever. Kristin and I watched for a time, then went to the street of stalls and bought an orange and some small clay dolls. We bought Michael an armadillo with a bobbing head.

Back in the square they were throwing down pine needles. The procession would be outside. When the enormous flower-and-leaf-covered coffin with its canopy was brought out, it was followed by all the male saints on their individual platforms, each carried by a group of men. The procession wound slowly, solemnly around the plaza in front of the church. Separately, female saints on high platforms were carried in the opposite direction by women in white. I thought of the *paseos*, the processions of young men and women circling each other at night in plazas all over Mexico. The saints themselves were oddly mismatched, draped in flowered silks and hung with mirrors, but of various sizes and shapes. They sat on their platforms made of upright manzanita plants, and as the female saints met the coffin each was made to bow three times, the tiny dolls dipping in such a dignified way that the sight was moving, the way a performance of puppets sometimes is. It was like an enormous puppet theatre, only these puppets were connected to such furious faith. Each was showered with petals from above, where men and boys sat on the wall. The male saints bowed too, constantly. The way was long and hot and arduous. We stood close to the gate among hundreds of people with babies and children, all in heavy Chamulan wool. The noise of the metal and wood clappers was unsettling. There was incense. People were eating petals and leaves. The elders carried huge baskets of greens and held them on their shoulders for an hour or more. These baskets went everywhere, surrounding every part of the ceremony. It was ecstatically religious, although no one in the crowd cried or crossed himself, no one did the usual things except when Christ was actually lowered into the coffin at the doors of the church and all of those thousands of people knelt – down and up and down again.

We'd lost track of our friends, although we kept looking for them as we pushed our way through the crowd.

At one o'clock we decided to try to get to Zinacatan, where another procession was about to occur. But there were no taxis. These villages do not consort with each other, although both are Mayan and only a few miles apart. Even their languages are different. We walked up the road, looking for *collectivos*, but there were only open trucks full of Chamulans. Then we found a boy standing by a car. Perhaps he would drive us for some cash. But he was unbelievably drunk; he could hardly stand. While we talked to him, his hat flew off and Kristin went around the car to rescue it. He hadn't missed it. He could barely speak. So we walked on. How would we even get back to Sra. Rixy's strange house for women, where we had been taken in? And what kind of trouble would we be in with Sra. Rixy if we weren't back at a decent hour? If all else failed, we could walk the ten miles and the day would still have been worthwhile. I saw some long-haired types getting into a beat-up car, outsiders like us. I asked if they were going to Zinacatan and they said they were arguing about it, the two women and the kids wanting to go and the man not wanting to. Maybe our arrival settled the question, because grudgingly they let us in. They had friends in Canada. We took off for Zinacatan.

Kristin and I had not peed since morning. We both had our periods. Never mind. Zinacatan was miraculous. Both the men and women wore bright pink, and the village was white and grey and clean. This time we went right into the church, which wasn't crowded, although they were just bringing Christ down from the cross. There were long minutes of wrapping him in the coffin. In fact there were two coffins. The second one held another Christ from another village. There were only three saints, but we watched them move around the square. Suddenly we saw our friends again. They were with Leonard. They had come with a snotty couple, the ones who had taken our front seats in the dusty van two days before and were nose-in-air all day. Leonard wanted to stay at Zinacatan and offered us his place in their car. Mary Evlyn and Paula had gone to a back street to pee and found all the Zinacatecans doing the same thing. Kristin and I bought another orange and got into the car.

Back in San Cristóbal we followed a procession that seemed to be made up of members of the Ku Klux Klan. Perhaps they were

Judases in white. They carried torches through the streets and wore tall pointed hats. But this Mexican demonstration of faith seemed pale in comparison to the Mayan mysteries. We ducked into The Bazar to hear the musicians and found the whole NaBalom volunteer gang there, so we ordered a bottle of mescal, which went down very quickly. We were all very jolly, toasting everything in sight and singing. I had more fun than was warranted with all these strangers so much younger, some of them Mexican, one of them German, two Americans, four Canadians.

We finally drifted out and dispersed, and when we got back to Sra. Rixy's the gate was locked, so we stood there helplessly. The whole house was dark. Then the dog began to bark, the baby began to cry, the lights went on and the señora came out angrily. The mother of the baby stood there in her shawl, too, and Kristin and I rushed to our room, where we stood in the dark until everything had quietened again.

We set the alarm. It was our last night in San Cristóbal. I felt very sad. I was thinking, I am so crazy about this child and also this country and this week with both. How to give it up? Another little death. I want want want. I want to hold everything at once. Everything. This dark old town and the mountains and the forests full of Indios and the women in the wool wraps and bare feet selling things in the square.

In the night I was a little sick, but the dog barked when I got up to go to the bathroom so I went back to bed and slept. I had lost our Mexicana tickets. Another story. But I dreamed they were found.

SUSAN SWAN

# Corfu: Visiting Lawrence Durrell's White House (from My Greek Journals)

Tuesday. August 11, 1992. It's the Festival of St. Spiridion, cele-brating the Island Saint who was so virtuous his corpse smelled sweet and sprays of red roses broke from his tomb. All the hotels will be booked, but I'm taking my chances on finding a room any-how and going up to Kalami to see Lawrence Durrell's White House. I don't have my jeans with me or anything practical like a sleeping bag, so I may have to camp out on the beach in my white satin nightgown and green silk blouse and festival party hat. I am sure Durrell and his old friend Henry Miller would approve. Durrell lived in the White House with his first wife, Nancy, in 1937. He had gone back to Corfu (where he'd first lived with his mother and his brother Gerald), and it was there in Kalami that he'd written *The Black Book*, his first well-received novel before *The Alexandria Quartet* made him famous in the late 1950s. In *Prospero's Cell*, Durrell's non-fiction account of those Kalami days, he talks about his writing in a room over-hung with cypress and olive trees and says that this old fisherman's house was set "like a dice" on a stone promontory shaped like a "mons pubis."

Mons. That's Durrell's word, and I'm thinking how accurate he was as my bus rumbles along the east coast of Corfu, passing

The house I rented in Afionas

roadside cafés where British tourists with hideous sun-burnt backs cluster under red-and-white Amstel umbrellas, drinking beer and eating the pub snacks advertised on the signs over their heads. This part of Corfu – fifty years after Durrell – is known as the land of the lager louts. Telephone poles and satellite dishes sprout above the hotels and tavernas, and college boys in peaked caps speed past me in jeeps with rollbars. But Durrell was right: the way the shoreline curves out into cypress-laden promontories and then back again into small coves is lushly female. And beyond the jammed coastal road, the water is a Great-Lake blue in honour of my visit. I am staying at the other side of the island, in the small village of Afionas, on the rugged west coast. It's a male landscape, while this undulating shore, despite the tribes of British tourists, is a feminine fiefdom.

I am living alone in Afionas and working on revisions of a novel of mine (*The Wives of Bath*), and I've been reading both Durrell and Miller again – their nonfiction this time. It's been decades since I read the novels of either writer, years that have challenged my opinion of the two men. First of all, I'd read the accusations by Durrell's daughter, Sappho, in *Granta* (Autumn 1991). In her journals she'd hinted at an incestuous affair with her father, and then committed suicide. As for Miller, he'd come to represent the apex of sexist braggadocio. For all that, I am still deeply connected to the old rogues, a pair of literary granddaddies with unfortunate habits, because they both loved and lived well in a country that has become my second home. Greece is a "magic precinct," Miller wrote over forty years before the film *Shirley Valentine* – marvellous things happen there that don't happen anywhere else in the world.

Now the bus has stopped in front of a hairpin turn. Cars and motor scooters spurt out from the other side of the mountain. We are part of a long queue, waiting for our turn to go around the bend, one of many in the road ahead. Finally, the traffic moves again and I get off a few miles up the highway at a small sign that says Kalami. I walk the half-mile down the rolling hill, past overgrown villas and cone-shaped cypress trees, to Kalami cove. The cove is very small and the beach is shady at this time of day. It's already four o'clock in the afternoon, and I have to find a room for the night. I ask a group of young Italians on the road ahead for directions, and they point me to the first taverna on the beach. A young woman with a missing front tooth tells me there are no vacancies, but she knows Durrell's White House. She says it's a restaurant now, and she points to a run-down white building on the other side of the cove. Remembering Miller's advice to wing it in Greece, I order an Amstel and a Greek salad and consider my prospects. If there aren't any rooms, I'll buy one of the pink plastic life rafts on sale at the store next door and sleep on that.

It was a long walk down the hill and it's hot – *zeste*, the Greeks say. One of the old men I always see drinking ouzo in

Greek tavernas is sitting at the bar beside me. He is staring openly at my hair. I've done it in cornrows for the heat. We begin to talk in broken English (I notice I speak broken English, not broken Greek, in my effort to be understood), and there's a commotion behind us. Heads turn. The Italians I saw on the road are walking into the taverna. I count seven of them. Some wear Sony Walkman headsets, and all of them are short and noodle thin with well-clipped hair. The Italians from the small Ontario town I grew up in were called "greasers." Their hairdos were long and oily, Elvis style, and they wore tight orange and red bathing suits and bounced soccer balls back and forth with their heads. I remember my friend's mother telling us not to look at them. In Corfu, as in many parts of Greece, the Italians exude style, and the young men, always fashionably dressed, travel in packs and banter with each other like hyperactive children. They cruise women in a swarm. Usually there's no real threat – it's just the Mediterranean hustle. The Greeks are low key and the Italians are noisy, but they all come on to you. The real danger comes from the North Americans and the Europeans: they're the ones who rape, not the Greeks. Greece has the lowest rape statistics of all the Western countries. In Greece, a rape can start a village vendetta against the rapist.

I'd had my first run-in with an Italian two weeks before. I had been dancing at a Mykonos club with my daughter when a group of them surrounded me and I began to play with them, pushing some of them out of my way and putting my elbows on the heads of the short ones. Suddenly, two of them danced me outside and one of them started to kiss me and tug at my clothes. The more I pushed him off me, the more daring he became. Like an overexcited puppy, he kept grinding his collegiate erection against me, thinking my resistance was part of our game. For the first time in Greece, my little warning bell had gone off: here's a man who could get carried away. I twisted out of his grip and ran off down one of the narrow alleys in the old Venetian quarter.

Now the Italians at Kalami are coming my way. Smiling at me as if I were an old friend. Not a good sign. The tallest one comes forward, shoving cigarettes and a beer at me. "Marlboros? Amstel? Pepsi? Ouzo?" As he stands there grinning, one of his friends steps up behind him and pours a beer over his head. The other young men shriek and call out words at us in Italian. He looks for a moment like he's going to weep. So I take one of his cigarettes because I feel sorry for him. (A mistake – done in by my Canadian manners.) He sits down beside me, the beer still dripping off his head. As he mops it off himself with a napkin, I tell him as courteously as I can that I am forty-six and have no interest in male company. (An old alibi to get me off the hook.) He smirks and orders us a round of beers. His friends behind us keep looking our way and shouting encouragement in high, screamy, insistent male voices.

Scowling at all of them, I get up and leave the taverna. It's five o'clock. There are three more tavernas on the beach. I start to hunt for a room again. I hurry anxiously along the small road at the back of the beach and the tavernas, stopping at cottages and one or two small modern apartments. The area feels overgrown like a culvert. And it's shabbier than I expected. I feel a little let down. Nobody has any rooms for the night. At number seven up the road, a man says "No problem" when I ask him if I can sleep on the beach. Then he suggests I try the villas at the top of the road, the new complex with trendy coach lamps on either side of the front door. It's a bit of a hike, but I start off anyway. Halfway up the hill, I hear voices, high-pitched male voices. I turn around and see the pack of Italian men. "Marlboros? Amstel? Pepsi? Ouzo?" one of them shouts. The young man I talked to in the bar calls to me, explaining that they are going to make spaghetti for dinner and want me to come. I shake my head and continue up the hill toward the villas. I can see them at the curve in the road below me, like a flock of crows, waiting. Then I forget about them. I am a long way from the beach now. I pass an olive grove on my left and decide that's where I'll sleep if there are no rooms in the villas. I'll just sneak up here after dark when the Italians have gone to bed and cover myself up with the silk shirt I have in my bag.

The sign at the front door says COMPLETO. I ring the bell anyway and there's no answer. I go down the hill slowly, hoping the Italians aren't still waiting. They're not. But I notice the sign at the end of the olive grove that says tenting or camping is strictly forbidden by Law 392. The olive grove is out. Maybe it'll be the floating mattress on the beach after all. I turn in at the White House. Just as the gap-toothed girl had told me, Durrell's old house is now a restaurant. Only the top floor of the building has rooms to rent, but there are no vacancies there either. A sign on one of the white walls says the speciality of the White House is crêpes and Greek yogurt with Corfu honey. I settle in with another Amstel on the large terrace overlooking Kalami cove. A Greek army boat is slowly inching its way across the strait to Albania, perhaps looking for Albanian refugees. They aren't wanted in Greece. I see smoke on the hills of Albania, and the young waiter George Mavroyas, who grew up in a nearby village, tells me that the Albanians are burning the hillsides in order to grow new grass. We discuss my plan to sleep on the beach, and he says I shouldn't worry about Law 392. Nobody will report me. He looks thoughtful. The mosquitoes, though. Then he smiles again. I'll just be a little uncomfortable, that's all. Nothing to worry about really. At that moment a small Greek fishing boat noses into shore in front of the terrace, and a mother and two children get off. They are glad to see me. They've rented the Durrells'

White House for the month of August. Every morning at ten, a tour boat goes by, the mother says, and points out Durrell's former residence. The children love it. They rush to the balcony and wave at the tour boat and the tour boat waves back. I could rent the house next summer if I want, the mother says. The phone number and the phone and fax number of the travel organization are printed on the side of the White House.

They go upstairs to change out of their bathing suits, and I'm alone on the terrace except for two cats who are playing with empty prawn shells. It's about seven o'clock. I'm in that no-man's-land of time in the Greek day – the hours before dinner gets underway around nine P.M. I try to imagine Durrell and his wife, Nancy, swimming like dolphins in the water just a few yards away. That's how Miller described them at Kalami in his travel book *The Colossus of Maroussi*. Likely Miller slept in the room just above me, drinking Metaxa brandy and writing letters of passion and enthusiasm – something he liked to do even if he was in the same house with the people he was addressing. But it's hard to relax. I know there's another pest besides mosquitoes that might bother me if I sleep on the beach: the Italians. I construct a scenario. There I am, in my white nightgown and green silk blouse, and there they are, standing above me. They won't do much, they'll even pretend to guard me. I've had that happen before on the beach in Afionas. For an entire afternoon, a group of Italian men sat around me in a wide circle, saying not a word. They watched me and looked sternly at anyone who came near. Then they left in a rubber dingy. My benign scenario – i.e., the Italians as nightly sentries – doesn't comfort me. One of them changes into the young man in Mykonos who got out of hand. Do I really want to go through that again? And then, God damn them, I feel racist talking about Italian men this way. As if they are children or monkeys who might go off half cocked . . . uh-huh, that pun is intentional. But this is Greece. As Miller says, marvellous things happen here. I shouldn't be so worried. I decide I will sleep on the beach.

An hour passes. People slowly filter into the bar and terrace. And suddenly it's crowded. It's also dark, and for the first time Durrell's presence is tangible. George the waiter has shown me his portrait in the bar. Durrell looks like any tousled-hair young man riding a motor scooter. George introduces me to a Welsh choirmaster who has been coming to Kalami since 1964. He says it hasn't changed a bit, and I believe him. Usually he drives down each summer through Yugoslavia, but the war there has made that impossible. This time he's come by Italy. He likes it because it's just the way it was when Durrell lived here. I eat my dinner, stuffed vine leaves, prawns, and yogurt with honey that comes disappointingly in a can. And all at once I feel a terrible, ghostly, watery feeling, as if Durrell had left his heart behind in this little seafaring cove. Maybe what I'm feeling is nostalgia. I stare morosely out over the promontory, at the moonlight casting shadows like spidery fingers behind the cypress trees. Only four miles away in the moonlight lies the hulking shape of Albania. It seems as far away as China . . . a tragic outpost, like Kalami itself – only a few hairpin turns away from the land of the lager louts on the coast road. Albania is a lost political kingdom, and Kalami is a little outpost of literary nostalgia just outside the empire of junk culture. Perhaps the culture of the lager louts will never bother to come down to the cove of Kalami but will simply move on to the future resorts that will be built farther up the coast road. And eventually Durrell's small paradise will be more surrounded than ever.

This sense of nostalgic sadness pervades Corfu towns too. The sadness of exile and failure. The Venetians, the Turks, and the British all tried to impose their ways on the Greeks, but nothing is left of their efforts except a few tourist ruins. The Greek culture endures because you can't change the Greeks – they change you. In other parts of Greece, you feel closer to the old classical culture – not the layers of other civilizations which have tried to feed off it for their own purposes. You come to Greece for that sense of direct connection to the ancient world, and in Corfu resent having to approach it layer by layer through other cultures that have come there before you. In Corfu you feel foremost the atmosphere of those other seekers. It is their story, like Durrell's sadness, that is waiting here for you, like a ghost nobody expected to see on the stair. And yet when he was living here, Durrell wasn't famous. And he hadn't had his daughter, Sappho, by his second wife, Eve. And the Second World War hadn't happened. So why should Durrell be sad at a time in his life when he was young and free?

It's 8:45, and down at the beach people are still swimming. That comforts me a little. Perhaps people will swim off and on all through the night and I won't be alone with my band of Italians. And then I see them coming down the road to the White House. They head toward me shouting and walking as if they are bouncing, bouncing right up into the air. Full of energy from their spaghetti. Suddenly I feel exhausted. They are heading this way, and I know what that means. Trying to avoid them in the bar while the other tourists watch. Getting up the psychic energy to tell them to fuck off and leave me alone. George the waiter will help me dismiss them, but how can George the waiter fend them off during the night? I can't ask him to do that. Their voices shriek louder and louder. People's heads turn in their direction. Any second now and they'll be here. I pick up my bag and try to leave quickly out the front entrance so they can't see me. I feel ashamed. "Nobody's going to kick me off my front porch," my grandfather used to say. Well Durrell's terrace isn't my porch. Never was, I tell myself.

I go down the steps and realize they'd already spotted me. They alight around me in front of the White House. Like scavengers. One of them grabs my cornrows and George races down the steps and pulls me back up onto the terrace. He screams at them in Greek. They retreat a little, but one of them still looks as if he is bouncing high up into the air. Inside the bar, George orders me a taxi. It comes in five minutes. A miracle. It turns out the driver was just coming down the coast when he heard the call. Afionas, I tell him, and he looks shocked until I assure him I am willing to pay the fifty bucks it will cost to take me the thirty miles of twisty road to the other side of the island. And then I thank George, who leads me out the back entrance, away from the Italians, and I speed along the tops of the Corfu bluffs, and I feel again Durrell's ghostly watery sadness. We speed up the bluffs under Corfu's largest mountain, the Pantocrator, and pass Greeks celebrating their fragrant St. Spiridion in tavernas in little mountain villages, until at last the taxi stops in my own village square. It's after midnight. I pay the driver and rush up through the silent and deserted street of the small village to see the moon from the vantage point of the donkey parking lot. (The field at the top of the cliff behind Afionas is where the farmers tether their donkeys for the night.) Does my vista compare to Durrell's? I stand for a long time, staring at the grand bay of Agio Georgios and the stern limestone bluffs whose sparse growth of olive trees looks like five o'clock shadow on a man's face. Of course my view compares. In Greece, every man and every woman is a citizen of their own village.

Back in Canada I understand Durrell's sadness. It's so obvious, I wonder I didn't see it before. Considering what I was doing myself. Durrell had gone to Corfu to write books, and he was on his third novel, *The Black Book*, writing with urgency and some desperation. It was the first novel of his that would win critical

Relaxing in a taverna, above the beach at Afionas

praise, but he didn't know that back in 1936. Listen to Durrell in a letter to Alan G. Thomas dated spring 1936: "I've been very down on the job lately over this fucking book which won't go as it should. It's difficult. If I ever finish it to my satisfaction I shall feel that virtue has gone out of me. Real virtue. It's like fine crochet, done at one level of emotion. Very queer and difficult for an up and down chap like me." In my own journal, a few days before I'd gone to visit Durrell's White House, I'd written, "My aloneness here in Afionas is beginning to get to me. I woke up anxious about my novel this A.M. Not sure the hump shoulder my narrator calls Alice works as a device for encouraging my narrator to tell her story." There are dozens of pages like this one in my journal, paragraph after paragraph of a writer's fret over this problem or that.

How could I have missed it? Durrell's despair – the ghostly sadness I sensed that evening at his White House – had nothing to do with Corfu, or the later wrecked marriages, or a troubled relationship with his daughter, Sappho. That was to come later. Durrell's

anguish was a writer's agony, working on his first angry and sexu-
ally explicit novel, wondering if the critics would like it – if
anybody would like it – and knowing it was an important test.
Durrell was only twenty-four then, about the same age as the pes-
tering band of Italians I'd met in Kalami. What I felt was an emotion as old as Greece itself: the writer's terror that he will not be
understood.

# JUDITH THOMPSON

## No Soy Culpable

"I AM INOCENT."

That's one of the first things we saw after stepping off the plane in Mexico City: a Wanted poster on the wall, with three walleyed, wide-faced men, and someone had written "I am inocent," with one *n*, in pen across the poster. As we walked into the Mexican air, we were approached by several Mexican men bellowing at us in broken English to come with them. But our tourist guide-booklets advised us to hire only official taxis, so that's what we did.

In the back of the rickety old taxi, which bumped and sped along the road to Mexico City, I felt stunned and slightly dreadful, the way I used to feel as a child with a new babysitter, or at a strange cousin's house. There was just that tiny chance that things would never be the same. I have not travelled much at all in the past twenty years because, I am embarrassed to say, I have been afraid to. I have used valid excuses: no money and no time, and one, two, and then three children, but the truth is that I inwardly resist any travel at all, even to Kingston, three hours away from Toronto. I have turned down trips to Russia and Sweden and England, because of this fear.

Of what?

Not flying, not danger, and certainly not the unfamiliar.

I am hungry for the unfamiliar. And I got lots of it in Mexico City. I was awestruck right away by the sight of the coloured tin and cardboard shacks on either side of the road. They were piled and crammed into an above-ground underground city. There were hanging plants and bright and white clothing dancing from lines. And although I guessed that these were the homes of the poorest Mexican people, and represented all that was atrocious in the Mexican system, they were beautiful, because people had made them to live in. Just after that, my breath was taken away by a fifteen-foot Marlboro Man on top of a building, astride a bucking, twenty-foot horse. With a cigarette hanging out of his mouth. I remembered that the actual Marlboro man is dead, of lung cancer. Canada and Mexico have America between them, and all over them.

The streets of this city of ten million were almost deserted. And although there was a scattering of intriguing, unfamiliar, twisted trees, there were almost no flowers. The air had poisoned them. It was early July, and I had come ready for heat with six sundresses. And one light sweater. And sandals, with no socks at all. I hadn't consulted even the weather channel. I was going to be slightly chilled the whole time. And damp. It rains every day in Mexico City in July, from around four in the afternoon on.

I was with a group of Canadian artists and arts administrators invited by the Mexican government and sent by External Affairs; we were lodged in luxury at the Stouffer Presidente, a big concrete warehouse for rich persons, which offered us rooms at less than half price. The hotel is located in Polanco, a wealthy area with embassies and Benettons and internationally renowned museums and astonishing Spanish-style mansions with twenty-foot wrought-iron fences and turrets and tiled courtyards, and, of course, round-the-clock security guards. The Stouffer Presidente itself had at least thirty policemen armed with semi-automatics patrolling the hotel twenty-four hours a day. This made me feel safe and threatened at the same time.

UNICEF was hosting a Conference of Mayors at the Stouffer Presidente. Mayors from around the world had been invited by UNICEF to attend a conference on child poverty. Every morning we would see them gathered, waiting for their bus in their wildly varied national dress, talking joyfully to one another. It gave me a glimmer of hope, until I learned that the Stouffer Presidente is owned by the Nestlé corporation, the same corporation that has been practically forcing baby formula on Third World mothers, deceiving them into thinking that mother's milk is in some way inferior. Odd. Like holding a conference on the well-being of mice in a boa-constrictor.

In the hotel there was a tour business, of course, and because my companion was writing about Hemingway, I agreed to go to a bullfight. I have always abhorred the idea of bullfights, but I told myself it was time to see what it was that I abhorred. After all, I couldn't stop it by not going, and by going I would have a deeper understanding, maybe, of the whole thing. So, we bought our tickets for fifty dollars American each, I still can't believe we paid that, and we were picked up by a shiny dark-red minivan. My companion and me, a Filipino mayor and his wife, a bullfight nut from Illinois and his wife, two rather gruff young Korean men, and a couple of others I don't remember. It took us about twenty-five minutes to get to the stadium. Okay, I thought to myself, in Canada that would have cost us eight to ten dollars. We were taken into the stadium for free, while others paid two pesos. Okay, we were at ten to twelve dollars. Canadian. The stadium was almost empty. This was because it was the winter season, and we would see only the novice toreadors. The stadium was all eroding cold stone, and we bought cushions to sit on. We sat for a very long time while our guide told us about McDonald's and other large corporations spreading around rumours that the tortillas made and sold by street vendors caused cholera. Suddenly there was a fanfare, and the young toreadors came on. They were stylish, in colourful, skin-tight pants and bolero jackets and theatrical capes, and they did what looked like a minimalist modern dance, full of pose and attitude. It was quite striking. Then the bull was released. It stood in the centre, still for a moment, and looked around. I thought its heart was beating fast. One of them poked it. It moved. Another poked it again. It ran. It was poked again, and it ran faster, around the edge of the circle. Every time it slowed down it was poked again. Occasionally it fake-lunged at one of its tormentors, but mostly it just ran in circles. Finally one of the toreadors took up his big decorated party stick and plunged it into the bull. I gasped. Our guide, sensing my dismay, explained to me that it was important to bleed the bull, because otherwise it would suffer a heart attack. Because of the fear. I looked back at the bull, standing quite still as the swordstick thing dangled from its side, and thick blood dripped from the wound. The bull was at this point still strong, and running hard, with dark, terrified eyes, and all I could think of was a young woman in Ontario who was kidnapped and murdered. I thought, God have mercy, is this what it was like? At the beginning, when she was pulled into the car, and she was still strong, and fighting, and not sure what was going on, and had some hope? Neither she nor the bull could have known that their death was a certainty. We knew that the bull would die, because we had been told that we would see five bulls die. The bulls always die. My breakfast came up into my mouth and I asked the guide to drive me back to the hotel, considering the exorbitant amount of money I had paid to his company. He refused, so I told my companion I was leaving, and I left. The tourist guide-book said that it is deeply insulting to leave the stadium; it said the savage wild beast in the ring bears no relation to its barnyard cousin in North America. But it looked exactly like the bulls I see at my cousin's dairy farm outside of London, Ontario. Sitting in the taxi, I reflected that the slaughterhouses of North America are no kinder than the bullrings of Mexico, and yet I participate in the slaughter. I hold a leather shoulder bag. Many of my shoes have been leather. At least at the bullfight the public confronts its participation in the slaughter of animals.

In the next few days, whenever I had time away from the con-ference, we filled ourselves with the unfamiliar. Here are some moments that have stayed with me:

Young clowns wearing orange wigs and big red feet and tear-drop big-mouth make-up, just standing on streetcorners. They didn't juggle, or blow up balloons, or sing silly songs. They just stood. When I smiled at one of them, he stared at me as if to say, "What are you smiling at you stupid bitch," and looked away.

There were mothers sleeping in the small parks with their chil-dren all wrapped up in the same shawl/blanket. It looked to me as if they had walked for twenty to thirty miles to come and sell their dolls and scarves to the tourists. But there weren't any tourists, there was only us.

A little boy of about four watched me as I looked at old photo-graphs of the Mexican revolution. I smiled at him, and he very quietly asked me, I guessed, for money. I gave him a few pesos, which he quickly pocketed, and then he disappeared.

There were dogs everywhere. Old and dusty, lopey Mexican dogs, just wandering, mostly on their own, about the city. Often they would lie in the middle of the sidewalk, and people would step

*Cameron Wallace*

As I look at this image of a mother and child,
I wonder if there is a photo of my own daughter
and me somewhere in Mexico City

over them. We stepped up to a very expensive restaurant, which was closed, to admire the shrubbery, when I noticed an ear perk up. I looked more closely and saw three dogs sleeping, completely hidden by the small bushes.

From the windows of our velvety, noiseless bus, we saw a tiny girl, about two years old, tottering on the edge of the curb in a crinoline dress, screaming. Cars were speeding by. We looked for the mother and finally saw her, at the far end of this "island," holding up her homemade dolls in the hope that passing cars would stop, and buy. She had no expression in her face at all, and in the whole five minutes we watched, she did not look at her child once. The child would learn, we decided, in a matter of months, not ever to cry.

The Zocolo, or main square, bordered by the National Palace and the Cathedral and other magnificent old seventeenth-century (I think) buildings. The Zocolo was occupied. Farmers from the country were living in large tents, in the middle of the square, and protesting Free Trade, among other things. The farmers were very striking, dressed in the same style of clothing that their fathers and grandfathers and great-grandfathers had probably worn. When we came out of the National Palace after seeing the unforgettable historical murals of Diego Rivera – depicting, among other things, the torture of the Incas by the conquering Spaniards – hundreds of farmers, male and female, stood facing us silently, holding up a banner with large, black letters. Their silence was penetrating.

Trapped in a labyrinthine market wide enough only for one and a half of us, full of shoes and bowls and jeans and sponges; thousands of stalls, sheets and curtains dividing them. Freshly made tortillas with curried chicken and meat and onion and bright green sauces, and pale green fruit in plastic bags, and apples cut into pieces and covered in paprika, mango or melon carved into the shape of a rose and sold on a stick; pineapple, freshly squeezed juices, and Chiclets and Diet Coke, and tamarind nectar.

Back from the conference at four o'clock one day, we caught a taxi to the pyramids, about twenty miles out of the city. The taxi driver was a nice older man who had been to Chicago in the seventies at the invitation of an appreciative tourist, but he hadn't liked it because all the houses, he said, were the same colour. He wondered how people could live in a place where buildings were the same colour. Mexicans paint their adobe houses bright blues and pinks and oranges.

Once at the pyramids, we were tackled by a dozen or so vendors of hideous, mass-produced trinkets: "I made it myself in my home." We had just learned that the pyramids closed at five and it was already ten to, so we ran, hoping to climb to the top. It seemed very important to climb to the top. We had been told that these were ancient Mayan pyramids, built to honour the sun god and the moon god. I had read about the human sacrifices; young girls who were carried up to the top of the pyramid, calm and content in the knowledge that they were dying for their people. I wondered if they had any fear at all, of the knife above their heads, I wondered if they fainted and cried when the knife plunged into their chests, and the priest carved out their hearts as an offering to the sun god. Did their mothers have even a moment of doubt? Suddenly, a dozen guards blew their whistles and shouted at us in Spanish. They were ordering us off the pyramids. The sheepish taxi driver, who of course hadn't told us about the five o'clock closing, whisked us away to a nearby shop which sold silver. He clearly had some arrangement with the owners. We reluctantly accepted their offer of free tequila and lemon, knowing that we couldn't afford to buy anything. We looked around, and ooohed and aaahed, and then said we'd like to go back. They did not smile when they said goodbye.

The night before we left, we saw a Mexican play, which was not on our itinerary. It was about a family that lived in the tin and cardboard shacks by the airport. Although we could not understand the words, the play was clear. There is nothing beautiful about the lives of these people who must live in boxes, with no water and no heat and no toilet. They are full of despair, and hatred for themselves and others. Many of the young people sniff a substance which makes them blind and demented. The mother must put her son on a leash and throw a can around his neck in the hope that kind strangers will deposit coins. She drags her son and her most precious possession, a tortilla cooker, along with her to the street. But if McDonald's and the other big U.S. corporations have their way, nobody will buy her tortillas anymore. At the end of this powerful play, the cast stood silently behind a banner which read something like "The Terrible Silence." The tiny audience clapped, and we all left full of shame.

On our last night we were taken to a bar/nightclub on the second floor of an old run-down house in a fairly busy area. It was called Paquita's, after the woman who owned the place and sang for her patrons on the weekends. The place was a disappointment at first, mainly because the snack food had been altered for our palates. Instead of the real Mexican food we had all begun to love, we were served slabs of bland generic cheese and canned ham, and supermarket tacos with no hotsauce. "Salsa piquante, por favor," we cried, and finally got it. The first two singers were passable, and we continued our lively sangria-drenched conversations over the music. But the third, this was Paquita. In our sickening middle-class way, we began to snicker quietly – she wore a harsh, sunset-coloured, skin-tight lamé dress to the ground, slit up to the crotch, and silver lamé platform shoes, more make-up than a drag queen on St. Laurent, and she was a good size 22. But the moment she started to sing all snickering stopped. The suffering, the intelligence, the life of the woman filled her voice and her face; her eyes looked through us behind our faces and found us.

When were changing planes in Houston, Texas, the Customs man said he had a brother up in Canada, in Ottawa. He said his brother told him that Canada was going to hell because of open immigration, that all these so-called refugees were draining the blood of the country and making men like his brother poor. Our smiles froze, and we answered him with our silence. I was frightened of this man. I knew that if I had answered him with the torrent of words gathering at the back of my teeth, he could have stopped us, and searched our luggage, and perhaps planted drugs or pistols in our bags. So we said nothing, and he waved us on through. In the plane to Toronto, I squirmed with guilt about my silence, and its inadequacy. Its Canadian-ness. Then I remembered the farmers in the Zocolo, gathered, facing us, using their silence.

I bought a tape of Paquita, and when I play it for friends they laugh, and say they've heard her in gay bars, or isn't she great, but they don't get it. I guess they'd have to see her eyes.

What was I afraid of? I think, judging from my feeling of relief as we landed at Pearson, I was afraid that I would not be able to get back. I was afraid that all technology would fail, and I would be stranded, a stranger in an unfamiliar place, with no voice to speak with, no words to be understood. Now I peruse the travel section of the paper and I fantasize about far-off places. I know, almost, that Canada does not disappear when I leave it. And I know that I do not disappear when I leave Canada.

# JANE URQUHART

## Returning to the Village

I wanted to be in a place that was both familiar and foreign, a place distant from the dailiness of life and yet filled with the warmth of domesticity, and I knew I could only do this by return-ing to the village.

The village was across an ocean, deep in the green heart of a country whose larger landscape I had come to understand by collecting a series of bright, startling images and whose language I knew only superficially. The village, however, I knew well. I had lived there seven years before with my husband and two-year-old daughter for one serene year. I had walked its narrow streets and gazed down into the valley from its gates. I had followed the paths that branched out from its walls towards an ancient cross, a medieval forest, a wash house, an enclosed garden. I had bought bread each morning at its single *alimentation* and lit candles in its dark, cold church. Because my husband worked each day in a studio which was separate from the house and my daughter attended *École Maternelle*, I had been, during the daylight hours, almost always alone in my explorations. It was the place where the writer in me – such as she is – was born.

The following few years had been filled with excitement and activity: people, parties, bouts of blurred travel. Now I wanted separation from the world, solitude, wanted to rediscover what it was that had set the words spinning in the first place. I needed to begin another book, and for this reason I felt it was necessary that I return to the village alone.

Because I chose late November to make this pilgrimage, it was already dark when I arrived in the village on a Thursday afternoon. I collected the key and six brown eggs from the farming family across the street, and opened the familiar oak door. The interior of the house was just as I remembered it; the tiles in the kitchen, the cream-coloured walls, the old stone sink, the crack in the bedroom ceiling. I lit room after room, expecting to be confronted with some evidence of change. There was none. Spoons in drawers, goblets in cabinets, the grain on the oak stairs, the pattern on the salon rug, mirrors and pictures on walls, the figures of birds worked into lace curtains were just as they had been.

This was a privilege and I knew it; to bring one's own altered body and psyche into a space, architectural or natural, that has remained constant over the passage of almost a decade is not an experience easy to come by in the last quarter of the twentieth century. I thought of Wordsworth's "Tintern Abbey," of Yeats' "Coole Park and Ballylee"; poems of memory and reassessment that had needed the reassurance of familiar visual stimuli to trigger them. I had had to travel thousands of miles to get to the remembered, abandoned place, but I was blessed in that I had access to the return. I counted my blessings as I faced the fireplace.

The idea of the fireplace as a theatre had been planted in my mind seven years before by the owner of the house when he had left instructions regarding the fires which were to be lit there. "Use lots of paper, lots of kindling," he had written, "and place the logs slightly to stage right." So began my relationship with this small corner of the universe, a corner which would grow in importance when the winds of January rattled the shutters and removed loose tiles from rooftops. Never housing a predictable entertainment, often difficult to cause to perform, this hearth and its fire became, over the course of that distant year, my own territory. I cursed the fire and I coaxed it. Often it had sent me choking to the windows or scrambling through outbuildings searching for materials which would guarantee flame. It was seldom well behaved, its unfolding plot rarely uncomplicated until I had been at it for some time. It wasn't until the winter was almost over that I realized that I had been working at the fire in precisely the same way that I had been working on my writing, experiencing, each day, the frustration, the fascination.

I awakened on the first morning of my return, as I had awakened every morning years before, to the sound of the family across the street beginning their day – the moan of a cow, the sound of a milk

House z Shadow  TE        urquhart 1978

pail striking cobblestone – and to the bells of the monastery on one side of the village and the convent on the other. In the intervening years I had thought a great deal about the convent, which had remained a hidden and mysterious female alternative, its activities made known only by the songs I had heard when I passed by its walls, or by a glimpse of its garden through a locked iron gate. Now I was grateful for its regularity: the fact that I knew that its bells would ring at the time of the day when bells should ring, that rituals were being performed, rituals I had never witnessed, mere steps from my door. All around me, I realized, a symphony was celebrating the sanctity of industry, continuity, inevitability. A tractor was fired up in a stone barn; children departed, chattering, for school; a milk truck arrived, picked up the fruits of the farmer's daybreak labours, and pulled away again; and I, the only pulse in the house, placed my bare feet on a familiar floor. Then I wandered through the house, pushing back the shutters, while behind me a series of rooms opened itself to the light.

After breakfast I took my remembered spiral walk around the village: outside the walls, inside the walls, through narrow streets, down alleyways, ending at the church square in the village's heart. I had brought along a basket which I filled at the *alimentation*. The woman there remembered me, mostly because of the "petite fille" who had sometimes accompanied me in the past. "Elle est comme ça," I said, holding my hand in front of me at shoulder level. The woman raised her eyebrows in astonishment.

In the early afternoon, after I had washed my few lunch and breakfast dishes, I entered the salon and began my daily struggle with the fire. Then I turned to the round walnut table, pulled out the green chair, sat down and opened my notebook. Behind me was a case filled with English books – a good thing because I knew I was not ready to write. I pulled the two large volumes of *Scott's Last Expedition* from the shelf and spent the remainder of the afternoon attempting to survive the sea voyage to Antarctica on the one hand, and on the other trying to encourage the reluctant fire. Blizzards swept pages, huge waves crashed over the icy decks of the *Terra Nova*, familiar fire tools clanked against marble, the wind banged in the chimney. Two decorative female faces looked solemnly up at me from the end of the andirons, twin girls I had become intimate with a decade before. A large log, eaten through the centre by fire, collapsed between them and was replaced by a chunk of softwood which burst almost immediately into flame. During the ocean storm, Scott was sick with anxiety concerning the fate of the animals on board. In the end he reported, sadly, that two ponies had been lost and one dog.

On the third day I decided to clean the house, which had been vacant for some months and was, as a result, somewhat dusty. This was a great pleasure in that it allowed me to run my hands over the surfaces of desks and cupboards, bureaus and tables that

I hadn't consciously thought about for a long time but which, nevertheless, had remained in my memory so that the act of cleaning them, now, became a sort of ceremonial reunion. I recognized wood grains – sometimes even the reflections of window-panes in wood grains – that I had known well in the past. I reacquainted myself with several small pieces of statuary; their sad, resigned gestures and vulnerable expressions. In the kitchen I was able to see again the way a damp cloth caused the old blue-and-red tiles to shine until an opaque tide rolled over them from the direction of the radiator. All of this calmed and comforted me.

In the afternoon, and at a respectable distance, I followed a party of dark-robed, contemplative seminarians on their daily walk out the narrow road that led eventually to the Camp de Caesar. They could not possibly have been, but they looked the same as the clusters of their brothers I had seen bicycling down poplar-lined lanes into the valley or taking this exact walk seven years before. I turned around, however, and began the trek back, stooping down now and then to collect sticks for the fire. There were several wonderful views of the village from this road, particularly now that the low winter sunlight shone on its walls. At one point a path I remembered plunged into the now leafless forest, and I walked down it to the place I had called my secret thicket. Here, there was an ancient stone bench and a view of the valley, the monastery, and, on the next ridge of hills, the neighbouring village. I sat down, and, not for the first time since my arrival, I confronted my former, younger self: her fantasies, expectations, disappointments, and obsessions.

That evening, while the fire behaved admirably, I sat in the gentleman's chair, stage right, and did not even look at the round

# III

walnut table where so much writing had taken place in the past. Things were not going well in *Scott's Last Expedition*; shrieking winds, frostbite, snow blindness. But none of this stopped Ponting from taking his glorious photographs or Scott himself from report-ing both disasters and triumphs in his clear, eloquent prose. But after he had left Cape Evans, the tone of his writing changed, became more forced and practical. Poetic images disappeared and at times the sentences became harsh, almost brutal. The weather, it seemed, was always against him, and he wasn't progressing as quickly as he had hoped. Sometimes he and his men were trapped for days inside tents while something white and furious took hold of the rest of the world. At Camp Shambles the rest of the beloved ponies had to be shot.

It was almost midnight. Before finishing this tragic history I wanted to clear my head, so I left the house for the village streets. All lamps were extinguished, except mine; all shutters were closed, including mine. The streetlights, in the interests of economy, had always been and were still switched off at nine P.M. There was a partial moon, and this, plus a carpet of brilliant stars, was my only source of illumination. But unlike Scott and his party I was safe, surrounded by a culture and civilization that had been left to me like a gift by preceding generations. Some of the narrower streets were so dark that I couldn't see my own feet, but I realized by my sure-footedness how intimate I had become with their surfaces, their dimensions, their distances. There was frost in the air; I could see its minimal shine on rooftops. But there was no ice underfoot. When I entered the house again, all the furniture seemed to greet me. I cut myself a chunk of bread on the old board in the kitchen, adding another incision to the thousands etched there, some by my own previous, younger hand.

After great hardship Scott and his men eventually reached the Pole only to discover that they had been pre-empted by Amundson and the Norwegians. Returning, they found the weather had worsened. Petty Officer Evans had died, and Oates, sensing that his weaknesses were slowing the party's progress, had staggered off into a blizzard in order to relieve the others of the burden he felt he was becoming. And Scott, himself, would never again walk into familiar rooms or gaze out windows at familiar landscapes. After penning his last few feeble words, he lay down in his tent and prepared to freeze to death.

The following morning I opened my eyes to shafts of strong sunlight, which penetrated the shutters and made narrow golden bars on the floor beside the bed. I had slept through the convent bells and the morning activities of my neighbours. When I opened first the windows, then the shutters, I was amazed to see that while everything in the village was crisp, frosty, and clear under a cloudless sky, the whole valley surrounding it was filled with a thick fog. I imagined what the village would look like from a distance, perched like a heavenly city on a prairie of soft cloud. The rest of the world, I realized, had simply disappeared.

In the afternoon, after setting a log slightly to stage right, I opened my notebook on the round walnut table and began to write.

*The drawings in this piece are by Tony Urquhart.*

ARITHA VAN HERK

# Death in Vienna

Forget the Vienna Boys' Choir, the famous Sachertorte, the Lipiz-zaner stallions, and the Vienna Philharmonic. This is a city shud-dering under its own weight of delicious disaster, suffocating within the leaden frames of façades uneasily balanced between Baroque, post-Gothic, and Renaissance. The eye is met, at the turn of every corner, with a façade, imposing or chaste. Look ahead and there is some heavily sculptured portal looming, look over your shoulder and there is another bearing down. But the façades speak also to a ghoulish obsession with the deaths of a covetous old city. Everywhere, amid the revered and polished past, is the tension of rank and privilege, and the over-protective assurance of the once Holy Roman Empire.

I am in search of, not waltzes or Sachertorte, but death in Vienna. And in the heavy air that filters the sun, there is the reas-surance that these streets cherish an inevitable lugubriousness, all winding alleys or passages inevitably eccentric, unhappy, and prone to early cul-de-sac. What has been pulled down or buried casts a reflection as true as what is present, alive, breathing.

In order to remember death in Vienna, it is necessary only to seek an eye in the lids of the glazed windows that repeat themselves in the blind façades of the various *palais*, cast in the eyebrowed blink of their blindness. Visiting Vienna is a cliché. Embedded in its own intricacy, cast in the spell of Baroque and post-Gothic figurations, Vienna streets gleam with the polish of a historical city gone tourist, taking itself by the hand on a Disneyesque excursion. Surrounded by its ageless assurance of culture and knowledge, elegance personified in the aristocratic length of fingers and the quick scars cut into the cheekbones of the old duellists, I am stumblingly clumsy. For there are but eighty museums and eighty-two libraries (with eighteen million books) here, hardly worth the week that I am spending, a brief glimpse into time cupped in the hands of containment.

I am here to check the many, many paintings of Judith with the severed head of Holofernes held in the Kunsthistorisches Museum, paintings by Vouet, Liss, Cranach, Bloemaert, Solimena, Varotari, Saraceni, and Veronese, although I am distracted by some powerful representations of Salome carrying John the Baptist's head on a platter. Staggering from the dim labyrinth of connecting rooms, down the marble staircase, past Canova's *Theseus Slaying the Centaur*, two massive males struggling into their own demise, down into Maria Theresa Square, I am struck again by the vocality, the lively texture of death in this grotesquely crypt-like city.

Transported so, I actually expect to see Gustav Klimt and Sigmund Freud walking down a street together, arm in arm. I dream here in Vienna, dream that I am losing letters, that other people are opening my mail. Strangely, in the dream, I am not upset, I assume that those who scan the words meant for me do not care and that my intensely personal letters mean nothing to them. And I dream that I am drinking coffee, beautiful small cups of dense coffee, a *kleiner Brauner*, with a knobbled glass of water beside, or thick heavy floats of *Einspänner*, the long silver spoon erect in the foam. I do not know if Klimt and Freud ever met, although, given their time and this arrangement of dead pasts brought together, all things are possible.

Walking lazily down Wahringerstrasse one evening, guiltlessly windowshopping, because the stores are closed, I bump into some-one I have not seen for fifteen years, a fellow student from one of my university classes. We hedge, defensive with one another, but clearly curious: Vienna, this maelstrom of the decadent? Nothing modern or even radical about it, evidence of conservatism in the businessman reading the newspaper and the occasional ker-chiefed housewife. Although we have coffee together, a *Fiaker*, coffee with rum, we refuse to tell one another what we are doing here, permitting the city to cloak us in its mysterious shroud. We might be meeting in an elegantly decadent purgatoria between death and resurrection where we do not have to answer for any-thing, past lives or other secrets.

My dreams of lost letters lead me to 19 Berggasse, in the Ninth District, where, climbing the stairs to the mezzanine, I imagine that I will be told an answer to my dream of intercepted letters, an interpretation of my correspondence as an open and disregarded file. I am interested not in *The Aetiology of Hysteria* but in *The Interpretation of Dreams*, crazily New Age as the desire seems. But Freud's penetrating stare does not seem at all present, despite his hat and walking stick in the foyer. Only the steamer trunk looks vaguely promising, although it is supposed to be the baggage that emigrated him to England when he was driven out in 1938. And in the roughly worn plush of the waiting room, I imagine being a patient, twisting on the stained chairs in my own desire to remem-ber and forget, to lay bare my twilit unconscious. Why am I dreaming about losing my letters, about other people reading my mail? I receive no mail here in Vienna, there is not enough time to forward mail, and I am only here for a week on my way back to Trier, where I am living and working for the summer. The legs of the chairs are traps, the potted palm is particularly ominous, the table bends itself between in a nervous arc, the last urge of hysteria, and the worn Persian over the scratched parquet floor looks to have held the nervous shufflings of the feet of a thousand bad dreams. But the consultation room is empty, the famous couch and all the books are in London, a residence in exile, ideas transported to another site; so although I sit on the edge of one chair (a forbidden act), I am unable to confess my paranoia about letters.

This is all dream. I refuse to enter the Sigmund Freud House, although I pass it almost every day on my long walk from my Ninth District hotel to the core of the city, where I am hunting for imaginations of death, mementos mori of mosaic and foundation. I resolutely take another way and walk past the Krankenhuisen, an enormous complexity of hospital buildings associated with the university. They point the way toward a whole broadsheet of graveyards, the *Hernalser Friedhof*, the *Dornbacher Friedhof*, the *Ottakringer Friedhof*, despite being at opposite ends of the city from the Eleventh District, where I resort to the comfort of the *Zentralfriedhof*, 593 acres of some three million graves, with its transplanted – oh, yes, they were dragged back – remains of Beethoven and Schubert, and the decorous begravement of Schnitzler, Hugo Wolf, and Johann Strauss, Jr., before I trudge on to the *Friedhof der Namenlosen*, "for those have no name," suicides and accidents washed ashore from the Danube.

All this amid the overwhelming rush of permanent impermanence – Mozart, that poor bastard, living in twelve different lodgings in ten years, and finally sweating his way to his own requiem in musty Rauhensteingasse. I do not go to Figarohaus, either, the CBC plays too much Mozart, and I am not about to have an orgasm at the thought that I am standing in the same room where both Haydn and Beethoven paid respectful visits. I am more interested in the adjoining street, Blutgasse, named for the Knights Templar who were massacred here in 1312. There is plenty of blood that has been washed away by Vienna drizzle, and I am dabbling my Canada finger in that liquid.

So much for a place that insists on an *Uhrenmuseum*, an hour museum, a time museum, a clock museum, with a thousand clocks, from Gothic to the present, all ticking and tocking their relentless way toward tomorrow, almost in line with the *Ankeruhr*, the animated clock built by an insurance company. In its Art Nouveau determination, a host of rulers and their consorts, long since dead, with Joseph Haydn bringing up the rear casually (as if Vienna were not a city built on salt and music), parade above the rebuilt square of the Hoher Markt, every noon. While the tortured fall of bodies in the Plague Column, the Baroque *Pestsäule* in the Graben, become exquisite adornment, rending their illness through the cloud pillar above what are now heartlessly exclusive parfumeries and salons de coiffure.

And in my dreaming search, behind the *mise en scène* of their secretive or forceful façades, I find tombs in every church, with their inhabitants reclining in sculptured relief, gestured toward heaven by tearstained angels. Tombs and the breath of arranged marriages, the Augustinerkirche, with its first Gothic, then Baroque, then re-Gothic interior witness to deathly weddings: of Maria Theresa to François of Lorraine; Marie-Louise to Napoleon by proxy; Franz Joseph, the last of the authentic Hapsburgs, to Elizabeth. Behind the grating in the far wall of the Lorettokapelle are the fifty-four silver urns containing the embalmed but certainly dead hearts of the imperial house, from 1637 to 1878. They are guarded day and night, a priest tells me, staring into my face as if searching for the origin of my macabre questions. It is astonishing what people will do, try to steal the very urns (which are discreetly cemented), scratch the silver, pray to them, and this, *now*, today, when scepticism about empire must be at its peak. But that is not all, oh no, not even close to sufficient, for the other organs and entrails rest in the catacombs beneath the Stephansdom, and the bones, yes the bones, are in the *Kaizergruft* of the Kapuzinerkirche. Talk about spreading yourself around in life and in death, ensuring there will be something left over to commemorate, something for both poor and modern to contemplate. The Imperial Burial Vault in the Capuchin Church has been the crypt of the Hapsburgs since 1633, and it could be said to be still operative, given that the most recent sarcophagus is of the Empress Zita (late widow of Karl), who died in 1989. Beneath every cellar is a cellar, and beneath that another, ongoing cryptology, the odour of mildew and dust hanging like a cloak. I go down the stairs hesitantly, after ringing a reluctant bell and being admitted by an even more reluctant doorkeep, who seems to feel that he has a right to inspect visitors before permitting them to offer him the small entrance fee. The air feels damply metallic, as if particles of lead float from the welded caskets. And here at last is my sepulchral art, elegantly grim, the smell of damp stone and cold earth over the metal casings of the enormous sarcophagi. I clutch my jacket close to my chest and try not to breathe too deeply, in this ecstasy of grotesque dreaming. The crypt is almost an apartment, spacious and roomy, with a foyer and antechambers, careful excavations of space laid out like rooms. In this company, its cellared treasure, rests the old Vienna that refuses to die, comfortably macabre, as gothically inclined as the city that continues, lost in its own vaultings. We in Canada associate vaults with money and banking, forgetting that the burial chambers of finance have their own means of eating flesh. An ornamental eating of flesh, those sarcophagi, from the plain copper box of Joseph II, who introduced the hygienic practice of sack burials, to the elaborate pewter mouldings of Maria Theresa and her consort, semi-reclining above their own remains, regarding one another with amused perfidy past the suggestive gesture of an angel. A double bed this is, enormously elaborated by the hanging folds of iron drapery, grieving angels, crowned skulls. All the Austro-Hungarian folly is gathered here in a neat encapsulation of bones: those emperors surrounded by multiple wives, those killed ungently in battle, those who died in their dutiful beds, and those who were murdered or suicided, guarding their secrets to a last and solidly encased silence. The bones of both Emperor Maximilian of Mexico and Marie-Louise, that unfortunate consort to Napoleon, are here, resting with their ancestors and their sculpted angels. Do they dream, I wonder, do they worry about letters held in state vaults, ready to fall into the hands of rapacious readers? They were too historical to visit Freud, to benefit from his interpretations of their dreaming life. And their staircase goes down, rather than up.

But it does not stop here, the deliciously macabre Vienna. I must walk a long way from the Ninth to the Fourth District to reach the *Bestattungsmuseum*, the Museum of Undertaking as art and profession. From the pomp of coffin covers to the reusable coffin introduced to save money, in this most expensive of all lively acts – dying – the *Entreprise des Pompes Funèbres* keeps a careful watch on who is permitting which pall, and who will be accompanied by white horses or black. All that fear of being buried alive, making sure the dead are really dead, stabbed to the heart to ensure that they won't wake up entombed, although the little cord hanging close to the body's hand should be a comfort, if a corpse does recover, come back from that tunnel of white light, one tug and a bell will ring, a grave attendant will come running

**WIENER**
A-1020 WIEN
GROSSE SPERLGASSE 24
TEL. 0222/214 46 78

**KRIMINALMUSEUM**

VEREINIGT MIT DEM
MUSEUM DER BUNDESPOLIZEIDIREKTION WIEN

TÄGLICH AUSSER MONTAG 10.00 – 17.00 UHR

How to find death in Vienna

with a shovel, will begin to dig. I ask if there is a record of this ever happening, and the city employee solemnly nods. And before the dead are swallowed by the cryptic moment they are propped in a chair for a photograph, one magnesium flash. This not a few steps from Schubert's *Sterbehuis*, house of death, where he raved and sang his delirious way to an end conquered by typhoid and syphilis.

I stop at the Circus and Clown Museum for relief, but that, too, is sadly tinged with rancid greasepaint and the thickly postered and costumed; tinsel and spangles are a coating for decay, despite the acrobatic heritage of gesture and the dance. To the *Wiener Kriminalmuseum*, the Crime Museum, operated by the police and full of the peculiar taste of those driven to desperate acts, and then, glad to have escaped unharmed, I hike to the *Riesenrad*, that ferris wheel revolving itself from 1898 on, almost a hundred years now, its slow-turning cars remembering *The Third Man*, Graham Greene and Orson Welles caught in a triangle of murder and its discontents. And after circling its spidery circle, resurrected from fire and movies alike, I take a long, long walk down the Hauptallee to the *Lusthaus*, a pleasure house for all, a two-storey octagonal pavilion like nothing so much as another crypt, a lust house, elegantly pedestalized to provide me and all the other *fin de siècle* ghosts with coffee again, first a *kleiner Brauner*, then a *Verlängerten*. And the water that I drink after each sip is a silent libation to this ur-grotesque city of gentle deaths and their rememberings.

After a week of such delicacies, I must pull myself onto the train, force myself to let go of such Gothic reaches. As the train – called Johann Strauss – pulls out of the Westbahnhof, I ease back in my plush seat, which reminds me of the chairs in Freud's house, and I remember my dream and that there will be letters waiting for me in Trier. I am alone in the compartment. Its six seats, decorously upright and side by side, tell me that the pall of the falling evening is escorting me to a different and smaller death. Even this, this brief compartment, is a moving coffin, the Viennese twilight covering now this most delightfully death-obsessed of all cities.

RONALD   WRIGHT

# The Painted Cave

They say you can never go back. You *should* never go back. To
those places you discovered when young, which opened your eyes
and stuck in your soul and have shone ever since like the road to
Damascus for St. Paul. Repeating such a journey, they say, is like
tracking down a first love and finding her blowzy and bellied and
worn down by the world.

1993. Janice wanted me to take her to France. She kept singing
that song about reaching thirty-seven and realizing she'd never
driven through Paris in a sports car with the warm wind in her
hair. Thirty-seven had come and gone with no sports car and no
Paris, not even a day trip from Dover to Calais with the shoppers
and lager louts. I'd run out of excuses, all the usual ones – France is
too expensive; France would be nice if the French didn't live
there; it's full of German/American/English tourists; Paris is just a
big city like any other (apart from the famous bits, it looks a lot
like Toronto); do you really want to spend all that money for the
thrill of drinking a ten-dollar coffee on the Champs-Elysées and
being insulted by the waiter? All right, says she, we can leave Paris
for another time. Why don't we just rent a car and drive south?

Anyway, how do you know what it's like? You haven't been there in twenty-six years.

So, you see, I'd run out of excuses.

In 1967, I'd hitchhiked through France with Roger, a friend from Cambridge. We were both eighteen and, aside from the geological intervals between lifts, we'd had a marvellous time. Hitching weeded out all those nasty French we'd heard about. Only nice ones gave rides and they were often very nice indeed. They bought us meals, introduced us to their families, put us up in their haylofts, and went out of their way to drop us at the *sortie de ville* where the chances of another ride were the least bleak. The trip had a buttery, croissant glow in my mind – unbroken sunshine, great forests, wild ravines, mediaeval towns with no suburban sprawl, long-haired girls who rode Peugeot mopeds and shook your hand and offered their cheeks for a kiss whenever you met on the street. I remember five-course meals with lakes of *vin ordinaire* for half a crown (about thirty-five cents), youth hostels that were endless parties, and squatting over Turkish-style loos with the door open and the sun streaming in and chickens going by. I remembered sleeping under the stars in a farmer's field and being woken up in the middle of the night by twin sisters – sixteen they were – who brought us bread and cheese and rosé and asked if we were beatniks.

Roger and I were neighbours our first year in digs, a crumbling Victorian row house where you had to feed a meter with shillings to boil a kettle, heat the bathwater, or toast your chilblains over a one-bar electric fire. I had the front room on the ground floor, he was directly above me, and on the top floor there was Clive, who had a thing about Greece and practised a bouzouki for long hours – until I threatened to fill it with concrete. We weren't very nice to our landlord and landlady, the Crabbes. We came in drunk, we stayed out all night (against regulations), and sometimes we had women in our rooms, which was even worse. Mr. Crabbe would report to our tutor that our bikes hadn't been in their usual spot, chained to the railings. I solved the problem with a second bike, assembled from various dead ones behind the college kitchen.

It was our first long vac, and like every student that year we were planning to hit the road – Clive to Athens, Roger and I to the Dordogne. We'd been studying the Old Stone Age and we wanted to see those places that had given their names to the earliest Europeans and the oldest art in the world: Le Moustier, Lascaux, Cro-Magnon. (Roger had clipped a cartoon from *Punch* – a family of middle-class Neanderthals, mum and dad hunched and defeated, bratty youngsters shouting, *Daddy! Daddy! Can we go and throw rocks at the Cro-Magnons today?*) According to French scholars, the first *Homo sapiens* worthy of the name was a Frenchman. This Cro-Magnon Man had appeared in the Dordogne valley thirty thousand years ago, and replaced the shambling and none-too-bright Neanderthal, whose name was suitably Germanic. The Germans, for their part, shifted the calumny farther east: when the first Neanderthal skeleton turned up in a quarry near Düsseldorf in 1856, it was dismissed as the remains of a Cossack mercenary.

First we needed equipment. Millet's, the war-surplus shop on Regent Street, kitted me out with a greasy combat jacket and a rubberized groundsheet that smelled like a condom, but their sleeping bags were expensive. I tried to scrounge one off a classicist I knew in King's – a young fogey who dressed like Fred Astaire and was rumoured to have a private income. He was a rowing blue and went on commando courses in the Scottish Highlands in January; he wouldn't be needing his gear over the summer.

"The only thing I can let you have is a rucksack and a map case, assuming you plan to do some serious walking," he said, casting a disdainful eye up and down my combat jacket, threadbare cords, and suede boots.

"What I'd really like to borrow is a sleeping bag."

"Sorry. Can't help. I don't let stuff like that go out any more. Not since I lent it to Oliphant last year and the bastard had a wank in it."

Roger had better luck. One of his girlfriends, an arty blonde, was less fastidious. Roger seemed to know a lot of women, which always puzzled me. He was lean, almost emaciated, wore thick round glasses, and affected a donnish manner. Yet he boasted of great accomplishments in love, attributing them to a part of his body in surprising contrast to his general physique. The mystery was how he got to a stage where this asset could be brought into play. Somehow they fell for his cynical laugh, his ornate pipe-smoking ritual, his habit of swanning round the room to Mahler, his tawny port and Earl Grey tea. I suppose it was because Roger was in love with being a Cambridge man, and love always attracts more.

We got the cheapest flight we could find – Lydd to Le Touquet in an old Fokker that had been looted from the Germans after the war. The fare included a bus to central Paris. It was a rainy June night when we reached the French capital (in my memory the sunshine doesn't belong here). The streets were oily with neon and taillights and dark pools of shuttered buildings that hadn't seen paint in fifty years. In one of these we stayed – a flophouse straight out of Henry Miller. There were small brown stains on the sheets (bedbugs?), and Madame asked us not to use the shower because, as she put it in English, "he is very ill." Someone had been very ill in the bidet.

To find supper we had to do battle with the traffic swarming at every corner like a revolutionary mob. There were gangsterish Citroëns with long black snouts and running boards, sansculotte

Deux Chevaux with canvas roofs, three-wheeled vans made of half a scooter and a sheet of corrugated tin, and weird little cars that looked like miniature Volkswagens but weren't. All of them were monuments to the Gallic love of needless complexity. They had horrible piss-coloured headlights, because some automotive *philosophe* had declared that yellow light was better for the human eye than the white variety invented by God, they smoked and sounded like chainsaws, they had umbrella handles for gearshifts, they bounced up and down like kangaroos, their engines were in funny places, their tyres looked dangerously flat, and the latest big Citroëns, which had been styled by Flash Gordon, had an ingenious pneumatic suspension that would collapse without warning, like a soufflé.

This mechanical fantasia made England's Austins and Rovers look reliable and sane – to say nothing of the drivers. Every Frenchman fancied himself as a Dakar rallyist, no matter how old his vehicle, how scant its horsepower, how bald its tyres, or how spent its brakes. He did not wait calmly for traffic lights to change; he stayed in gear, revving manically, wreathed in engine and cigarette smoke, inching up and rolling back on his clutch in order to defend the tiny space allowed him by his foes, unafraid to nudge the cars ahead and behind so that above the lawnmower chorus you heard clacks and thumps like the sound of billygoats crashing horns. Then the light would change, pedestrians would scatter, burning Gauloises would be tossed from windows, bald rubber would spin madly on wet cobbles until the rallyists calmed down enough to get some traction, and they were off, laying a pall of blue smoke like a gas attack on the *pissoirs* and cafés along the boulevard.

1993. We pick up a rental car at Charles de Gaulle airport. It's a brand new Ford Escort. I drive and Janice peruses the *Guide*

*Michelin.* We are starting to get hungry. Since we have no French money, this means a stop at a bank before we can search for a restaurant. "I can't wait for my first gastronomic experience," Janice says, as if contemplating the prospect of a Latin lover. We stop in the city of Meaux, only to find that a neutron bomb has fallen, and the only thing moving in the whole place is a gang of Germans on the same quest. "Excuse me, do you speak English?" are the first words we hear. Monday in France is as dead as Sunday in Aberdeen. Deader, in fact – even the hotels are locked up for their *fermeture hebdomadaire*. Back to the main road, so hungry now that a sign promising *Frites à 400 Mètres* seems too good to be true. But it is true, the genial chef is willing to accept dollars, and my wife's first gastronomic experience is Coke and chips from a roadside van.

1967. Roger and I rode the *Métro* as far as we could, and set off down the N20, that straight Roman road running from Paris to the Pyrenees. For the first two days, progress was slow but steady. Then we got badly stuck between Châteauroux and Limoges. We'd had one lift all day – a few miles in a truck delivering auto parts. We waited at the edge of a small town until noon, gave up and had lunch, returned to our post, waited for another hour, then started walking. Soon we were in a landscape of vast wheatfields beneath a remorseless sun, trudging through the dry grass like characters from a Beckett play – Roger with a leather suitcase, and I with the classicist's rucksack – counting the plane trees planted along the roadside with the grim inevitability of the metric system. Every ten metres, a pool of shade; every hundred trees, a painted stone: Limoges 76, Limoges 75, Limoges 74, and so on. This put us in a foul mood. We began sticking our fingers up instead of our thumbs.

"Bloody hell!" cried Roger at an English family studiously

avoiding eye contact in a Morris Oxford. "We're your compatriots!"

"Mon Dieu!" he shouted when a prim bourgeois couple in a dumpy Peugeot slowed, stared, and accelerated. "We saved you from the Germans!"

And when he saw a big black D on the back of a Mercedes, he yelled after it, "Mein Gott! We saved you from yourselves!"

Just then I found the cigarettes. They were in the grass, a pack of Gitanes – almost full. A few steps beyond were some matches. They must have blown out of an open sports car. We sat down, lit up, and everything changed.

"I have a charmed thumb," I said. I stuck it out, and within five minutes an open sports car stopped – something red, French, and fast, with a young blade who looked like Alain Delon at the wheel. He wanted to show it off. We rode with him to Périgueux, which was a bit out of our way; then on a whim he turned onto a country track heading where we wanted to go – Les Eyzies, the "archaeological capital of the world." The arrow-straight N20 must have been a frightful bore for Alain Delon; he'd been waiting for a road like this – narrow and twisty, strewn with donkey carts, goats, drunken peasants. These he scattered with the horn as he whipped through the bends, tyres screaming like teenage girls at Charles Aznavour.

Roger, in the passenger seat, had gone strangely silent, his bony hand gripping the top of the door like a carpenter's clamp. I was behind, wedged in a compartment designed for a mademoiselle's hat box. Every now and then, after a particularly nasty moment, Alain would grin as if he'd just seen a competitor crash in flames, and Roger would return this with a corpse-like rictus that he thought was a sophisticated smile. We had begun to descend in hairpins to the Vézère River (a tributary of the Dordogne) when it happened. The sun was low on the rocky hills, and the valley was filling with shade. Suddenly the car pirouetted on a bend and shot towards the abyss. It stopped on the edge of a grassy bank, with a superb view and one front wheel in mid-air. *Merde!* Alain vaulted out of his seat without opening the door. And then his eyes widened in astonishment. The cornering stresses had not caused the Michelins to lose their grip; rather than let go of the asphalt, one had peeled itself entirely from the wheel.

"Where are you boys going to stay?" he asked us after he'd fitted the spare and resumed his tumultuous descent unabashed. We said there was a youth hostel. By then the dusk was thickening to darkness in the narrow valley pinched between limestone cliffs. He stopped passers-by and asked for the *auberge de la jeunesse*. It was on the outskirts of the village, not far from a bridge – an old stone farmhouse, built between the road and a great rock overhang that had once sheltered early man. It was closed, and looked as though it planned to stay that way. There were tall weeds in the gravel path, tiles missing from the roof, a padlock and chain on the iron gate.

Alain shook open a pack of Gauloises, offered them, lit up, and shrugged. "*Pas de problème.*" He finished his smoke, ground it beneath a shiny heel, and beckoned us to follow him over the wall beside the gate. He stalked around the building, trying doors, studying windows. At the back, where the cliff met the wall of a low outbuilding, he scrambled onto a roof, trotted casually along the ridge, and slipped into an attic window like a cat burglar. He emerged a few moments later to beckon us up. We found ourselves in a loft with a plank floor and piles of empty sacks. The place smelled of tarred burlap, flour, and hay. Alain Delon spread a few of the sacks around. "*Voila!*" he said, the proud host. "Just close up when you go." He left with a handshake and a roar of exhaust.

We stayed for a week, washing in the river, returning after dark. No one noticed or cared.

1993. The French have started to paint the outsides of their houses. The rows of plane trees have been bulldozed away for extra lanes, the driving is no more flamboyant than anywhere else, the cars look like normal cars, and the newer ones even have white headlights. Our problem is not speed but sloth – crawling along in the foul air behind caravan after caravan pulled by diesel-powered vans, at least half of which belong to the thrifty Dutch.

I'd heard that France was the last bastion of the arrogant and suicidal smoker. But French restaurants now have no-smoking sections, and in a *tabac* I see a man buying an oxymoron – Gauloises Lights.

Janice enjoys the road signs. She grew up in Quebec, where Anglicisms have been rigorously purged. Here you stop at *Stop* signs, you park at *Parking*, you camp at *Camping*, and you see congregations of Netherlands plates at every *Caravanning*.

1967. I'll always remember that first morning in Les Eyzies because it was the morning I discovered croissants. We climbed down from the youth hostel's attic and walked into town – a straggle of buildings along the road. There was one café, with two patrons. We sat down and observed the mysterious French breakfast ritual. A man in a shabby suit had a bowl resembling a small chamber pot full of hot chocolate. In this he would dunk large pieces of bread and swallow them like oysters; then he'd lower his moustache to the rim of the bowl and siphon up the contents with a sound like a bath running out. The other man's breakfast was a tiny cup of strong black coffee and a large glass of brandy. He was prim and erect, in a three-piece suit with a gold fob. We asked the waiter what there was to eat. Eggs and bacon? No. Toast and marmalade? No. Kippers? Don't even ask, said Roger.

The man drinking brandy came up and spoke to us in an impenetrable dialect.

"I'm sorry," I said, "our French isn't very good."

"I wasn't speaking French," the man said crossly. "I thought you were English. I am professor of English at the school." He was speaking our language, but in the manner of someone who has learned it only by sight. This was no mere accent, these were English phonetics based on pure guesswork.

"Zey weel heave *croissant* wan ze back air a reeve," the English teacher said laboriously.

Roger managed to decode it: "I think he's saying that a baker will be bringing croissants soon."

The English teacher nodded vigorously and shook our hands. "Ay em so hippy to mate you," he said, smiling; then he left to teach the youth of Les Eyzies.

The baker was a short fellow of fifty or so, with the face of a dissolute baby, bloodshot eyes, and a huge belly bulging inside a filthy singlet stained with sweat and ashes and tomato juice and heaven knew what else. Against this he lovingly clutched a dozen croissants.

"My God, you're squeamish," Roger said. "Try them. They taste wonderful." Indeed they did. We had them every morning of the week – with brandy – and not once did the baker change or wash his singlet.

1993. Good croissants seem to have become as rare in France as good fish and chips in England. Every morning so far, we've been presented with a brace of cold, damp, stale offerings. We can get better from Valu-Mart at home.

1967. Perched on a limestone ledge directly above the Les Eyzies café was a concrete Neanderthal, looking for all the world like a cartoon caveman, though without club, loincloth, or genitalia. He was naively modelled, whitewashed, and based on a number of misconceptions. Few men have had such a bad press as Neander-thal Man. When the scientific establishment at last acknowl-edged that the poor fellow wasn't a Cossack, they cast him in the role of the missing link – that elusive creature loping halfway across the page between ape and us. It was assumed that he stooped, had no power of speech, and walked on the outsides of his feet like a gorilla. But, as more bones were discovered, this view did not hold up. The most "apelike" skeletons were shown to be sufferers of severe arthritis; the Neanderthals' brain was found to be larger than our own; and evidence came to light that they had cared for their sick and had buried their dead with religious rites – with flowers and ochre and animal horns. Perhaps *Homo neanderthalensis* was not really so primitive after all, merely a Euro-pean adaptation to the cold of the last Ice Age. Perhaps he deserved to be promoted to a sub-species of *Homo sapiens*. And if that were so, perhaps he (or she) and the Cro-Magnons had inter-bred. Perhaps even the French were descended from Neanderthal Man.

But no one wants to claim him for an ancestor; he is doomed forever to be a Caliban. Because, no matter how touchingly the Neanderthal buried his dead, the Cro-Magnon buried him with a brilliant, full-colour advertising campaign for their superior accomplishments. It was this that Roger and I had come to see – the great cave paintings of Lascaux and Font-de-Gaume, paint-ings that for realism and aesthetic power have never been sur-passed. But we had a problem: Lascaux, discovered during the Second World War, had been closed to the public in 1962 because the million descendants of Cro-Magnon Man who had tramped admiringly through it had, with their breath and lights and care-lessness, threatened to obliterate in fifteen years what nature had preserved for fifteen thousand. However, we learned that this *fer-meture* was not absolute: Lascaux was opened from time to time for the right people. Roger, whose French was better than mine, began to cultivate the English teacher, who had hinted that he knew someone at the site. We were serious Cambridge students, Roger emphasized, producing a letter of introduction from our tutor. Every morning at the café, we put up with the teacher's assaults on our language. On our last day in Les Eyzies this diplomacy bore fruit. We didn't really qualify as the right people, but if we told no one and went through quickly, an exception could be made.

The cave had two or three doors, as airlocks, and beyond them a damp, penetrating chill – the chill of a vault where meat or wine is aged. Caves are always another world, as alien as the sea, but here we were transported back in time to the golden age of hunting, when the ice was melting across Europe and the big game yet remained, when human beings were few and left no trace on the world but this. We saw animals that no one has seen alive in at least ten thousand years – woolly rhinoceros, cave bear, perhaps even sabre-tooth cat. We saw the wild ancestors of cattle and horses boldly drawn in ochre, haematite, and charcoal with extraordinary movement – hoofs splayed, nostrils flaring, backs rippling with agony and power after penetration by a hunter's lance. There was a strikingly modern, airbrushed look in the freedom of the figures, in the way pigment had been blown from tubes, the way natural contours of the rock had been cleverly used for relief. These paintings were in no way primitive or naive; their naturalism was more assured than in any European art until the Renaissance, and they were fifteen thousand years older than a Leonardo. Not even the Renaissance painted animals with such energy and charm. Civilized art has honoured man not beast; here it was the other way round. The only human figure was crude and lifeless, as if paralysed by the charge of a magnificent wounded bull.

1993. It's late afternoon when Janice and I reach Les Eyzies, sedately, in our Ford Escort. I hardly recognize the place; the straggle of houses has become a town. There are hotels and restaurants everywhere, and a long traffic jam crawling past gift shops selling Limoges pottery, plaster saints, and Swiss army knives made in China. I couldn't begin to guess where the baker lived, where the café stood, where the one expensive restaurant was – where Roger and I, on our last night, treated the English teacher to a fancy dinner that turned out to be sheeps' brains.

We've booked ourselves into a country hotel at vast expense, but I see the old youth hostel – still shadowed by the overhanging cliff at dusk. Today it's a private house.

Lascaux, as before, is closed – closed now for more than thirty years. Early the next morning, I go to buy tickets for Font-de-Gaume, the only important painted cave still open, but it's booked solid for a fortnight. The woman at the office says, "If you hurry, you might be able to get into Lascaux Two."

Lascaux Two? Yes, the *Guide Michelin* confirms that a concrete "facsimile," a "remarkable reconstitution," has been opened near the original cave. Janice wants to see it.

"But it's a theme park, a fake," I say. "It's like going to the Louvre and being shown a reproduction of the Mona Lisa. It's like Euro-Disney and Gauloises Lights."

"Never mind," says she. "It's better than nothing."

We arrive early – half an hour before opening time – having learned to expect crowds in the Dordogne, despite the recession. But already the crowd is five blocks long, and more unruly than the mob outside our local flea pit for *Jurassic Park*. There's only one thing to do – forget it.

They are right, you see: you never can go back.

## About the Contributors

Graeme Gibson

**MARGARET ATWOOD** was born in Ottawa in 1939 and grew up in northern Quebec and Ontario and in Toronto. She has published over twenty books, comprising novels, short stories, poetry, and literary criticism, and has won numerous awards. Her most recent novel is *The Robber Bride*, co-winner of the 1994 Trillium Award. She has travelled extensively and has lived in Boston, Vancouver, Edmonton, Montreal, Berlin, Edinburgh, London, and the South of France. She lives in Toronto.

Paul Casselman

**PIERRE BERTON** works in all branches of communication. He has written revue sketches for the stage, plays for radio, documentaries for radio, films, and television, a daily newspaper column, a musical comedy for the stage, and thirty-seven books. He has won three Governor General's Awards for creative non-fiction. His latest book is *A Picture Book of Niagara Falls*.

**DIONNE BRAND** was born in Trinidad, and came to Canada in 1970. She has published six books of poetry, including *No Language Is Neutral*, which was nominated for the Governor General's Award. Her latest work of non-fiction is *No Burden to Carry*, a collection of oral histories. Her work in documentary film includes *Long Time Comin'*. She lives in Toronto.

*Germaine Beaulieu*

**NICOLE BROSSARD** of Montreal is the author of numerous books, including *Daydream Mechanics*, *French Kiss*, *The Aerial Letter*, *Mauve Desert*, and *Picture Theory*. Twice winner of the Governor General's Award, she was also awarded the prestigious Prix Athanase-David for the whole of her work, and the Harbourfront Festival Prize. She is currently working on a novel.

*K.W.O.I.*

**JUNE CALLWOOD** is a journalist with twenty-four books to her credit. A member of the Canadian News Hall of Fame, she is past chair of the Writers' Union of Canada and past president of PEN Canada. She has been tirelessly involved in community work, and has received the Order of Canada. She lives in Toronto.

**GEORGE ELLIOTT CLARKE,** a native of the Black Loyalist settlement of Three Mile Plains, Nova Scotia, is a poet, scholar, and critic. His second book of poetry, *Whylah Falls* (1990), received the 1991 Archibald Lampman Award. He lives in Ottawa.

**LEONARD COHEN** was born in Montreal in 1934. His creative career spans nearly forty years, during which he has produced an impressive body of work: nine books of poetry, two novels, and eleven albums. His most recent book is *Stranger Music: Selected Poems and Songs.* His latest album is *The Future.*

**ROBERTSON DAVIES** has just completed his eleventh novel, *The Cunning Man;* in addition, he has written fifteen plays and eighteen other works. His novels have been translated into eighteen languages and he has received many honours, including Companion of the Order of Canada.

© Elisabeth Feryn

**TIMOTHY FINDLEY** has for over three decades been a writer of fiction, drama, and documentary. His novels include *The Wars*, *Not Wanted on the Voyage*, *Famous Last Words*, and *Headhunter*, his most recent. Just missing a disaster-bound flight in the 1950s kept him out of the air for thirty years, but now he can be found in cars, trains, and planes.

Donald Winkler

**SHEILA FISCHMAN** is one of Canada's foremost literary translators and has brought to English-language readers the work of, among others, Roch Carrier, Michel Tremblay, Marie-Claire Blais, and Yves Beauchemin. She has twice won both the Canada Council Translation Prize and the Félix-Antoine Savard Prize, offered by Columbia University. She lives in Montreal.

Brian Smale

**GEORGE GALT** is a journalist, critic, editor, and the author of two travel narratives, *A Journey Through the Aegean Islands* and *Whistle Stop: A Journey Across Canada*. He lives in Toronto.

*Matthew Mann Gibson*

**GRAEME GIBSON** is the author of four novels, including 1993's *Gentleman Death*. He has been active in cultural politics since the early 1970s, and served as president of PEN Canada, from 1987-89. He has won the Toronto Arts Award for writing and publishing, received the Order of Canada and the 1993 Harbourfront Festival Prize. He lives in Toronto.

*Henry Fiks*

**ALISON GORDON,** journalist, broadcaster, and crime novelist, covered the Toronto Blue Jays for the *Toronto Star*. *Foul Balls: Five Years in the American League* is her story of that experience. Since 1988, she has published three Kate Henry mystery novels: *The Dead Pull Hitter*, *Safe at Home*, and *Night Game*. She has been a member of the PEN Canada board since 1989 and is the organization's 1993-94 president. She lives in Toronto and is completing her next novel.

*CBC File Photo*

**PETER GZOWSKI** is a writer who also spends time behind a CBC microphone, as the long-time host of "Morningside." He has won seven ACTRA awards. A former editor at *Maclean's*, he is currently a columnist for *Canadian Living*. His many books include *The Private Voice, Canadian Living,* and, most recently, *The Fifth (and Probably Last) Morningside Papers.*

*Tyler Hodgins*

**JACK HODGINS** is a teacher and fiction writer who lives in Victoria, British Columbia. His works include *The Resurrection of Joseph Bourne,* for which he won the Governor General's Award, *Spit Delaney's Island, The Invention of the World,* and *Over Forty in Broken Hill,* a travel book. His most recent work is *A Passion for Narrative: A Guide for Writing Fiction.*

*R.D. Huggan*

**ISABEL HUGGAN** is a Canadian who, since 1987, has lived outside Canada with her husband and daughter in Kenya, southern France, and, most recently, the Philippines. She is author of the award-winning *The Elizabeth Stories,* and her most recent book, a collection of stories, is *You Never Know.*

*Ruth Kaplan*

**JANICE KULYK KEEFER** was born in Toronto, has worked at universities in Canada, England, and France, and has travelled nowhere near as much as she would like to. Her most recent books are *Travelling Ladies* and *Rest Harrow.* She teaches at the University of Guelph and lives in Eden Mills, Ontario.

**THOMAS KING's** short stories have been widely published throughout Canada and the United States, and a film based on his novel *Medicine River* has been made for CBC television. His latest books are *Green Grass, Running Water*, a novel, shortlisted for the 1993 Governor General's Award, and *One Good Story, That One*, a collection of short stories. He is currently chairman of American Indian Studies at the University of Minnesota.

**MYRNA KOSTASH,** born a second-generation Ukrainian-Canadian in Alberta, works as a full-time freelance writer of creative non-fiction. Her most recent book is *Bloodlines: A Journey into Eastern Europe*. She is active in PEN Canada and is the current chair of the Writers' Union of Canada.

**ALBERTO MANGUEL,** anthologist, critic, translator, journalist, and novelist, was born in Argentina. Before arriving in Canada in 1982, he worked in such places as Milan, Tahiti, Paris, and England. His books include *Black Water* and *Black Water II*, *The Gates of Paradise*, and a novel, *News from a Foreign Country Came*. His latest anthology is *Meanwhile, in Another Part of the Forest*. He lives in Toronto.

Shirley M. Adamson

**DAVID MCFADDEN** was born in Hamilton, Ontario. He is the author of two recent books of poetry, *Gypsy Guitar* and *Anonymity Suite*, and a travel book, *A Trip Around Lake Ontario*. "Mr. Looney" is from *An Innocent in Ireland*, to be published in early 1995 by M&S.

F. Mistry

**ROHINTON MISTRY** was born in Bombay, India, and came to Canada in 1975. He is the author of a collection of stories, *Tales from Firozsha Baag* (1987), and a novel, *Such a Long Journey* (1991), which won the Governor General's Award, the Commonwealth Prize, and was shortlisted for the Booker Prize. He lives near Toronto and is completing his next novel.

Chris Buck

**DANIEL DAVID MOSES,** poet and playwright, is a Delaware from the Six Nations lands along the Grand River. He lives in Toronto, where he writes and works with Native and cross-cultural arts organizations. His plays include *Coyote City*, *Almighty Voice*, and *His Wife*. His poetry is collected in *Delicate Bodies* and *The White Line*. He is also co-editor, with Terry Goldie, of *An Anthology of Canadian Native Literature in English*.

Jerry Bauer

**ALICE MUNRO** was born in Wingham, Ontario, and divides her time between Clinton, Ontario, and Vancouver Island. Her short-story collections have been published all over the world and have won her many prizes. Her most recent collection of short stories, just completed, is entitled *Open Secrets*.

**MICHAEL ONDAATJE** was born in Sri Lanka, and came to Canada in 1962. A novelist, poet, anthologist, filmmaker, Ondaatje has won numerous awards for his work. His books include *Running in the Family* (a memoir), *The Cinnamon Peeler: Selected Poems*, and the novels *In the Skin of a Lion* and, most recently, *The English Patient*, which won the Booker Prize, the Governor General's Award, and the Trillium Award. He lives in Toronto.

Chick Rice

**P. K. PAGE** is a poet, prose writer, and painter who has travelled widely and has received numerous awards for her work. Her books include *Evening Dance of the Grey Flies*, *The Glass Air*, and *Brazilian Journal*, a memoir. *Hologram* is her forthcoming book of poetry. She lives in Victoria.

**NINO RICCI** was born in Leamington, Ontario. From 1981 to 1983 he taught English at a boarding school in south-western Nigeria. His novels are *Lives of the Saints*, which won the Governor General's Award and Smithbooks/Books in Canada First Novel Award, and *In a Glass House*. He lives in Toronto, where he is at work on his third novel.

**DAVID ADAMS RICHARDS** was born in Newcastle, New Brunswick. He is the author of eight novels, including *Nights Below Station Street*, winner of the Governor General's Award, *Evening Snow Will Bring Such Peace*, which won the Canadian Authors Association Award, and his most recent, *For Those Who Hunt the Wounded Down*. He received the Canada-Australia Prize in 1993. He lives in Saint John, New Brunswick.

**CONSTANCE ROOKE,** critic, editor, academic, and short-story writer, is Associate Vice President (Academic) of the University of Guelph. She was the editor, for ten years, of *The Malahat Review*, is the author of *Fear of the Open Heart: Essays on Contemporary Canadian Writing*, and editor of the anthology *Night Light: Stories of Aging*. She is a member of the board of PEN Canada.

*Jean Marc Desrochers*

**SALMAN RUSHDIE** was born in Bombay in 1947. His five novels include *Midnight's Children*, *Shame*, and *The Satanic Verses*, and his fiction has been awarded the Booker Prize and the Whitbread Prize. His most recent fiction work is *Haroun and the Sea of Stories*, and a collection of his essays and criticism, *Imaginary Homelands*, was recently issued. In early 1989, Ayatollah Khomeini of Iran issued a *fatwa* against Rushdie, calling for his death on the grounds that *The Satanic Verses* is blasphemous towards the Muslim religion. Since that time, he has been forced to live in hiding. He is one of PEN's honorary members.

*Beverley Rockett*

**JOHN RALSTON SAUL** is a novelist and essayist living in Toronto. A former president of PEN Canada, his latest book is *Voltaire's Bastards: The Dictatorship of Reason in the West*, and his most recent novel is *The Paradise Eater*.

**CAROL SHIELDS** lives and writes in Winnipeg. She has won many awards for her books, which include *Swann*, *The Republic of Love*, *Happenstance*, and *The Stone Diaries*, which won the Governor General's Award and was shortlisted for the Booker Prize. She won the Marian Engel Award in 1990.

Rafael Goldchain

**LINDA SPALDING** grew up in Kansas, studied at the University of Colorado, and lived, for fourteen years, in Hawaii. She came to Canada in 1982. Her short stories have appeared in several magazines, and she is the author of two novels, most recently *The Paper Wife*. She is the editor, with Michael Ondaatje, of *Brick, A Journal of Reviews*. She lives in Toronto.

Anne Levinsky

**SUSAN SWAN** is a novelist and professor of Humanities at York University. Her fiction has been published in Canada, the United States, Germany, Holland, and Britain. Her most recent novel, *The Wives of Bath*, was shortlisted for the 1993 Guardian fiction prize and Ontario's Trillium Award. She lives in Toronto.

**JUDITH THOMPSON** was born in Montreal in 1954 and grew up in Kingston, Ontario. She has written plays for the stage, for radio, and for television. Her stage plays include *White Biting Dog*, *The Other Side of the Dark* (both of which won Governor General's Awards), *Crackwalker*, *Lion in the Streets*, and *I Am Yours*. Her recent television plays are *Life with Billy* and *Turning to Stone*. Judith Thompson lives in Toronto. She teaches drama at the University of Guelph.